REFERENCE RESOURCES:

A Systematic Approach

by
JAMES M. DOYLE
and
GEORGE H. GRIMES

The Scarecrow Press, Inc.

Metuchen, N.J.   1976

Library of Congress Cataloging in Publication Data

Doyle, James M   1944-
    Reference resources.

    Bibliography: p.
    Includes index.
    1. Reference services (Libraries) 2. Information
science. 3. Research. I. Grimes, George .H., joint
author. II. Title.
Z711.D65   025.5'2   76-7080
ISBN 0-8108-0928-1

CONTENTS

FIGURES

INTRODUCTION

Today's library user has a wealth of information resources available to him. Locating desired information and
using it effectively are not simple undertakings, however.
This is particularly true for the untrained user. Even when
aware of basic library resources, the user usually does not
know how to use them efficiently or how to relate them to
other reference resources.

It is the authors' belief that the user of library resources, whether untrained or an experienced librarian/in-
formation specialist, must possess an awareness of the theory
of how information is created and how it "flows" through the
various formats of print material found in most research libraries. Once aware of the "bibliographic chain" of formats
through which information flows over time, the user must become familiar with and use systematic procedures for identifying and locating desired information. The final element in
a successful information search is knowledge of general reference resources and of resources in the academic disciplines.

We hope that this book will assist all types of information searchers to: 1) understand the nature of reference
resources and the structure of their expression in various
print formats; 2) use a systematic approach to conducting resource searches; and 3) identify specific resources which will
meet their information needs.

The book is intended to be used by two basic audiences: 1) librarian/information specialists preparing for a
professional career; and 2) the average intelligent adult who
is pursuing an information need. The book is intended as a
"searcher's manual" in the second context.

We would like to thank those colleagues who agreed to
review and critique various parts of this book in its early
stages. We also appreciate the efforts and suggestions of
Lois Bailey of the University of Detroit Library and Jodi

Smith of the Wayne County Intermediate Schools who did such an excellent job of typing the manuscript.

We hope that you find our ideas and work of value. Indeed, we hope that you enjoy the systematic pursuit of knowledge as much as we have enjoyed developing the ideas contained herein for your consideration.

James M. Doyle
Public Services Librarian
Macomb Co. Community
  College
Warren, Mich.

George H. Grimes
Consultant, Learning Resources
Wayne County (Michigan)
Intermediate Schools

Part I

THE STRUCTURE AND IDENTIFICATION
OF REFERENCE RESOURCES

The Bibliographic Chain
-- Phases in the Bibliographic Chain
-- Links in the Chain
Human Resources
Institutional Resources
Work-in-Progress Reports
Unpublished Studies
Periodicals
Reports and Monographs
Indexing and Abstracting Services
Bibliographic Lists and Essays
Annual Reviews and State-of-the-Art Reports
Books
Encyclopedic Summaries

The Searching Process
-- The Searcher
The Librarian/Information Specialist
The Experienced Information Searcher
The Untrained Library User
-- Conducting the Search
General Considerations
A Model of the Searching Process
-- Steps in the Searching Process
Question Statement and Definition
Structuring the Search
Synthesis
Analysis
Decision Making
Evaluation of Effectiveness

THE BIBLIOGRAPHIC CHAIN

The process through which an item of information progresses as it moves from its creation within an individual's mind to its potential resting place within an encyclopedic summary of a given subject field has been characterized as the bibliographic chain (Doyle and Grimes). The progressive links in this chain are:

Information residing in human resources
Information being created by institutions
Work-in-progress documents
Unpublished studies
Periodicals
Reports and monographs
Indexing and abstracting services
Bibliographic lists and essays
Annual reviews and state-of-the-art reports
Books
Encyclopedic summaries.

Even the most cursory scanning of the above list reveals that the bibliographic chain, as its name indicates, is a chain of print information formats. The term format is used to describe the various physical packages which house information. Reference resources exist in print form, in the main, and most scholarly knowledge production is communicated through the printed page. Other informational formats include: films, recordings, television, multi-media packages, and museums and other institutionalized settings which house information of intellectual significance. The substance of these other media forms is normally identified, discussed, and analyzed in print, however. Print is the basic form of intellectual exploration and access, though not necessarily of intellectual content. The bibliographic chain accordingly deals with reference resources in terms of their natural occurrence in print.

Not all items of information complete the entire bibli-

ographic chain sequence. Many are subsumed under other
topics en route and disappear from view. Others are combined with related information and are thereby transformed in
substance or emphasis. Items which have the necessary validity, significance, uniqueness, and appeal travel the full
distance through the chain.

Progression through the bibliographic chain is tied to
time. An item of newly created information which is sufficiently useful moves chronologically from the status of a distinct idea through the other stages of the bibliographic chain
to its ultimate destination in the generalized knowledge of an
encyclopedic summary of a particular subject field.

In its initial concept a piece of information is perceived as a rather distinct entity whose full implications are
only partially realized, if at all. As this piece of information becomes progressively integrated with other new bits of
knowledge and with pre-existing knowledge, it loses its unique
identity and becomes a part of our intellectual fabric. It
may generate its own unique set of ideas, but it usually
emerges as another dimension or facet of some previously
existing concept. If this newly integrated bit of information
duplicates, but does not improve, the previously existing concept, it will, hopefully, sink into oblivion. This is, unfortunately, not always the case.

Phases in the Bibliographic Chain

Each stage in the bibliographic chain represents a
further integration of distinct information into the general
knowledge mass. There are three separate but interrelated
phases represented by the links in the chain.

Phase I includes packages of information only in the
most general sense. This phase includes:

> Human resources
> Institutional resources.

At this time the information basically resides within
the minds of people either individually (as with a researcher)
or in groups (as with the staff of a project). These resources
include the thoughts, observations, deductions, investigations,
assumptions, and unplanned discoveries of individuals.

Phase II includes materials in print form with intellectual content. Includes here are the formats of:

Work-in-progress documents
Unpublished studies
Periodical articles
Reports and monographs
Annual reviews and state-of-the art reports
Books
Encyclopedic summaries.

These formats contain information which has moved from the area of pure intellectual activity or working notes into some more formalized physical format.

Phase III includes printed materials which have no particular intellectual content of their own, but which help locate actual information. These are basically surrogate publications. Included are:

Indexing and abstracting services
Bibliographic lists and essays
Annual reviews and state-of-the-art reports.

Annual reviews and state-of-the-art reports may also provide some actual content in addition to performing identification functions and are, therefore, included in both Phases II and III.

An obvious discontinuity exists between the nature of Phases II and III. A strong argument can be mounted for the separation of Phase III into a parallel progression. The authors choose not to do this, however, as the basic logic of the bibliographic chain is the progression of an item of information through various informational formats sequenced according to time. The question of whether it is the substance of the idea itself or references to it which are being dealt with is an important, but subordinate, consideration. The critical question is, "How can an information seeker gain access to an idea of information pertinent to his or her needs and interests?" The chain as represented in Figure 1 is the most effective answer to this question in the authors' judgment.

The Links in the Chain

Let us now examine each link in the bibliographic

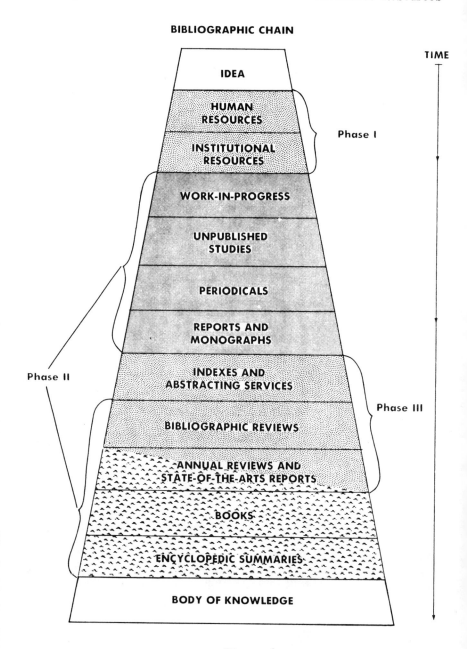

Figure 1

chain in more detail.

Human Resources. A human resource is an individual who can supply certain skills and competencies without necessarily speaking for any particular organizational structure. Generally, human resources are researchers, scholars, or consultants who might be connected with universities; research and development departments in business and industry; independent researchers and those involved formally or informally in conceptualizing and generating ideas; and local, state, and national government agencies addressing the concerns of the citizenry in general.

The "invisible college" is significant in idea generation and formulation. An idea seldom springs full blown from the mind of one person. Interaction with others in the same area of endeavor is a prime source of intellectual stimulation. Individuals also seek and utilize information for idea generation from the various formats included in the bibliographic chain.

Even though the invisible college acts as a stimulant and an arena for trying-out and revising ideas, the idea still must be retained within an individual for the nurturing and incubation necessary for fruitful emergence into the world of intellectual exploration.

Institutional Resources. Institutional resources are those formalized organizational structures to which an item of information or an idea moves once it has shown that it has the capability of standing on its own, apart from the human resource which generated it. There are two general subcategories of institutional resources--agencies and projects.

Agencies are organizations which have an ongoing administrative structure and staff, and both short- and long-range programs. The agency may have a profit or nonprofit orientation and single or varied interests. Its essential character is that it is intended to be an ongoing entity.

Projects, unlike agencies, can be identified by their relatively short and circumspect nature. They usually deal with a rather restricted focus and may be one aspect of a larger, more permanent organization or effort.

Work-in-Progress Documents. Work-in-progress refers to those resources which give access to the current work of researchers and scholars. This work could be at various

stages of development, but not to the point where it is ready
for publication within the next links in the chain. This type
of information often aids people working in parallel or com-
plementary areas, allows for interaction within the "invisible
college," and helps avoid unnecessary duplication of effort.
Work-in-progress documents are often in typescript form.

Unpublished Studies. Unpublished studies are research
materials that have reached a completed state but which are
not intended for formal publication, at least in their present
form. This category includes an organization's internally
produced reports, informally circulated items, graduate essays, theses, and doctoral dissertations.

Periodicals. Periodicals include magazines, journals,
newsletters, commercial loose-leaf services, and similar
serial items which appear at regular intervals. These publications contain articles of various lengths and levels of interest. Journals may publish lengthy and sophisticated articles
that are de facto reports. Magazines and newsletters may
publish only descriptions, abstracts, and condensations. The
range of content treatment in this category of information format is extremely varied. The common characteristic is the
periodic nature of the publications. Periodical articles usually appear simultaneously with unpublished materials or
shortly thereafter.

Reports and Monographs. Once unpublished studies
have been evaluated and revised, they are often formally published as reports or monographs. These are intended for
general, rather than informal circulation. They are frequently part of an irregular series published by professional associations, universities, commercial publishers, and research
and development agencies. Reports may be available on an
open access or restricted basis, depending on their nature,
content, and intent.

Indexing and Abstracting Services. Indexing and abstracting services are the first of the surrogate information
formats. They have no intellectual content of their own, but
are location tools which "stand in the stead of," and provide
access to, actual reference resources.

Indexes usually appear within a few months of the
serial literature that they control, but the time lag is greater for abstracting services. Abstracts must be prepared
after the item is read, a time-consuming process unless done

by the author or publisher at the outset. Indexes and abstracting services usually provide subject, author, and title access.

Bibliographic Lists and Essays. Bibliographic lists are bibliographies in a given field or on a given topic, usually annotated and selective. Bibliographies may be published separately or as a part of a larger work for reference purposes.

The bibliographic essay is a special type of bibliographic list which provides an overview of an area by synthesizing the content of the area in narrative form, and providing citations to the sources of the ideas or information provided. The bibliographic essay differs from annual reviews and state-of-the-art reports in that it may deal with a field or topic over time rather than during a restricted period. The main intent, however, is to lead to other reference resources.

Annual Reviews and State-of-the-Art Reports. These are surrogate publications which do have intellectual content. Their intent is to collect all current and pertinent published material (since the last review or report) in a given field or discipline, and synthesize it into a report on the major accomplishments, problems, and trends in that field for the period of time covered. Their purpose is to give an overview and citations for further reference and exploration. It is this second aspect which places them in the category of location tools. The first aspect provides some measure of intellectual content, though without benefit of the perspective and process of trial over time which results in the content of an encyclopedic summary.

Books. Books are usually a revised version of formal report literature which reflects further study, with additional background information and interpretation added. The time lag is generally greatest in the area of scholarly books on research topics. Books are the most frequently used of the reference resources because their major intent is to communicate something of importance to an audience of some size or to provide an in-depth comprehensive treatment of a topic of some significance.

Encyclopedic Summaries. This is the last major link in the bibliographic chain, and the one in which the time lag is greatest. Encyclopedic summaries are designed to give a

broad overview of a whole field.   Due to infrequent publication
and updating policies, in addition to the lead time involved in
their production, the content of encyclopedic summaries is
usually three or more years out of date at the time of publication.   This factor is not a critical one, however, since
only those items of tested significance should appear in an
encyclopedic summary.

THE SEARCHING PROCESS

Boswell once wrote that "knowledge is of two kinds: we know a subject ourselves, or we know where we can find information upon it" (Boswell, Vol. I, p. 558). The vast amount of technical information that has accumulated since Boswell's day almost precludes knowing a subject ourselves; the skill of finding information by oneself, therefore, is critical to functioning in modern society.

The intent of this book is to introduce a new and more practical method of locating reference resources.

The map is a good analogy to the operation of the literature searching process. In any attempt to locate a given place, a map is an essential asset. The map provides an approximation of the terrain separating the traveler and his goal, scaled down to a convenient size. With this tool the traveler can determine the sequence of moves necessary to reach the desired destination most economically.

The literature searching process, or the "documentary itinerary" as it has been called (Uytterschaut, p. 14), which we will now explore constitutes a map or a sequence of moves whereby the literature searcher may progress from an expressed need for information to the ultimate goal--the information itself.

The bibliographic chain discussed previously is a map (model) which provides a basic understanding of reference resources. Later the bibliographic chain will be incorporated into a practical guide, in flowchart form, to the searching of scholarly literature. Together, the concept of the bibliographic chain and the process flowchart will, it is hoped, provide an understandable and effective guide to the location of needed information.

The authors hope that this model and flowchart will serve two purposes. The first is to suggest an information

seeking procedure to the individual who is conducting a personal search for information with only incidental assistance
from trained library personnel.   The second purpose is to
provide what we believe to be a completely new approach to
the training of librarians and information specialists in reference bibliography.   Robert Taylor once advised library
schools to "... reexamine course content in reference work.
It is possible, for example, to orient these courses more
toward the dynamism of communication, i.e., [question] negotiation, rather than concentrating solely on the static content
of reference collections.... " (Taylor, p. 191).   The authors
hope that their model, in concert with the searching flow
diagram, will help move the library profession toward this
goal.

The Searcher

     The literature searcher may be an inexperienced be-
ginner working largely alone, an experienced scholar independently pursuing time-tested research strategies, or a highly trained librarian or information specialist working with
colleagues or subject area specialists.   Let us consider the
orientations of these varying types of reference resource
searchers.

     The Librarian/Information Specialist.   The ideal train-
ing of a librarian/information specialist includes both a thor-
ough grounding in the philosophical tenets of the profession
and the technical training and practice necessary to carry out
professional activities.   An area of academic expertise is also
desirable.   Technical preparation separates into two types of
training: one is that necessary to become a specialist in the
resources of the library/information field; the second is to
gain general intellectual control over the main information
points of entry of the major subject disciplines.   The preceding is based on Katz's comments on the implications of
reference work for librarians (Katz, p. 68).

     Another concern related to the librarian/information
specialist's effectiveness is his or her attitude toward reference work.   "William James has observed that '... the
deepest principle of human nature is the desire to be appre-
ciated.'   If every reference librarian would keep this thought
in mind, reference work would be considerably easier.   Re-
gardless of the type of question or the type of user, funda-
mentally the [reference] interview is an appreciation of man
and his behavior" (Katz, pp. 44-5).

The Experienced Information Searcher. The second major category of searcher is the experienced scholar who is competent to do in-depth and sophisticated reference resource searching in his or her own field of specialization. Most libraries, especially academic and special libraries, have patrons in this category. They are the "invisible" users who know what they want and generally how to obtain it. They are invisible to the librarian/information specialist because they normally act quite independently of the librarian. Additionally, the library professional is keyed, both by vocation and avocation, to aiding persons whose knowledge of access to reference resources is inadequate for their purposes.

In spite of the self-sufficiency of the experienced information searcher there are two ways in which the bibliographic chain concept and searching schematic may be helpful. These formulations:

--serve as a structure for the knowledgeable, but less efficient, searcher by providing an organizational pattern and list of resources which will reduce searching time considerably.

--provide the person skillful in searching the literature of a particular field with a guide when he or she is delving into an unfamiliar field's literature.

The Untrained Library User. Some writers feel that the psychological threat that a huge research library presents is more of an inhibiting factor to the uninitiated than the untrained user's lack of knowledge of library resources. "Perhaps the necessity for such psychological detective work [question negotiation] comes, in part, not so much from the patron's inability to express himself, as from his feeling that he is not really entitled to request specific information" (Schiller, p. 8).

Even when the inhibition problem is surmounted, however, it is still apparent that novice users have a significant task in interfacing their needs with the materials that are available in the libraries they have chosen (or are forced) to depend upon. In his paper on this subject, Robert Taylor identifies four levels of information need on the part of the user (Taylor, p. 182). These levels are:

--Visceral - When the user needs information but doesn't yet realize it.

--Conscious Need - When the user first realizes a
need for information and heads for the library.

--Formalized Need - When the user can intelligently
express the need (this stage is usually reached during the reference interview).

--Compromised Need - This occurs once the librarian/
information specialist has "renegotiated" the user's
expressed need, based on what is actually available.
At this point the user quite literally takes what he
can get (that is, what the librarian/information
specialist has convinced him that he really needs).

Taylor points out that "Question negotiation is a game
of chess where the librarian is at an advantage because he
knows the files. Really we redefine the search strategy"
(Taylor, p. 186).

In terms of how the user searches, Allen's research
with engineers indicates that the first criterion seems to be
accessability; that is, "What can I get with least effort?"
(Gerstberger and Allen). A preferred user's search pattern,
as described by Utterschaut (Utterschaut, p. 4), is to locate
the basic works of the leading authors in the subject field in
question, hoping to locate pretailored bibliographies quickly.
(An analysis of user information processing behavior is included in Part II of this book.)

Clearly then, a person's sophistication at reference
resource searching is dependent on training and experience.
Because of the wide variation in these factors, skill and di-
plomacy are required on the part of librarian/information
specialists during the user's initial contacts with the literature searching process.

Conducting the Search

General Considerations -- In pursuing the "documentary itinerary" outlined by the bibliographic chain, there are
some commonsense guidelines that should be kept in mind:

--Create an efficient and consistent system of notetaking. Such a system will not only prevent the
recording of useless information, but guard against
the omission of needed information as well. Noth-
ing is more frustrating and annoying than a frantic
last-minute search for missing volume and page
numbers, full author names, and so on.

--Allow sufficient time for the search, based on the depth and comprehensiveness of the information desired. Careful question definition should provide an idea of the time needed to complete the search.

--Scan the reference resources available first, then proceed with the detailed search. The greater the bulk of information available, the more selective the search should be.

--Don't select an information source because of its length rather than its worth. There is rarely a correlation between quantity and quality in research literature.

--Don't emphasize an author because of his frequency of publication rather than the depth of his research.

--Remember that all search leads cannot be productive. Recognize a dead end situation when it exists and move to a different approach.

The above is based in part on Katz's list of reasons for search failures (Katz, p. 68-71). If these items are kept in mind, the searcher's trip through the research literature should be considerably easier.

Before proceeding to consideration of a model of the searching process, some brief comments concerning major sources of information available in the average library may be helpful. Most research libraries contain three general types of information resources:

General Circulating Materials. An adequate catalog of these materials is normally available. This collection is the strong point of the typical library.

Specific Reference Works. Included here are specialized indexes, bibliographies, handbooks, and other items usually found in a well-stocked reference room. The card catalog does not usually give good access to these materials. The late Millicent Palmer, in an essay on library instruction, demolished the "myth of the card catalog" when she pointed out that finding reference works in the subject catalog "is merely a gamble, even with inside tips provided by cross-references and/or the Library of Congress list of subject headings, which one wins against high odds. Ironically, an area of its greatest unreliability is in its subject coverage of bibliographic systems, most of them scholar produced.... Even to an experienced searcher, the card catalog cannot reveal these search and evaluation systems nor their relationships" (Palmer, p. 9).

It is necessary to pool the knowledge of the user, the subject area specialist, and the librarian/ information specialist concerning the resources of the field in question to gain complete access to subject area reference resources.

Specialized Collections. Federal, state, and local documents; information and pamphlet files; and archives are examples of this type of material. Specialized collections are normally poorly indexed in the card catalog. Access by broad category or specific item are most productive.

A Model of the Searching Process. Conducting a search of information from reference resources is basically an exercise in the application of practical logic. The information searching procedure flows in an orderly sequence which includes these steps:

1. Determination that a need for information exists
2. Statement of the question in its initial form
3. Delimitation and redefinition of the question
4. Statement of the redefined question
5. Structuring the search
6. Selecting most suitable information sources
7. Analyzing information sources selected
8. Obtaining additional information if necessary
9. Synthesizing information
10. Analyzing information
11. Decision making
12. Evaluation of the effectiveness of the search.

The flow diagram (Figure 2) illustrates the steps in the searching procedure. The steps listed above are keyed to the diagram by index number.

Steps in the Searching Process

Question Statement and Definition. The question

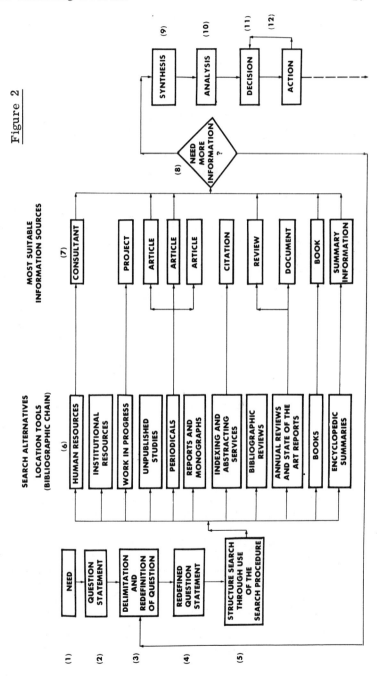

Figure 2

INFORMATION SEARCHING PROCESS

statement and definition phase of the search includes three
steps:

> Initial Question Statement
> Delimitation and Redefinition of the Question
> Redefined Question Statement.

One of the most important activities in the searching
process is the reference interview. As Katz (p. 46) points
out, the reference interview consists of two parts: question
negotiation and formulating the literature searching strategy.
The searching strategy will be dealt with in the next part of
this discussion.

Defining the reference question, or the process of
question negotiation, is a critical factor in the searching
process whether the user does it for himself (introspective-
ly) or whether it is done through a reference interview with
a librarian/information specialist.   In either case the questions and steps are essentially the same.   This is true of
simple "ready reference" or detailed research questions.
"The essential difference is not a matter of technique, but
of depth of knowledge, judgement, and evaluation" (Katz,
p. 66).

Taube (p. 90) suggests three types of questions a
searcher may want to ask when seeking information:

> --Index question ("What documents are available on a
>   topic?")
> --Content question ("What subjects are covered in the
>   documents?")
> --Association questions ("What other topics are rele-
>   vant to the subject under research?").

Within this context a conscientious effort to define a
reference question should involve the following:

> Initial Question Statement. -- A written statement of
> the question should be made.   This statement should
> be rewritten until it is clean and succinct in relation
> to the need being satisfied and the area of investiga-
> tion dealt with.   It is a good practice to make a sep-
> arate list of key terms which are descriptive of the
> content of the question.   The question and key terms
> should be compared to check their compatibility, and
> appropriate adjustment made in the question statement
> as indicated.

Delineation and Redefinition of the Question -- Question delimitation and redefinition can be accomplished through asking these questions:

--What is being sought? Specifically, what is the topic? What keywords are descriptive of the information desired?

--What types of information resources are desired? Human resources? Institutional resources? Print materials? What bibliographic format? Media materials?

--What relevant information is already available?

--What is the level of interest? Practical? Theoretical? An overview? An in-depth treatment?

--What type of person needs the information? Student? Practitioner? Layman?

--What time limits are appropriate in regard to the age of the information? Current or retrospective information? If retrospective, how far back? How immediate is the need for this information?

--What physical formats will be most convenient? The original document? Duplicated copies of a part of the document? Microfilm copy? Media formats such as film or an audio recording?

--What is the scope of the information sought? An overview of all relevant resources? Referral to selected resources? A synthesis of relevant information? An in-depth analysis of relevant information?

--What other limitations are there? Geographic location of the desired resources? Financial limitations? Foreign language limitations?

--How will the resulting information be applied? Scholarly inquiry? Administrative decision-making? Research and development activities? Personal exploration? To fulfill academic requirements? Professional growth?

Redefined Question Statement. -- In order to produce a redefined statement of the question, the substance of the question should be discussed with either a person knowledgeable in the area under consideration, a librarian/information specialist, or preferably both. The question should be carefully rewritten following application of the questions listed above and interpersonal exchange. A standard index in the subject area under consideration should be consulted and indexing terms descriptive of the content of the question should be selected and listed. If a thesaurus of the technical language of the subject area being dealt with is available, the key descriptive terms should be selected from that source. At this point the "art" of reference work comes into play. The searcher must develop a "feeling" for the initial question before it can be translated into specific searching terminology. In many cases this terminology is not obvious in the initial question statement.

A logical procedure which can be employed to structure a search from key descriptive terms is Boolean algebra. Boolean algebra deals with the formal relationships and possible logical combinations of searching terms. In this procedure, searching terms are divided into classes of like and dissimilar items. The relationships between these items (searching terms) can then be viewed as to their separateness, intersection, overlap, and concentric configurations. The operations involved in these relationships are termed OR (logical sum) or AND (logical product) operations. An example of an OR operation is the relationship of special education to the general student population. Special education students are a particular class of student. An AND operation would be involved in the overlap between aspects of two different classes such as the hard-of-hearing and the field of education, as illustrated by a question dealing with education of the hard-of-hearing. Boolean algebra is particularly useful because it provides a formal context for structuring information searches and because it deals with yes/no decisions which lend themselves particularly well to computer programming technology (Lancaster, p. 21)

The process outlined above may seem to be a laborious and tedious one. The effort put into question definition at this point is usually energy well spent, however. A clear idea of the goal in mind is the most critical ingredient in effectively reaching the anticipated destination.

Structuring the Search. Structuring the search involves:

> Selecting most suitable information sources
> Analyzing selected information sources
> Obtaining additional information if necessary.

The starting point for structuring the information
search is the redefined question statement and associated
descriptive terms.   If the descriptive terms are selected
from a standard indexing source or thesaurus for the subject
area under consideration, as suggested previously, it is but
a short step to identifying potentially valuable information
sources.

1.   Selecting most suitable information sources. --
The next necessary ingredient in structuring the search is an
authoritative and descriptive list of reference resources in
the area under consideration.   The Discipline resource packages found in Part III of this book constitute one such list.

2.   Analyzing selected information sources. -- A selection should be made of promising reference resources and
a systematic analysis of these resources carried out.   It
should be emphasized that Phase III resources are an excellent starting point for a search since the intent of these items
is to identify information in other sources.
A very useful device to assist in the search, as well
as to provide a record of the search itself, is the Search
Procedure Form.   An example of one such form for the area
of education is shown as part of Figure 2.   Prime searching
prospects can be checked on the form and then marked off
as they are actually consulted.   Notes can be entered on the
form regarding the value of particular resources.
The information sources identified should be consulted
and appropriate notes taken.   Keep in mind the cautions
listed at the beginning of this section regarding notetaking and
other considerations related to the searching process.

3.   Obtaining additional information if necessary. --
If sufficient or relevant information is not obtained in the
first search attempt, repeat the process on a broader scale.
At this point in the process it is wise to consult a librarian/
information specialist or person knowledgeable (human resource) in the subject area being dealt with.
In the event that sufficient information is not obtained
after the attempt to identify additional information, return to
the original question statement to see if it can be delimited,
redefined, or interpreted in a more productive manner.

Synthesizing Information.   Synthesizing information is
a personal process and the approach used can vary greatly
according to the intellectual style of the person carrying out
the search.   Synthesis by its very nature requires the appli-

cation of human intellect to the myriad items of information
gathered during the searching process.

The two qualities which an effective synthesis of information should possess are: 1) a distillation of the substance of knowledge related to the question at hand; and
2) citations for the sources from which this information is
obtained.   An excellent example of a synthesizing procedure
is the bibliographic essay, discussed in the earlier section
on the Bibliographic Chain.

Analyzing Information.   Information analysis is also
a personal intellectual activity.   It is basically an attempt
to draw objective conclusions from the information gathered
and synthesized.   One straightforward method of analyzing
information is to make a list of the conclusions or implications pointed out by the synthesis.   Another is to mark each
section of the synthesis which relates to a specific aspect of
the redefined question.   Analysis may be a purely intellectual
activity within the mind of one person or through interaction
with others.

The end product of the analytical process should be a
set of conclusions which lead to effective decision making in
relation to the originally posed question.   In many cases the
list of conclusions itself may be sufficient to complete the
search procedure.

Decision-Making.   Not all reference resource searches
culminate in a decision.   Many trivial or speculative questions simply require the location of specific facts or items.
In such cases, the searching process ends with the analysis
step.

Other questions, particularly those of an administrative or research and development nature, require decisions.
The nature of these decisions depends on the problem and
circumstances at hand, but in all cases there should be a
direct connection between the decisions made and the information gleaned from reference resources through the systematic
search process carried out.

Evaluating.   The ultimate evaluation of the effectiveness of a reference resource search is the usefulness of the
information found to the user's process of decision-making.
Since evaluation involves the measurement of the degrees of
success in meeting stated goals, a simple evaluation proce-

dure is to compare the type, quantity, and quality of information obtained with the intent of the question originally posed.
A longer-range, and much more difficult, task is to determine
the ultimate impact of the information on resolution of the
user's original need.   This is a most difficult process since
information is usually sought to help make decisions but is
not the prime factor in decision-making in many instances.

    If the original question posed is quantitative, or re-
lates to a specific item sought, the evaluation of the effectiveness of the search is simply whether the date, fact, answer,
quotation or other item of information was located and veri-
fied.

RESOURCE USE

The resource use process is a set of circumstances by which the information user realizes his need, seeks information, assimilates it, puts it to use and evaluates the effectiveness of that use. Information has been characterized as "... facts or figures ready for communication or use ... knowledge is an organized body of information; wisdom implies knowledge with information so thoroughly assimilated as to have produced sagacity, judgement and insight" (Kent, p. 20). Reference resources are those informational materials which contain knowledge or surrogate references to it.

In this section we examine the concepts underlying the field of resource use as well as the specific aspects of both personal and interpersonal information processing. A key concept in resource utilization, linkage, is discussed in detail.

A major source of ideas related to the use of information and knowledge is user studies. As Clemens has pointed out, "The final system function is user services ... an information system that does not relate closely to user requirements and user characteristics will be of little use and is not worth the money required to support it. It is necessary, therefore, that the system receive continuous feedback from the user on how well he's satisfied with the services provided, whether he feels he needs more information, and a variety of other questions" (Clemens, p. 15). The needs of the user are the dominant consideration in the design of information services. Despite this fact, there is still no effective, systematic method of identifying these needs. As Ely indicates, "Most studies on information needs do not distinguish among need, demand, or use." He further states that, "of the many studies that have attempted to identify user information needs, none has probed sufficiently to yield anything more than statements of 'nice to know' information and information seeking behaviors" (Ely, p. 15).

While Ely's comments are accurate as a generalization, some good users studies have appeared in the literature. Despite the general dearth of acceptable studies we will attempt to take an organized look at user characteristics as revealed by the best of the present studies available because of the central role of user needs in the resource use process. If user needs cannot be satisfied, the most carefully designed information system is for naught.

Basic Concepts in Resource Use

Most of the current systematic approaches to developing models of the resource use process are based on work done in science and technology, particularly within the field of engineering.

The classic model of the communications process is the "sender-channel-receiver" concept. A generalized description of this process is provided by Shannon. Shannon's model (Figure 3) can be applied to electrical, biological, psychological, and social interaction and, therefore, to the transfer of information and knowledge (Shannon and Weaver).

The activity of the transmitter in Shannon's model is usually referred to as encoding, and that of the receiver, decoding. Anything which interferes with transmission of the message is termed noise.

Ronald Havelock and his associates have produced the most comprehensive analysis to date of the literature on the dissemination and use of resources (Havelock). His analysis views resource use as a communications system. For the sake of consistency and cohesiveness we shall generally follow the pattern suggested by Havelock in exploring the field of resource utilization under the basic concepts of:

> System
> Message
> Barrier
> Input, Output, Throughput, and Feedback
>
> ... and the supplementary concepts of:
> Interface
> Channel and Medium
> Linkage
> Chain
> Network.

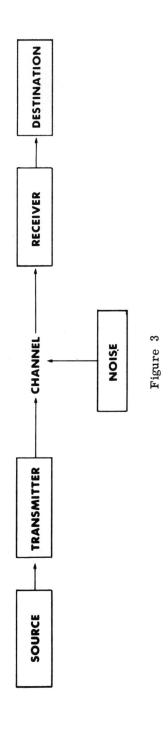

Figure 3

System. -- A system is a set of components which
act upon one another to bring about a state of balance, inter-
dependence, or wholeness. The important thing to remember
is that the parts of the system are in, or seek, balance.
The nature of the balance may vary greatly. The system
may be "loosely structured" or "tightly structured," or particular aspects of the system may be thus characterized.
Systems can also be described as stable or unstable, according to the dynamic properties of their parts. Unpredictable
components may also be an aspect of a system. When unpredictable components are not present the system is incom-
plete. For example, a motor vehicle can "exist" without
gasoline or a driver, but it cannot function unless these aspects are present in the system. The degree of interde-
pendence existing among system parts can be referred to as
the integrity of the system.

A distinction should be made between "static" and "dynamic" systems. In static systems components exist in a
more or less fixed relationship to each other. A dynamic
system's parts act upon one another. Examples of a static
system are: pieces of a pie, atoms that form a molecule,
a jig-saw puzzle. The pieces of a dynamic system push and
shove at each other. They try to force changes in their re-
lative positions, with the resulting pattern of action and reaction creating a balance of forces. Examples of dynamic
systems are: the internal structure of the atom, the solar
system, any circulation system, and a dialogue between people. Most systems have both static and dynamic properties.

Message. -- The message is the dynamic property of
the system. Within dynamic systems there must always be
at least two messages, which could be termed the "action"
and "reaction" messages. The reaction message returns the
system to a balanced state. When action and reaction messages occur in a routine and regular cycle, the system is
in a state of "dynamic equilibrium." New messages will up-
set the equilibrium and force a change in a static system.
Dynamic systems, however, may need a continuous input of
new messages to maintain their equilibrium.

Barrier. -- The static property of a system is the
barrier. The barrier guards the system's integrity and defines the "inside" and "outside" of the system. The barrier
stops messages. It keeps them inside or it keeps them outside. Most barriers, however, are permeable; that is, they
allow some messages to go through.

Input, Output, Throughput, and Feedback. -- Most
systems which occur in the real world are open systems,
that is, they receive incoming messages and transmit messages to the outside world.   Messages incoming through the
system barrier are termed input.   Messages leaving the system are termed output.

Messages which occur within the system are termed
throughput.   Throughput can involve a rather complex sequence of messages within a single system or within sub-systems.

When an output message acts in such a way that it
creates a new message having impact on the system, this is
called feedback.   Feedback is any input message which is
directly and casually related to the system's own output.   An
example of feedback is the action of a thermostat.   When the
temperature in a room drops, the thermostat senses the de-
crease and activates the house heating system.   When the
temperature in the house rises as a result of this action, the
thermostat then reacts to the new message and turns off the
heat.

Interface. -- Interface is a neutral term describing a
relationship between two systems or subsystems.   It indicates
that there is a relationship of some sort and carries no connotation of barrier, merger, or other specific state.   It is
the meeting place of two systems.   If two systems are sep-
arated by a barrier, then the barrier is the interface; if they
are merged, the point of merger is the interface.   An information user and resource person addressing a common concern
represents an interface situation.

Channel and Medium. -- A channel is the point at
which a barrier is permeable.   If a message passes from
system A to system B, the region between A and B through
which the message passes is the channel.   A channel is in
reality a specific type of interface.   A channel may also be
a third intervening system or series of intervening systems
(as in the case of nerve cells acting between sense receptors
and the muscles of the human body).

Medium is essentially synonymous with channel and is
an alternate term used in some contexts.   The term medium
does carry the connotation of a channel having some character
of its own which may partially shape the message (e. g.,
print, audio, or visual media).

Linkage. -- Linkage is a term used to indicate that
two systems are connected by messages so as to form a
greater system.   If the barriers between the two systems
are permeable enough, messages can flow out of each to the
other.   Response messages (feedback) can also flow into each
system from the other, so that a link or state of linkage has
been created between them.   The basic role of a librarian/
information specialist is that of a "knowledge linker."

The term linkage suggests a pattern of interaction
between two systems rather than a single exchange of messages.   The human interaction inherent in the statement and
definition of an information need, as discussed earlier, is a
good example of a linking situation.

Chain. -- A chain simply carries the metaphor of the
link one step further.   It postulates a "chain of knowledge"
flow of information.   It includes messages flowing from information resources to the user, as well as feedback from
the user to the resources.   The chain is composed of a series of links between individual systems.

Network. -- In reality the flow of knowledge is a very
complex situation.   There are actually many chains and links
which cross each other, run parallel to each other, and are
interconnected.   This complex interweaving is termed a network.

Personal Information Processing

Shannon's generalized model of the communications
process (discussed in the previous section) is too simplistic
to account for the complexities of human communication.   A
person performs many communications functions almost simultaneously.   He may be both a transmitter and receiver
of messages at any given time.   A further elaboration of
Shannon's model is necessary, therefore, to take into consideration the multiple aspects of human communications.
Osgood has devised such a model which proceeds from Shannon's formulation.

The Osgood Communications Unit (Figure 4) depicts
the individual as a transceiver, thus incorporating in one
unit the ability to be both a source and destination of messages (Osgood, p. 1).

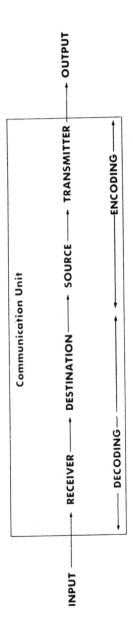

Figure 4

The Osgood Communications Unit describes the functions basic to personal information processing. In psychological language the term input in the Osgood model means "stimulus," receiver becomes "reception" and "perception," destination and source are "cognition," transmitter is "motor organization and sequencing," and output is "response." Osgood makes the point that engineering models such as Shannon's do not take into consideration the meaning of the signal (message), a critical observation in relation to resource use.

In addition to the functions depicted in the Osgood model, two other psychological concepts which are critical to personal information processing are need and behavior.

Need. -- Need connotes man's motivations, aspirations, and feelings of want. Individual human needs are the "why" of resource use. Needs are significant messages from the human system. They create instability within the person and lead to a cycle of behavior which must ultimately correct this instability. This cycle alternates between arousal and satisfaction.

Behavior. -- Like need, behavior forms a subsystem within the individual. The behavioral subsystem also follows an alternating pattern, oscillating between search and consumption. Search activities "... relate to the struggle by the organism to find problem solutions, whether they be in the form of food, shelter, clothing, comfort, praise, facts, formulae or scientific knowledge" (Havelock, ch. 2, p. 12). The closing stage of the search activity is consumption. Representative consumption activities are eating, enjoying, accepting, absorbing and learning.

The need (arousal/satisfaction) cycle and the behavior (search/consumption) cycle are essential to the maintenance of life itself. The question of an effective information searching process which we are addressing in this book is merely a specific expression of these basic aspects of the human condition.

Information Seeking and Use. -- In the real world the need and behavior cycles are very dependent upon each other. They are open subsystems which together form a greater system. The components of this larger system in sequence are: 1) arousal, 2) problem awareness, 3) searching, 4) consumption, 5) solution, and 6) satisfaction. Comparing this sequence with that of the information searching procedure discussed previously we find:

Human Behavior	Information Seeking Process
1. Arousal (need)	Awareness of need
2. Problem awareness	Question statement and definition
3. Searching (behavior)	Structuring and conducting the Search
4. Consumption (behavior)	Synthesis and analysis
5. Solution	Decision-making
6. Satisfaction (need)	Evaluation of results

As with most communication systems, there is danger of impeded message flow due to internal barriers present in the above sequence. A main point of possible impedance lies in the translation of the aroused need (Step 1) into an operational problem statement (Step 2). Similar dangers occur between the other stages of the sequence. If the solution resulting from the process has suffered from insufficient or interrupted information flow, the cycle can be repeated with the application of more vigor and urgency at the points of difficulty.

Havelock states that, "Although all of these internal psychological issues are important, the focal issue for the student of dissemination and utilization is the search process, for it is through the search process that new knowledge is brought to bear on real life problems" (Havelock, ch. 2, p. 14).

There are two types of search processes, internal and external. In the internal search process the individual acts as a self-sufficient closed system. He contains within his own memory all of the facts necessary to arrive at a solution to the problem and, therefore, has no need to seek outside knowledge or resources. In the external search process, on the other hand, memory search alone is not sufficient and the user is forced to turn to the outside world for help. He must then make contact with other resource systems. In an external search a message must be created which, when transmitted, will efficiently communicate the user's need to others. The receipt of this information by others (i. e., information specialists) will allow them to search out information relevant to the user's stated need.

Interpersonal Information Processing

Since human communication is a social activity, any

adequate model of it must include at least two of Osgood's
Communication Units, a source unit (sender) and a destination unit (receiver) (Figure 5).   A message connects these
two units.   Messages are of two general types: immediate
(e.g. face-to-face conversation) or mediated (e.g. written,
audio, visual).

The first two links in the bibliographic chain are immediate sources of information (human and institutional resources); the rest of the links in the chain are mediated
formats (mainly print).

Resource use is an interpersonal process; therefore,
an understanding of the nature of senders and receivers is
necessary.   Carrying the concepts of need and behavior into
the interpersonal communications process, the receiver is
analogous to need and the sender to behavior.   The same
basic steps which take place within an individual as he satis-
fies an internal need for information must also take place
when the needs of a receiver are satisfied with the assistance
of a sender.   In each case the same dangers of impediments
to efficient knowledge flow are present.   The interpersonal
process is, however, much more complex since there are
two sub-systems and sets of messages to be coordinated.

The flowchart of interpersonal information processing
provided next (Figure 6) illustrates how the functions of an
external information search are related between the user (receiver) and resource person (sender).

This rather idealistic view of the user/resource person linkage does not include an indication of the variety and
types of impediments which may occur in the resource use
process.

Both direct and indirect factors impede the flow of information in interpersonal linkage.

Indirect Influences. -- Indirect influences on interpersonal information processing are those factors which predis-
pose an individual to be amenable to the influence of others.
Although usually beyond the control of the resource person,
indirect influences are critical aspects of any interpersonal
relationship.   Significant influences of this type are:

                Participation
                Cohesiveness   (cont'd on p. 39)

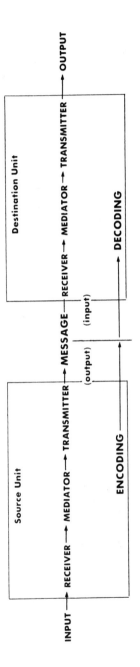

Figure 5

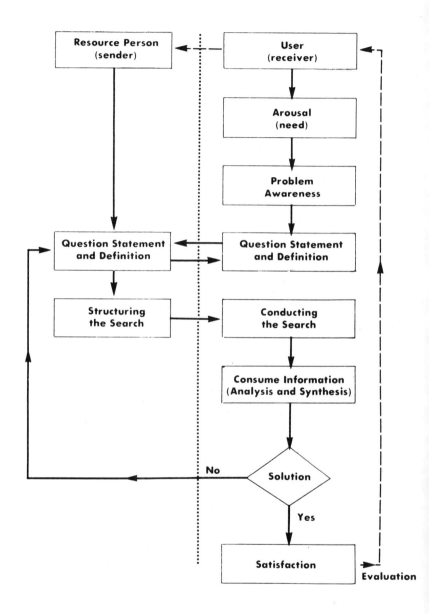

Figure 6

Group Resistance
Conformity and Social Support
Social Interaction
Similarity of Attitudes
Status
Community and Family Norms.

Participation. -- Participation through active involvement of individuals affected by the results of the decision-
making process is a powerful influence on creating acceptance
of new ideas and change.

Cohesiveness. -- Research on cohesiveness indicates
that individuals who are strongly attached to other members
of the group will be greatly influenced by the norms of the
group. If the norms of the group are similar to the direction of the influence being exerted, the likelihood of acceptance is very great. If, on the other hand, the direction of
attempted influence is different from group norms, the group
and individuals within the group will resist the change.

Group Resistance. -- The counterpart of group cohesiveness is group resistance. With proper presentation of
ideas, group resistance can be overcome. The usual cohesiveness and norms of a group can be used to sensitize individuals to an idea that they would normally resist. Group
discussion and involvement in decision-making are important
factors in this process. Other factors which seem to be
significant in influencing action in the face of group resistance are: a) peer support for acceptance of outside resources; b) public commitment to the decision involved; c)
the consensus of the group as perceived by the individual;
and d) the development of new norms while maintaining group
cohesiveness. To effectively overcome resistance, the norms
and cohesiveness of the group must be acceptable; and discussion, involvement, and other methods should be used to promote acceptance of the idea.

Conformity and Social Support. -- Conformity and
social support are closely related to the cohesive attraction
that one group member has for another. Where there is
moderate group acceptance there will be a greater likelihood
that individuals will accept a new idea. Some group members may publicly accept an idea under these circumstances,
however, while privately disagreeing with it. Individuals
who are highly acceptable to the group tend to be more open
about disagreement with new ideas and are likely to deviate

from group norms. Peer support for a particular approach
increases the probability that the approach will be used. Additionally, under conditions of crisis, change can be made
and accepted which would be rejected under other circumstances.

Social Interaction. -- Social interaction can have a
great effect on the adoption of new ideas, and, in fact, is
probably the most important influence on the adoption of in-
novative concepts and behaviors. A major school of thought
about the overall process of accepting new ideas revolves
around the concept of social interaction. Termed the Social
Interaction Perspective or "agricultural model" of change, it
involves the steps of: a) awareness of the innovation; b) interest in finding more information; c) evaluation of the information found; d) trial of the ideas involved; and e) adoption
or rejection of the procedure (Rogers). Interpersonal interaction is the critical element in this overall process. Studies
have shown that ideas are adopted by those who have close
affiliations with others interested in the same new idea, depending on the degree of interpersonal support that they receive.

Similarity of Attitudes. -- Similar background is a
key factor in promoting sensitivity to and openness with others. Individuals who have similar attitudes on a number of
issues have a strong tendency to like each other and interact
more. They will also try to resolve serious disagreements
that may occur. Also, individuals who interact with each
other and have similar attitudes are more open to influence
by others.

Status. -- Individuals seek out others with status
levels similar to their own. Studies of opinion leaders indicate that personal influence and communication on a wide
variety of matters are generally limited to individuals of
about the same status level. Moreover, as status differences
become greater, the tendency to stay within one's own status
level becomes stronger. In cases of influence across status
lines, a higher status person is much more likely to influence
a lower status person than vice versa, unless the higher status person is perceived as trying to exert undue influence.
In the latter situation the lower status person may resist the
attempt at influencing.

Community and Family Norms. -- The community and
family affect the adoption of new ideas. Community norms

can be characterized as falling along a traditionalism-to-modernism continuum. Acceptance of "modern" norms permits people to make decisions from a wide variety of choices. "Traditional" norms severely limit the freedom of the individual to make independent decisions because only a restricted number of alternatives is available.

The individual's family is also a major influence in acceptance of ideas. Family members serve as reference points, consultants, information screeners, links to new knowledge, sources of support in tasks to be done, and decision-makers in the adoption of new practices.

Direct Influences. -- Direct influences are those interpersonal influences that directly affect the knowledge utilization process. Major direct influences are:

Credibility
Legitimacy of Role
Role Perception and Definition
Language
Being out of Phase
Feedback.

Credibility. -- Credibility is the extent to which a sender is perceived as a reliable and believable source of information by the receiver. When a sender is considered to have status and is trustworthy there is a strong tendency to change attitudes in accordance with the attitudes of the source.

Credibility can be developed as a result of the receiver's perception of the sender's intentions. A receiver who is in an ongoing linkage situation with a sender will put much more trust in the information and advice provided by the sender.

Legitimacy of Role. -- The extent to which a general class of individuals is perceived as being helpful, knowledgeable, and creditable is an important factor in trusting their advice and judgment. The outstanding example of perceived legitimacy of role is the medical doctor. Doctors are considered to be expert and valuable until clearly proven otherwise, simply on·the basis of the status of their position.

Role Perception and Definition. -- The "user" determines the way in which the sender and receiver are perceived.

In order to fulfill either of these roles adequately, individuals must be able to see themselves as being resource persons or users. For example, if individuals do not see themselves as users they may see no need for outside resources.

Language. -- A sender and receiver may simply be speaking different languages, literally or figuratively. For example, the sender's message may be loaded with technical terminology which is unfamiliar to the user, or may be in a foreign tongue.

Being out of Phase. -- It is possible that the sender may be giving a solution to a problem before the receiver has fully phrased his problem; or the sender may not have an answer available to the receiver's concerns.

Persons learn of others' expectations and acceptance from the ways in which others behave toward them. If these perceptions of expectations are faulty, a breakdown in communication can occur.

Feedback. -- Feedback is critical to a person's capacity to judge the effect of his or her own action. It is the compass which keeps the resource person on course, or gives the clues to chart a more productive course if need be.

There are two types of feedback: 1) task-environment rewards, and 2) interpersonal rewards. Task environment rewards are feedback from the general environment and involve a time delay. Interpersonal rewards are feedback from fellow group members and are usually immediate. Because interpersonal rewards are essentially immediate, they have the greatest impact on performance. Often in the resource use process, however, the time-lag between a decision to adopt a procedure based on available information and the realization of results from the decision occurs considerably later.

Feedback comes quicker to the resource person than to the user. The resource person may get immediate interpersonal feedback from the user on his performance, but the user may have to wait a significant period of time to determine whether the resource person's input has been helpful in solving his problem.

Linkage. -- As indicated earlier, linkage means that two systems are connected to form a greater system. The

interrelationship of the resource person and user is an example of linkage. Key aspects of linkage are that:

1. The user must be meaningfully related to outside
    resources, and must interact with the outside re-
    source system in such a way that he will get back
    something that will help him find a solution to his
    problem.

2. The user must enter into a reciprocal relationship
    with the resource system. To completely under-
    stand the user's need, the resource system must
    be able to "get inside of" this need and to simu-
    late it.

3. The resource person must be able to draw upon
    remote resources if necessary. He must be able
    to communicate the user's need to others who are
    also resources themselves.

Linkage is a complex process, and one with many
subtle nuances. It is the basic mechanism which connects
the librarian/information specialist and the user. For this
reason it is central to our consideration of the resource use
process.

USER CHARACTERISTICS

User needs and characteristics should be the basic consideration in the design, development, and operation of information systems. Most studies of information needs are quite weak, however, and yield little more than statements of "nice to know" information. Despite the general dearth of acceptable studies, there are some fine efforts in the examination of user needs and characteristics. We shall consider five of the most productive studies and projects. They are:

> Information Requirements of the Social Sciences (INFROSS) Project (Bath University Library Group, England)

> Center for Research in Scientific Communication (Johns Hopkins University)

> Project on Scientific Information Exchange in Psychology (American Psychological Association)

> Research Program on Organization and Management of Research and Development (Massachusetts Institute of Technology)

> Syracuse University Psychological Abstracts Retrieval Service (SUPARS).

As indicated by their titles, most of these projects deal with information use in the sciences and technology. One should be cautious, therefore, in directly transferring the results of these studies and projects to specific situations in other fields. Generalizations about the character of information needs and use patterns can however, be made.

A prime source of further information on user needs and characteristics is the Annual Review of Information Science and Technology (Cuadra); the chapter on "Information Needs and Uses" in particular.

Information Requirements of the Social
Sciences (INFROSS) Project

This project is operated by the Bath University Library Group in England. Its prime focus is on the needs and uses of reference resources among social scientists (Line).

A questionnaire was the primary information gathering technique of the INFROSS study. It was circulated to a sample drawn from all social science researchers in England. The resulting data showed that:

--periodicals and monographs were used the most by British social scientists, followed by government documents, proceedings, research reports, and computer print-outs.

--colleagues and experts in the field external to the researcher's institution were the most used informal channels.

--bibliographies and references in books and journals were the most used methods for locating references, followed by consultants, abstracts or indices, and colleagues within the researcher's institution. There was very little use of library catalogs.

--personal collections of books are directly related to the use of libraries. Those with the smallest collections are the least likely to use formal methods of obtaining references. Those who own the most volumes are the heaviest users of libraries. (Apparently people tend either to buy books and use libraries or not to do either one.)

--older and more experienced researchers tend to use the library less than others. Older respondents are also more tolerant of library inadequacy.

--researchers wanting methodological and conceptual information are more easily satisfied, whereas those wanting historical and descriptive information are least likely to find library collections adequate.

--abstracting and indexing periodicals are the most popular method of keeping current. The most

common method of keeping track of currently published materials and research-in-progress is through
personal contacts.

--very few researchers delegate the searching process
to others, but older respondents were more likely
to do so.   Researchers in non-university settings
delegated much more searching than did those at
universities.   Retrospective searching is delegated
more than current searching.

Center for Research in Scientific Communication

Several significant studies of communication within the
scientific community have been done by Johns Hopkins University.   The activities of the Johns Hopkins Center for Research
in Scientific Communication address many of the same questions in the same way as the Project on Scientific Information
Exchange in Psychology of the American Psychological Association (discussed next).   The APA studies are of earlier
origin.

An example of the parallel effort of the Johns Hopkins
and APA programs is the investigation of communications
flow at the Eighteenth International Congress of Psychology.
The body of the Johns Hopkins and APA reports is identical,
although some of the conclusions and recommendations differ
in emphasis.   The Johns Hopkins' report also includes a
study of the Sixth World Congress of Sociology.   Results of
the Johns Hopkins' study indicate that:

--while a substantial proportion of the papers at both
meetings were reviews or syntheses of studies,
there was a tendency for the reviews to contain
more current material than is found in reports of
single studies and experiments.   (Apparently a review author is willing to add material that might
be too premature or speculative to stand by itself.)

--authors were the primary beneficiaries of interaction at the two congresses.

--presentation at an international meeting has greater
effect on an author's work than is true of presentation and interaction at a national meeting.

--an important function of international meetings is

that of developing and extending informal communication networks on a worldwide basis.

One of the great values of the Johns Hopkins studies
is to demonstrate the differences in communication needs that
exist among disciplines.   These studies show that:

--one-third of the authors at the Sixth World Congress
of Sociology planned final publication in book form,
while approximately one-fifth of the authors at the
Eighteenth International Congress of Psychology
planned such publication.

--social scientists are less likely than natural scientists to disseminate their work informally or at
meetings prior to publication.

--physical scientists seem to do the most intensive
dissemination of information in the shortest period
of time and in the most effective manner for assimilation.

--social scientists disseminate more diffusely, over a
longer period of time, and in a manner less con-
ducive to successful assimilation.

--the time required, from completion of research to
presentation in the formal literature, is substantially
longer in the social sciences than in the natural sciences.   This is due in part to the higher rates of
rejection by social science journals (Garvey, et al.).

The general pattern of dissemination of knowledge in
the scientific community is that scientists:

--disseminate their research first at colloquia and by
preprints.   Colloquia and preprints permit the scientist to obtain advice and criticism informally from
other specialists in the field.

--later disseminate their research at professional association meetings.   (These meetings appear to
serve the function of bringing scientists with similar
interests together, thus allowing informal inter-
change.)

--use publications as the final mode of dissemination.

Studies of the "invisible college" hypothesis have emerged from several sources, including Diana Crane of the Johns Hopkins staff. Crane postulates that the growth of a scientific area is initially generated by a few innovators and early adopters who then attract other practitioners and students. These interactions account for the rapid increase in the number of participating persons in the area (Crane, 1969; Crane, 1972).

One study found that almost three-quarters of the respondents in one survey were directly or indirectly interconnected with one another in a large network. There was a core group in this network, however, which was characterized by the greater number of: papers produced, persons citing their work, and persons who read their work. Information transmitted to these individuals could be transmitted through informal contacts to 95 per cent of the other persons in the network (Crawford).

One statement suggests that the definition of the invisible college can be developed along the following lines:

--The number of people in the invisible college of a given area is approximately the square root of the number of people active in the area.

--The works of the members of the core invisible college are highly related and of high quality. The members are interconnected through cross-citations in their works and through interactions of various types.

The invisible college is increasingly being understood as a self-generating phenomenon created by the scientific community (Price).

Project on Scientific Information Exchange in Psychology

This American Psychological Association (APA) project is a comprehensive study of the information flow in a specific discipline. The project has sponsored a number of investigations which are being used to suggest organizational policy changes and innovations in information use within the APA. Several of the key studies will be reviewed here.

Those who made presentations at the international

conference were asked to rank 16 different kinds of publications, scientific meetings, and personal communications by how well they furnished needed information (American Psychological Association, 1963).

--American participants gave the highest ratings to journals, discussions with colleagues, books, and correspondence, in that order.

--Foreign participants placed books above discussions and rated discussions and correspondence lower than the Americans did.

Use of books was the subject of another APA study. A questionnaire was used which was returned by more than half of the APA members (American Psychological Association, 1965). It was found that:

--almost three-quarters of the respondents cited one or more books as relevant to their most information demanding activity.

--book users rated not only books but all written media higher in importance than did book non-users.

--most of the books cited by participants had been discovered through a colleague's recommendation, prior knowledge, browsing, or other informal means.

--half of the participants indicated that "theory" was a particularly important aspect of the book, "data" was important to 42 per cent of the respondents, "general points or conclusions" to 38 per cent, and "method or procedure" to 37 per cent of those participating.

Interpersonal communications functions during different phases of a research project were the subject of another study. It was found through interviews with psychologists in two major research environments that:

--interaction with colleagues, instructors, directors, and students was necessary in converting ideas into action.

--consultation with many people on design, methodology, procedure, and apparatus took place during the planning and progress of the research.

--the most valued type of communication with colleagues took place when research was nearing completion, when the interpretation of findings was involved, and when applications and extensions of
work were being planned.

--critical appraisal of at least a few colleagues was
sought when research was being readied for presentation.

An APA study of psychologists' needs for technological
innovations analyzed their interest in audiotapes and other
audiovisual media (American Psychological Association, 1966).
It was found that:

--seventy-five percent of the respondents indicated
that they would use audiotapes if they were made
available.

--the preference among various types of media were:
live (face-to-face audience), videotapes, audiotapes,
books and manuals, and journals and abstracts in
that order.

Research Program on Organization and Management
of Research and Development

Thomas J. Allen and his colleagues at the Alfred P.
Sloan School of Management, Massachusetts Institute of Technology, have conducted on ongoing series of studies of the
communications process in research and development laboratories.

One of the earlier investigations undertaken by the
MIT program was of the preference for various communications channels by scientists and engineers (Allen, 1964).
Engineers in eight laboratories were questioned as to the
time allocation of their activities. It was found that:

--information gathering is the most important at the
start of each project.

--literature searching and outside consultation con-
stituted the most important activity during the initial
period.

--literature searching diminished as the project continued and was replaced by interpersonal communication.

--staff consultation was the dominant activity near the end of the project.

In analyzing matched project teams working on the same design activity (Allen and Cohen) it was found that:

--higher-rated teams had relatively stable communications patterns throughout the project.

--lower-rated teams spent far more initial time gathering information than later, and fluctuated more in their communications pattern throughout the project. (The inference seems to be that lower-rated teams were less well prepared at the outset of the project and/or may have suffered from the effects of premature closure.)

The concept of perceived utility of information was studied by Allen and Gerstberger (Allen and Gerstberger); this study showed that:

--ease of access and use are stronger factors than technical quality in determining which information channels are used. This is also true of which channels are used first.

--experience in using an information channel results in high use of that channel.

--acceptability of information relates more to perceived technical quality than to accessibility or ease of use.

--when a choice has to be made between easily accessible information and that of high technical quality, the decision was to accept the technically superior information.

In terms of the types of information used by research and development personnel, another series of studies (Allen, 1967) found that:

--scientists lean more heavily on literature sources, while technologists depend on oral sources. (The difference appears to stem from the scientists'

thrust for new knowledge as contrasted with the
technologists' desire to produce "things that work. ")

--there is a two-step flow of information in research
and development laboratories. There are "gatekeepers" who are more in touch with outside developments, activities, and the literature than their co-
workers. These gatekeepers allow entry of information into the organization and assist with its dissemination within the organization.

The concept of the informational gatekeeper is explored further in a follow-up study (Allen, et al., 1971).
The MIT group has found that in a given working team there
are identifiable communication "stars. " These persons, as
compared with their colleagues tend to:

--use external information sources much more frequently.

--engage in give-and-take communications more frequently with others in the same office or department.

--form a closer communication network among themselves.

Syracuse University Psychological Abstracts Retrieval Service (SUPARS)

The Syracuse University Psychological Abstracts Retrieval Service (SUPARS) is an example of an information system developed to study user patterns and needs (Atherton).
This on-line computer-centered retrieval system was tested
through 75 telephone communication terminals situated across
the Syracuse University campus. SUPARS allowed remote
access to bibliographic citations and abstracts for over 35, 000
documents derived from Psychological Abstracts. An elabo-
rate publicity campaign was conducted during the period of
operations. It was found in terms of SUPARS participants
that:

--most wished to obtain an exhaustive review of an
area.

--more than 40 per cent wished to survey the literature in general.

--about one-third wished to keep up-to-date in one or two content areas.

--about 20 per cent wanted to find a specific abstract.

Two-thirds of the SUPARS users had no previous experience with computer terminals and three-quarters had no experience with computer-based retrieval systems.

In-depth interviews were conducted with a random sample of SUPARS users to determine the effectiveness of the system. About half of the sample population indicated that they had successfully retrieved what they had wanted to find.

SUMMARY. -- Common characteristics found in the preceding user studies are:

--ease of access and use are stronger factors than technical quality in determining what information resources are used. If a choice between ease of access and technical quality must be made, however, the material with higher technical quality will be chosen.

--peer groups and the "invisible college" are very important informational sources and influences. Peer groups, colloquia, and conference presentations are major means of gaining feedback on work in development.

--interpersonal interaction with colleagues functions differently during different phases of a research study. Ideas are converted into action through informal interaction with colleagues and others. Consultants are employed during the design and operational phases. The most critical interpersonal communication takes place when findings are being interpreted and applications and extensions of the work are being planned. Critical appraisal of a few colleagues is sought when the research is being readied for presentation.

--there are information stars or "gatekeepers" who control a major portion of the information flow within organizations. These persons use external

information sources more frequently, engage in more
frequent give-and-take communications with others
in the same office or department, and form a closer
communications network among themselves.

--abstracting and indexing services as well as personal
contacts are perceived as the best methods of keeping current in a field.

--the more specific the nature of the request the
easier the satisfaction.

--the more specific the content of the area (e.g.,
physical science), the quicker the dissemination of
information within the field.

PART III

AN OPERATIONAL MODEL OF
THE SEARCHING PROCESS

An Operational Model
--An Example of the Searching Process

Discipline Resource Packages

--Social Sciences
      --General Social Sciences (Sociology, Anthropology,
        Political Science, History, Geography)
      --Psychology
      --Business and Economics
      --Education
      --Law

--Humanities
      --Philosophy and Religion
      --Language and Literature
      --Fine Arts

--Science and Technology
      --Physical Sciences (Astronomy, Chemistry, Earth
        Sciences, Engineering, Mathematics, Physics)
      --Life Sciences (Agriculture, Anthropology, Bio-
        logical Sciences, Health Sciences, Paleontology)

--General Works
      --Almanacs
      --Biography location tools
      --Book location tools
      --Book Review location tools
      --Dictionaries
      --Encyclopedias
      --Periodical location tools
      --Statistical sources

AN OPERATIONAL MODEL

We have considered the structure and identification of reference resources in Part I, and discussed knowledge utilization and user behavior in Part II. Part III will delineate an operational model of the searching process and provide Discipline Resource Packages for identification of reference resources related to particular user questions.

Before examining an example of a specific user question, review of the steps in the searching process would be helpful. They are presented in more detail in Part I. These steps are:

1. <u>Determination of a Need.</u> - Need connotes man's motivations, aspirations, and feelings of want. Needs are the "why" of the resource use process.

2. <u>Initial Question Statement.</u> - A statement of the question should be written and rewritten until it is clear and succinct. A separate list of key terms related to the question should be made and compared with the question statement for consistency.

3. <u>Delineation and Redefinition of the Question.</u> - The following questions should be asked regarding the initial question:
    What is being sought?
    What types of information resources are desired?
    What relevant information is already available?
    What is the level of interest?
    What type of person needs the information?
    What time limits are appropriate?
    What physical formats will be most convenient?
    What is the scope of the information sought?
    What other limitations are there?
    How will the resulting information be applied?

4. <u>Redefined Question Statement.</u> - The initial question statement should be discussed with a librarian/information

specialist, subject area specialist, or both. The question
should be rewritten following this discussion and application
of the questions indicated above. A list of indexing terms
descriptive of the content of the question should be selected
from appropriate indexes or thesauri.

5.   Structuring the Search. - The appropriate Discipline Resource Package and associated Search Procedure Form should
be used to structure the search.

6.   Selecting Primary Information Sources. - Referring to
the information provided in the appropriate Discipline Resource Package, the reference resources which seem to have
the greatest potential to provide information relevant to the
question are checked on the Search Procedure Form.

7.   Analyzing Selected Information Sources. - Those items
selected as primary information sources are scanned in either
full or abstract form and their content noted.

8.   Obtain Additional Information If Necessary. - If sufficient
or relevant information is not obtained in the first search attempt, repeat the process on a broader scale. The assistance of a librarian/information specialist or subject area
specialist may be helpful at this point.

9.   Synthesizing Information. - There are many approaches
to information synthesis. The two prime qualities of an effective synthesis, however, are: a) distillation of the substance of the knowledge related to the question, and b) citations for the resources from which the information is obtained.

10.   Analyzing Information. - Information analysis is an attempt to draw objective conclusions from the information
gathered and synthesized. This is essentially a subjective
and personal process. The end product of the analysis
should be a set of conclusions which lead to effective decision-making in relation to the originally posed question. ·

11.   Decision Making. - Not all reference resource searches
culminate in a decision. In many cases a list of conclusions
is sufficient for closure; in others a decision on specific action can be made. In all cases where a decision is to be
made there should be a direct connection between the decision
made and the information gleaned through the searching process.

12. Evaluating. - The ultimate evaluation of a reference resource search in the utility of the information in decision-making or the degree of effectiveness of the resources in gathering the information sought. Determination should be made, therefore, of the effectiveness of the searching process in producing a useful and valid decision, or in finding information. The judgment as to the degree of this effectiveness should be fed back to the assisting librarian/information specialist to help improve future searching activities.

The entire reference searching process is shown in the following block flow diagram. The diagram shows the specific materials which might be selected and used in relation to a particular reference question.

The Information Searching Process

1.   Need

2.   Initial Question Statement

Due to the rising costs of providing equal educational opportunities to all students, cost effective uses of technology to educate a variety of learners must be throughly investigated. One such technology is the transmission of instructional program content via satellite.

$\longrightarrow$

Are telecommunications satellites an effective means of providing instructional programming for students across wide geographic areas?

$\longrightarrow$

3. Keywords

| telecommunications |
| satellites |
| television |
| radio |
| instructional programs |
| information systems |

4. Delineation and Redefinition

- What is being sought?

- What types of information resources are desired?

- What relevant information is already available?

- What is the level of interest?

- What type of person needs the information?

- What time limits are appropriate?

- What physical formats will be most convenient?

- What is the scope of the information sought?

- What other limitations are there?

- How will the resulting information be applied?

5. Redefined Question   6. Primary Informa-
    Statement   tion Sources

| Is there sufficient current information available in the form of reprints and articles, for purposes of a feasibility study to be conducted by a national educational research organization? | Review the information on the Bibliographic Chain in Part I, review the various discipline resource packages, and select the most promising search alternatives on the appropriate Search Procedure Form. |

$\longrightarrow$

Keywords:

telecommunica-
    tions
satellites
information net-
    works
educational tele-
    vision
electronic com-
    munications
instructional tech-
    nology

Search Procedure Form	EDUCATION
NAME OF USER	**DATE OF INQUIRY**

REDEFINED QUESTION STATEMENT

KEYWORDS

WORK IN PROGRESS

☐ Contemporary Authors
☐ Pacesetters in Innovation

☐ Research in Education

UNPUBLISHED STUDIES

☐ DATRIX
☐ Dissertation Abstracts International

☐ Masters Abstracts

PERIODICALS

☐ American Documentation
☐ American Education
☐ American Educational Research Journal
☐ American Libraries
■ Audiovisual Instruction
☐ Automated Education Handbook
☐ Bulletin - National Association of Secondary School Principals
☐ Child Development
☐ Children
☐ College and University Reports
☐ Comparative Education Review
☐ Congressional Quarterly Service
■ Croft Newsletter Services
☐ Education
☐ Education Court Digest
☐ Education Recaps
☐ Educational Administration Quarterly
☐ Educational Leadership
■ Educational Technology
☐ Educational Product Report
☐ Government Contracts Guide

☐ Guide to Federal Assistance for Education
☐ Harvard Educational Review
■ Joint Council on Educational Telecommunications DATA Base Service
☐ Journal of Applied Psychology
☐ Journal of Educational Psychology
☐ Journal of Educational Research
■ Journal of Research and Development in Education
☐ Journal of Teacher Education
☐ National Elementary Principal
☐ Phi Delta Kappan
☐ Psychological Review
☐ Report on the Education of the Disadvantaged
☐ Review of Educational Research
☐ Saturday Review
☐ School and Society
☐ Social Education
☐ Teachers College Record
☐ Theory into Practice
☐ Today's Education: the Journal of the NEA
☐ Urban Education

REPORTS AND MONOGRAPHS

☐ Abstracts of Papers
■ Cooperative Research Monograph Series
■ ERIC Document Collections

☐ NEA Research Reports
☐ What Research Says to the Teacher

INDEXES AND ABSTRACTING SERVICES

☐ Abstracts of Instructional Materials in Vocational and Technical Education (AIM)
☐ Abstracts of Research and Related Materials in Vocational and Technical Education (ARM)
■ British Education Index
☐ Child Development Abstracts and Bibliography
☐ CIRF Abstracts
☐ College Student Personal Abstracts
☐ Current Contents - Education
■ Current Index to Journals in Education

■ Education Index
☐ Educational Administration Abstracts
☐ Exceptional Child Education Abstracts
☐ Perceptual Cognitive Development
■ Research in Education
☐ State Educational Journal Index
☐ Subject Index to Children's Magazines

BIBLIOGRAPHIC LISTS AND ESSAYS

- "Outstanding Education Books of 19" Today's Education, the Journal of the NEA
- Research Studies in Education

- Sources in Educational Research
- The Teachers Library: How to Organize it and What to Include
- Textbooks in Print

ANNUAL REVIEWS AND STATE OF THE ART REPORTS

- Annual Phi Delta Kappa Symposium on Educational Research
- Association for Supervision and Curriculum Development Yearbook
- Biennial Survey of Education
- Bowker Annual
- International Yearbook of Education

- National Council for the Social Studies Yearbook
- National Society for the Study of Education Yearbook
- Review of Educational Research
- ● Review of Research in Education

BOOKS (List appropriate subject headings as well as author and title for books selected. See Discipline Resource Package for list of basic titles.)

ENCYCLOPEDIC SUMMARIES

- Dictionary of Education
- Encyclopedia Britannica
- Encyclopedia of Education

- Encyclopedia of Educational Research
- Encyclopedia of Library and Information Science
- Who's Who in American Education

COMMENTS:

Additional sources:

"Communications Satellites: A New Hazard for World Cultures," Carroll V. Newson, Educational Broadcasting Review, April 1973.

checked Annual Review of Information Science and Technology (last two volumes).

also looked at Journal of Educational Technology Systems (several possible articles).

SEARCHER'S SIGNATURE	DATE COMPLETED

7.   Resources Located

Author: J. Russell Burke and Frank W. Norwood

Title: Satellite Developments and the ATS-6

Source: Audiovisual Instruction, May, 1975

Pages: 12-16

Abstract: The ATS-6 is available to demonstrate potential
applications of the technology evolving from the
U.S. space effort.   It is currently engaged in 23
experiments including education and health applications.

Significance and Possible Use:
A research and development effort in actual appli-
cation of satellite technology.   See in particular
India and Alaska experiments.

Author: Carroll V. Newson

Title: Communication Satellites: A New Hazard for World
Cultures

Source: Educational Broadcasting, April, 1975

Pages: 77-85

Abstract: Discusses the attitude of nations which are concerned about technologies to "promote the free
flow of ideas by word and image" (UNESCO Constitution) and the need for controls to avoid cultural erosion.

Significance and Possible Use:
Speaks to some of the political and cultural implications of educational programing by satellite.

7.   Resources Located

Author: Kenneth A. Polcyn

Title: Future United States Educational Broadcast Satellite
Experiments: The Rocky Mountain Region Experiment

Source: Educational Technology, August, 1973

Pages: 46-52

Abstract: Describes in detail the Rocky Mountain Experiment
using the ATS Satellite.   Covers governance, the
nature of the experiment, management, software,
and evaluation procedures.

Significance and Possible Use:
An in-depth look at the plans for one satellite-
based telecommunications activity in the area of
instruction.

Author: R. Priemer, S. Laxpati, H. Rolfe, A. Conrad

Title: On the Use of Communications Technology as an Alternative to the Urban University: Issues and Models

Source: Journal of Educational Technology Systems, Fall,
1972

Pages: 97-111

Abstract: Discusses the application of communication technology to the development and implementation of
urban universities in the future.   Integration of
communication technology is offered as a model
for delivering university services.

Significance and Possible Use:
Discusses uses of communications technology in an
educational setting with particular regard to the
delivery of instruction.

7.   Resources Located

Author: Robert A. Scanlon

Title: Improving Educational Productivity Through the Use of Technology

Source: Paper presented at the 1974 American Educational Research Association Conference.

Pages: 13p.

Abstract: Provides summaries of papers presented and discussions held during a symposium on "Improving Productivity of School Systems Through Educational Technology." Explores the potentials and implications of advanced technology-based communications systems for improving educational productivity.

Significance and Possible Use:
        Deals with the question of productivity.

Author: John A. Curtis

Title: Needed: A National Telecommunications Network for Education

Source: Engineering Education, May, 1974

Pages: 567-571

Abstract: The need for and advantages of a national educational telecommunications network are specified. The technology needed and set-up procedures are discussed. Recommendations for development are made.

Significance and Possible Use:
        Deals with the possibility of a national network.

7. Resources Located

Author: Edward W. Ploman

Title: A Survey of New Communications Technologies and
Their Uses

Source: Research Report from Committee for Out-of-School
Education and Cultural Development, Council of Europe

Pages: 50p.

Abstract: A survey focused on certain major developments in
various countries regarding the production, distribution, reception, and uses of communications technologies and media (including satellites).

Significance and Possible Use:
Gives broad view of communications technology activity.

Author: John Walkmeyer

Title: Planning Alternative Organizational Frameworks for a
Large Scale Educational Telecommunications System
Served by Fixed/Broadcast Satellites.

Source: Memorandum from Program on Application of Communication Satellites to Educational Development,
Washington University

Pages: 120p.

Abstract: Explores using satellites for development of large-scale educational telecommunications systems. Deals
with system-wide concerns and issues relating to
specific system components. Discusses consequences
of networking.

Significance and Possible Use:
Takes both a broad and narrow view.

9.   Synthesis

8.   Need More Infor-
     mation?

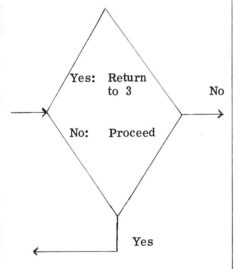

Yes: Return
       to 3

No: Proceed

No

Yes

Considerable thought
and experimentation
has taken place re-
garding the use of
satellites as a means
of providing instruc-
tion to students.   A
variety of specific
activities are taking
place through the
use of the ATS Sat-
ellite.   Technical,
educational, cultural
and political consid-
erations are being
explored.   No on-
going operational
programs are pre-
sently underway,
however.

10. Analysis

The variety and abundance of the current literature available would seem to indicate that there
is definite feasibility in the application of communications satellite technology to the delivery
of educational programming.   However, close
attention should be paid in exploring the
feasibility of the time framework being dealt
with, the specific population(s) to be served,
cost factors (both developmental and operational),
long-term cost benefit, and social/cultural implications.

11. Decision

> To proceed with
> a feasibility study,
> such study to be
> preceded by care-
> ful delineation of
> the audiences to
> be served, time
> framework being
> dealt with, and
> potential for cost/
> benefits to be de-
> rived.

→

12. Evaluation

> (To be done after
> the feasibility study
> is completed.)

→

DISCIPLINE RESOURCE PACKAGES

Discipline Resource Packages are, as the name implies, descriptive listings of reference resources arranged by subject area disciplines. They are intended as guides to the basic reference literature in the major areas of scholarly pursuit. As these are basic lists, those possessing specialized or advanced knowledge and research skills in a given discipline will probably not be satisfied with the extent of resources provided. The beginner or generally interested searcher, should find sufficient resources for his purposes, however.

The "disciplines" selected for the packages follow the usual organization of the world of knowledge represented by the Dewey Decimal System and the Library of Congress Classification System. The four major discipline categories, with an indication of sub-areas are:

- Social Sciences (General Social Sciences, Psychology, Business and Economics, Education, Law)

- Humanities (Philosophy and Religion, Language and Literature, Fine Arts)

- Science and Technology (Physical Sciences, Life Sciences)

- General (Almanacs, Biography location tools, Book Location tools, Book review location tools, Dictionaries, Encyclopedias, Periodical location tools, Statistical sources).

In all, there are eleven Discipline Resource Packages; one for each sub-area under the three major subject area headings, plus one for the general category.

The contents of the Discipline Resource Packages are arranged according to the Bibliographic Chain. The first two formats of the Chain, having to do with human and institutional resources, are not included, as the focus of this book is on the searching of printed library reference resources.

Most Bibliographic Chain formats within each Discipline Resource Package contain location tools for identification of relevant resources. Two exceptions are the categories of Periodicals and Books. These two formats are composed of citations to primary information resources themselves, rather than location tools. Annotations are not provided for these materials.

The General Discipline Resource Package is an amalgamation of those resources which do not fit under the categories of the Bibliographic Chain. This package is arranged, therefore, by the sub-categories indicated.

Each Discipline Resource Package includes: an introductory statement; a list of sub-topics, if appropriate; annotated lists of reference resources arranged by the Bibliographic Chain, including bibliographical information; and a Search Procedure Form for the area.

How to Use the Discipline Resource Package

Discipline Resource Packages provide the content for steps 5, 6 and 8 of the searching process (Structuring the Search, Selecting Primary Information Sources, and Obtaining Additional Information If Necessary). They lead to the informational substance for steps 7, 9 and 10 of the process (Analyzing Selected Information Sources, Synthesizing Information, and Analyzing Information).

The General Discipline Resource Package should be used for all searches, in addition to the subject area package or packages related to the content of the question being dealt with.

It should be recognized that the completeness of coverage of reference resources differs among disciplines. An examination of the various Discipline Resource Packages shows that social science resources, for instance, are sparse at the top of the chain and more complete in the later stages. Science and technology show the opposite pattern. It is unfortunate that gaps exist in the literature coverage of many fields. These variations in the range of existing resources between disciplines are a significant factor in structuring a search.

It should also be noted that only bibliographic information and in most cases an annotation are provided in the Discipline Resource Packages. The true value of a given resource can only be determined by examining the actual item itself.

Discipline Resource Package

GENERAL SOCIAL SCIENCES

Joan W. Gartland
University of Detroit

The social sciences may be defined as those disciplines which study the activities of human beings in groups through objective methods. They include psychology, business and economics, education, and law, which will be considered separately, and the following five fields which, for purposes of this book, will be treated under the broad heading, general social sciences:

> Sociology (including social work)
> Anthropology (including archaeology)
> Political science
> History
> Geography.

To do justice to the literature of these fields in a study of this size is, of course, an impossibility, but the following listings may serve the reader as starting points from which to further explore vast worlds of scholarship.

WORKS IN PROGRESS

Contemporary Authors
  A comprehensive source for biographical data on contemporary authors, many of which may not yet appear in traditional biographical sources. Entries are short, with personal, career, and work-in-progress information. A list of writings and sources of biographical and critical data are given when possible. The set is now in its 48th volume but many of the earlier volumes have been cumulated. Each volume is a separate alphabet but a cumulative name index is provided at the end of volume 48. (Gale Research Co., Detroit)

UNPUBLISHED STUDIES

CROSS-DISCIPLINARY

Dissertation Abstracts International
> The most complete source for abstracts of doctoral disserta-
> tions written in the United States.   Most U. S. universities
> contribute to this system operated by a private corporation.
> Unfortunately, several important universities do not partici-
> pate.   Microfilm or paper copies of the dissertations are
> available for purchase.   Until recently, the indexing has been
> spotty and of poor quality.   Fortunately, a much better (and
> very expensive) 37-volume cumulative index is now available.
> (University Microfilms, Ann Arbor, Mich.)

Guide to Lists of Master's Theses
> Dorothy M. Black's valuable guide brings together often hard-
> to-find lists of master's theses written through 1964 at uni-
> versities and colleges in the United States and Canada.   Lists
> are arranged both by subject and by specific institutions.
> Cross references.   (American Library Association, Chicago,
> Ill. , 1965)

Masters Abstracts
> This is a selective, classified and annotated list of master's
> theses produced by many, but by no means all, U. S. colleges
> and universities.   As with dissertations, microfilm or paper
> copies of the theses are available for purchase from the pub-
> lisher of the Abstracts.   Due to its selectivity, it is much
> easier to use than Dissertation Abstracts International.   MA
> is presently being published quarterly.   (University Micro-
> films, Ann Arbor, Mich.)

SOCIOLOGY

"Doctoral Dissertations in Social Work" Social Service Review, Sept.
1954- . (annual)
> Abstracts of dissertations completed during the previous July-
> June period, as well as listings of dissertations in progress.
> Based only on the work done in schools of social work with
> doctoral programs.   (University of Chicago Press, Chicago,
> Ill.)

Sociology Dissertations in American Universities, 1893-1966.   (Lun-
day, G. Albert)
> Arranged by subject under 26 topics.   Gives author, title,
> date, and institution by code.   Author index.   (East Texas
> State Univ. , Commerce, Texas, 1969)

ANTHROPOLOGY

Yearbook of Anthropology
          Lists dissertations in anthropology written between 1870 and
          1954. International in scope. Gives author, title, name of
          institution, and date. The periodical, Current Anthropology,
          continued the listing in its February 1966 and December 1968
          issues. (Yearbook of Anthropology, Wenner-Gren Foundation,
          New York, 1955)

POLITICAL SCIENCE

"Doctoral Dissertations in Political Science in Universities of the
United States," American Political Science Review, 1910-1967.
          Title of the listing varies. Lists dissertations completed and
          in progress since 1910 (with some interruptions). Since 1968,
          the listing has been published in PS, the quarterly newsletter
          of the American Political Science Association, Washington,
          D. C.

HISTORY

Dissertations in History: An Index to Dissertations Completed in
History Departments of United States and Canadian Universities,
1873-1960
          Arranged by author, this compilation by Warren F. Kuehl
          gives title, date and institution where work was submitted.
          The subject index permits the user to see what has been
          written on a given topic. (University of Kentucky Press,
          Lexington, Kentucky, 1965)

List of Doctoral Dissertations in History...
          This list, whose antecedents date back to 1906, has been pub-
          lished by the American Historical Assoc. since 1947. Since
          1958, it has included both dissertations in progress and com-
          pleted. Arrangement is by subject areas, with sub-topic divi-
          sions. Dissertations on all periods and countries from the
          participating institutions listed are included. Author index.
          At present, published triennially. (American Historical As-
          soc., Washington, D.C., 1947-   )

GEOGRAPHY

A Bibliography of Dissertations in Geography: 1901-1969: American and Canadian Universities (Browning, Clyde E.)
          1,582 dissertations, arranged by subject categories. Gives
          author, title, institution, and date. (Univ. of North Carolina,
          Department of Geography, Chapel Hill, N.C., 1970)

"Recent Geography Dissertations and Theses Completed and in Prep-

aration, " The Professional Geographer, 1950-   (Currently published
in the February issue.)
>Frequency and title of the listing has varied.   Arranged by
>author.   (Association of American Geographers, Washington,
>D. C.)

PERIODICALS

SOCIOLOGY

Aging (bi-monthly)
American Behavioral Scientist (bi-monthly)
American Journal of Sociology (bi-monthly)
American Sociological Review (bi-monthly)
American Sociologist (quarterly)
Current Sociology (3x yr.)
International Journal of Comparative Sociology (quarterly)
Journal of Marriage and the Family (quarterly)
Journal of Social Issues (quarterly)
Public Administration Review (bi-monthly)
Public Welfare (quarterly)
Race Today (monthly)
Social Casework (monthly)
Social Problems (quarterly)
Social Research (quarterly)
Social Security Bulletin (monthly)
Social Service Review (quarterly)
Social Work (quarterly)
Society (formerly: Trans-Action) (monthly)
Sociometry (quarterly)
Urban Affairs Quarterly
Welfare Fighter (monthly)
Welfare in Review (bi-monthly)

ANTHROPOLOGY (Including Archaeology)

American Anthropologist (bi-monthly)
American Antiquity (quarterly)
American Journal of Archaeology (quarterly)
American Schools of Oriental Research.   Bulletin (quarterly)
Anthropological Journal of Canada (quarterly)
Anthropological Quarterly
Anthropos (3x yr.)
Antiquity (quarterly)
Archaeology (quarterly)
Current Anthropology (5x yr.)
Expedition - The Magazine of Archaeology/Anthropology (quarterly)
Journal of American Folklore (quarterly)
Journal of Near Eastern Studies (quarterly)

POLITICAL SCIENCE

American City (monthly)
American County Government (monthly)
American Political Science Review (quarterly)
Atlas (monthly)
Canadian Journal of Political Science (quarterly)
Comparative Politics (quarterly)
Current History (monthly)
Dept. of State Bulletin (weekly)
Foreign Affairs (quarterly)
International Affairs (quarterly)
International Development Review (quarterly)
Journal of Politics (quarterly)
Orbis (quarterly)
Political Science Quarterly
Public Administration Review (bi-monthly)
Public Opinion Quarterly
Review of Politics (quarterly)
State Government (quarterly)
Urban Affairs Quarterly
Weekly Compilation of Presidential Documents
World Politics (quarterly)

HISTORY

American Chronical (monthly)
American Heritage (bi-monthly)
American Historical Review (5x yr.)
American Quarterly
Catholic Historical Review (quarterly)
Comparative Studies in Society and History (quarterly)
English Historical Review (quarterly)
Historian, A Journal of History (quarterly)
History Today (monthly)
Horizon (quarterly)
Journal of African History (quarterly)
Journal of American Studies (3x yr.)
Journal of Contemporary History (quarterly)
Journal of Modern History (quarterly)
Journal of Negro History (quarterly)
Journal of Social History (quarterly)
Journal of the History of Ideas (quarterly)
Mankind: the Magazine of Popular History (bi-monthly)

GEOGRAPHY

Association of American Geographers, Annals (quarterly)
Canadian Geographical Journal (monthly)
Economic Geography (quarterly)

Explorers Journal (quarterly)
Focus (monthly)
Geographical Journal (quarterly)
Geographical Review (quarterly)
Journal of Geography (monthly)
National Geographic Magazine (monthly)

REPORTS AND MONOGRAPHS

SOCIOLOGY

Duke University. Sociological Series. 1939-
> One of a number of monograph series in sociology published
> by leading American universities. For titles in this series
> and others, consult: Eleanora A. Baer, Titles in Series.
> 2d ed. (The Scarecrow Press, New York and London, 1964,
> 2 vols. + 3 suppls.)

ANTHROPOLOGY

American Anthropological Assoc. Memoirs. 1905+
> Such well-known anthropologists as Benedict, Herskovitz, and
> Kluckhohn have written monographs for this series. For
> titles see Baer, Ibid. (American Anthropological Assoc.,
> Washington, D.C.)

Columbia University. Contributions to Anthropology. 1910-
> Monographs by such eminent scholars as Benedict, Boas,
> Bunzel, Herskovitz and Mead. For titles in this series, see
> Baer, Ibid.

POLITICAL SCIENCE

American Academy of Political and Social Science, Philadelphia.
Monograph Series. 1933+
> As the name of the sponsoring institution indicates, this
> monograph series includes works both on political science
> and on other aspects of the social sciences. For titles in
> the series, see Baer, Ibid.

CQ Weekly Reports
> Gives up-to-date information on the activities of Congress,
> including the status of legislation, roll-call votes, committee
> activities, and coverage of current matters of concern in all
> branches of government. The Congressional Quarterly Al-
> manac draws on this material for its annual publication.
> (Congressional Quarterly, Inc., Washington, D.C., 1943-)

Harvard Political Studies.   1930+
>   One of a number of monograph series in political science
>   sponsored by American universities.   For titles in this and
>   other series, see Baer, Ibid.

HISTORY

American Historical Association.   Publications, 1932+
>   Monographs with American, British, and French emphasis.
>   For titles, see Baer, Ibid.   (University of Pennsylvania
>   Press, since 1950)

Smith College Studies in History, 1915+
>   One of a number of excellent monograph series in history
>   sponsored by American universities.   For titles in this series
>   and others, see Baer, Ibid.

GEOGRAPHY

American Geographical Society of New York.   Research Series.
1921-
>   These monographs take up many different aspects of geog-
>   raphy.   For titles in the series, see Baer, Ibid.

Northwestern University Studies in Geography.   1952-
>   One of several monograph series sponsored by American uni-
>   versities.   For titles, see Baer, Ibid.

INDEXES AND ABSTRACTING SERVICES

CROSS-DISCIPLINARY

The Gallup Opinion Index: Political, Social and Economic Trends
(monthly)
>   Gives results of polls on selected topics of current concern.
>   (Gallup International, Princeton, N. J. , 1965-)

Index to Periodical Articles By and About Negroes (annual)
>   The forerunner of this index was: Index to Selected Period-
>   icals Received in the Hallie Q. Brown Library (decennial
>   cumulation, 1950-1959) which indexed periodicals not indexed,
>   or partially indexed, elsewhere.   The 1960-1970 decennial
>   cumulation added, as part two, indexing done by the staff of
>   the Schomburg Collection, New York Public Library, and was
>   entitled Index to Periodical Articles By and About Negroes.
>   Arrangement is by author-subject.   (G. K. Hall, Boston)

Monthly Catalog of United States Government Publications, 1895-

Lists, by department and bureau, current government publications. Gives price and ordering information. Since January
1974, the indexing has been improved so that now there is
a subject, author, and title approach to entries   Annual index is published in the December issue. List of periodicals
published in February issues. Decennial indexes. A very
valuable source for keeping up-to-date on a multitude of subjects. (U. S. Government Printing Office, Washington, D. C.)

The New York Times Index, v. 1- , 1913- (semi-monthly with annual cumulation)
Subject index to the vast amounts of information covered in
the New York Times. Entries cite date, page and column in
which a particular item appeared. Cross references direct
readers to other pertinent headings. The New York Times
Index volumes for the years 1851-1912, a series which began
issuing in 1966, are reaching completion. (New York Times
Company, New York)

Public Affairs Information Service Bulletin (PAIS) (weekly)
Indexes books, periodical articles, pamphlets, government
publications, etc. A basic resource for research in many
fields, including: political science, economics, sociology and
foreign affairs. Annual cumulative volume. (Public Affairs
Information Service, New York, 1915-)

Social Sciences and Humanities Index (quarterly) (until 1965: International Index)
Author and subject index to over 200 periodicals in the field
of the social sciences and the humanities. As of June 1974,
continues in two parts: Social Sciences Index, which adds 186
periodicals to the 77 previously indexed, to make a total of
263 in the fields of anthropology, area studies, economics,
environmental science, public administration, sociology, etc.;
and The Humanities Index, which is enlarged to include 260
periodicals in the fields of archaeology, classical studies,
folklore, history, language and literature, performing arts,
philosophy, religion, theology, etc. Both indexes have separate book review sections. (H. W. Wilson, New York,
1916-)

SOCIOLOGY

Abstracts for Social Workers (quarterly)
Abstracts articles in social work and related fields such as
psychology, psychiatry, and sociology from over 150 periodicals. Arranged by topic, with author and subject indexes.
(National Assn. of Social Workers, Albany, N. Y., 1965-)

Crime and Delinquency Abstracts (bimonthly) Ceased, 1972. (formerly International Bibliography on Crime and Delinquency)

Abstracts (beginning with vol. 3) of published literature and
of research projects in the field.   Author and subject indexes.
(National Institute of Mental Health, Rockville, Maryland,
1963-1972)

Population Index (quarterly)
Annotated listing of books and articles in the field of popula-
tion studies, arranged by sub-topics.   Official statistical pub-
lications and new periodicals in the field are also included.
Indexed by geographical regions and by author.   (Office of
Population Research, Princeton Univ. , and the Population
Assn. of America, Princeton, N. J. , 1935-)

Sociological Abstracts, 1953-   (6x yr. ; frequency varies)
Abstracts journals pertaining to sociology.   International in
scope.   English summaries of foreign language articles.   Arrangement by broad subject areas, with subject and author
indexes.   (Sociological Abstracts, Inc. , New York)

ANTHROPOLOGY

Abstracts in Anthropology (quarterly) 1970-
Abstracts, in English, of articles in archaeology, cultural
anthropology, linguistics, and physical anthropology from a
wide range of periodicals both American and foreign.   Author
and subject indexes.   (Greenwood Press, Westport, Conn.)

Abstracts of Folklore Studies (quarterly) 1963-
Signed abstracts of articles relating to folklore which appear
in the periodicals listed at the beginning of each issue.   Abstracts are arranged by title of periodical.   There is an annual index for author, subject, and title.   (University of
Texas Press, Austin, Texas)

Art Index (quarterly) 1929-
Indexes foreign and American periodicals and museum bulletins by author and subject.   A good source for articles in
archaeology and art history and the history of arts and crafts.
(H. W. Wilson Co.)

Motif-Index of Folk Literature: A Classification of Narrative Elements in Folktales, Ballads, Myths, Fables, and Mediaeval Romances,
Exempla, Fabliaux, Jest-Books and Local Legends.   (6 vols.)
Motifs are systematically indexed in a decimal classification
system by subject.   Includes references to sources of information on motifs.   Volume 6 is an alphabetical index.   In-
valuable to anthropologists and students of folklore.   (Stith
Thompson.   Indiana University Press.   Rev. & enl. ed. ,
1955-58)

POLITICAL SCIENCE

Arms Control and Disarmament: a Quarterly Bibliography with Abstracts and Annotations (ceased pub., Spring, 1973)
> Prepared by the Library of Congress; world-wide in scope.
> Books, periodical articles, and documents are included. Author and subject indexes. Annual cumulation. (Government Printing Office, Washington, D.C., 1964-1973)

International Political Science Abstracts (quarterly)
> English or French abstracts of articles on various aspects of political science published in periodicals from many countries. Subject and author indexes. (Basil Blackwell, Oxford, England, 1951-)

Poverty and Human Resources Abstracts (quarterly)
> Includes abstracts of books, articles, pamphlets, government reports, etc. concerned with social problems. Additional lead articles. (Sage Publishers, Beverly Hills, Calif., 1966-)

HISTORY

America: History and Life: a Guide to Periodical Literature (quarterly) 1964-
> Abstracts articles on the history and culture of the United States and Canada from prehistory to the present. Subject arrangement. Recent volumes have combined author, biographical, geographical and subject index. Volume O, published in 1972, covers years 1954-1963, picking up pertinent abstracts on American and Canadian studies which were then covered by Historical Abstracts. (Eric H. Boehm, ed., ABC-Clio Press, Santa Barbara, Calif.)

Historical Abstracts: Bibliography of the World's Periodical Literature (quarterly) 1955-
> Prior to 1971, the abstracts covered the history of all countries from 1775-1945 except for Canada and the United States, which are the subject of America: History and Life, from 1964 on. In 1971, however, the series was expanded to two volumes: vol. one (part A) covering 1775-1914 (modern history), and vol. two (part B) covering 1914-1970 (the twentieth century). Abstracts include political, economic, cultural, social and intellectual history from journals the world over. The arrangement is by subject. Indexing is now combined author, biographical, geographical and subject. (ABC-Clio Press, Santa Barbara, Calif.)

GEOGRAPHY

Geo Abstracts (formerly Geographical Abstracts) (six series, 1966- ;

each pub. 6x yr.)
>Each of the six series is devoted to a separate topic: geo-
morphology, biogeography and climatology; economic geography; social geography; sedimentology; regional and community planning. Abstracts books and articles. International
coverage. (Univ. of East Anglia, Norwich)

BIBLIOGRAPHIC LISTS AND ESSAYS

CROSS-DISCIPLINARY

The ABS Guide to Recent Publications in the Social and Behavioral
Sciences
>The first volume of this series, published in 1965, is a cumu-
lation of the bibliography section "New Studies..." which appears monthly in the periodical, American Behavioral Scientist, covering the years 1957-1964. It includes books, periodical articles, some government reports, pamphlets, and un-
bound items in the social and behavioral sciences. Entries
are annotated. Arrangement is alphabetical by author, with
title, proper name and subject indexes. Covers approximately 6, 664 works. Laymen may find that using this index is
tedious, and that its selectivity is limiting. However, the
annotations are useful, and the work, along·with its annual
supplements, are worth investigating. (American Behavioral
Scientist, New York, 1965; supplements, 1966-)

Guide to Reference Books. 8th ed. (Constance M. Winchell) 1967
>This mainstay of all librarians is an essential guide to re-
searchers in the social sciences. Reference materials, fully
but concisely annotated, are arranged by broad subject areas:
general reference works, the humanities, the social sciences.
Cross references direct the reader to related works listed in
separate sections. About 7, 500 titles are included, with 1964
as the cut-off date. The work is updated by supplements
compiled by Eugene P. Sheehy. The latest of these, the
third supplement, covers the years 1969-1970. (American
Library Association, Chicago)

A London Bibliography of the Social Sciences...
>This work is the most extensive bibliography in the field.
International in scope, it includes books, pamphlets, and
documents arranged by subject. The original four volumes,
published by the London School of Economics and Political
Science, were based on the holdings of nine London libraries
and special collections. Since then, other libraries have
been added and works in Russian included. Kept up to date
by supplements. (British Library of Political and Economic
Science, London)

A Reader's Guide to the Social Sciences
>Introductory essay gives over-view of the evolution of the

social sciences during the past two-hundred years, followed
by bibliographic essays on history, geography, political science, economics, sociology, anthropology, and psychology,
each written by a different author. An excellent introduction
to the literature of these fields. (Edited by Bert F. Hoselitz,
The Free Press, Glencoe, Ill., 1959) (Rev. ed., The Free
Press, New York, 1970)

Sources of Information in the Social Sciences (Carl M. White and
Associates)
An indispensable guide to the literature of the social sciences
covering: the social sciences, in general, history, geography,
economics and business administration, sociology, anthropology, psychology, education, and political science. Includes
annotated lists and short bibliographical essays. Excellent
coverage of all types of information sources in the various
fields. (2d ed., American Library Association, Chicago,
1973)

A Classified Bibliography for the Field of Social Work
Arranged by subject, with two major divisions: counseling
and guidance, and social work. Approximately 5,500 books,
periodical articles, audio-visual aids, theses and dissertations, and government documents. Not annotated, except for
cues to the theme of films, etc. Valuable for bringing together titles from the different media. (Leo M. Tighe.
Premier Publishers, Santa Clara, Calif., 1959)

International Bibliography of the Social Sciences: International Bibliography of Sociology (annual) 1951-
One of four social science bibliographies which comprise the
International Bibliography of the Social Sciences, prepared by
the International Committee for Social Sciences Documentation.
It includes books, periodical articles, pamphlets, and government publications from many countries. Author and English
and French subject indexes. Originally published by UNESCO.
(Aldine Publishing Co., Chicago, Ill.)

ANTHROPOLOGY

A Bibliography of North American Folklore and Folksong
Volume one covers non-Indian Americans north of Mexico,
including Canada. Volume two covers American Indians
north of Mexico, including the Eskimos. Arrangement is
basically by regional areas, but there are also sections including general bibliographies as well as ethnic and occupational. Material covered includes folksongs, folklore, dances,
and music, both printed and recorded. Some annotations.
Two indexes: one for author and subject, and one for com-
posers, arrangers, and performers. (Charles Haywood. 2
vols. 2d rev. ed., Dover Publications, Inc., New York,
1961)

International Bibliography of the Social Sciences: International Bibliography of Social and Cultural Anthropology (annual) 1955-
    Prepared by the International Committee for Social Sciences
    Documentation in cooperation with the International Congress
    of Anthropological and Ethnological Sciences. Lists books
    and periodical articles; international in scope. Author and
    French and English subject indexes. Originally published by
    UNESCO. (Aldine Pub. Co. , Chicago, Ill.)

POLITICAL SCIENCE

The Foreign Affairs 50-year Bibliography: New Evaluations of Significant Books on International Relations, 1920-1970
    Intended as a selection of books on international relations
    which are landmarks in the field, this bibliography includes
    2, 130 reviewed books and 900 additional citations. A group
    of 400 scholars selected the entries which are international
    in scope. The reviews are critical and descriptive, often
    placing a book in perspective and comparing it with others in
    the field. Reviews are in English. Three-part subject ar-
    rangement. Author and title indexes. An excellent work for
    laymen and scholars alike. (Byron Dexter, ed. R. R.
    Bowker Co. , New York and London, 1972)

International Bibliography of the Social Sciences: International Bibliography of Political Science (annual) 1953-
    Includes books, periodical articles, pamphlets, and govern-
    ment publications from many countries. Author and French
    and English subject indexes. Prepared by the International
    Committee for Social Sciences Documentation in cooperation
    with the International Political Science Association. Original-
    ly published by UNESCO. (Aldine Publishing Co. , Chicago,
    Ill.)

The Literature of Political Science: A Guide for Students, Librarians, and Teachers. (Clifton Brock)
    An excellent introduction to library research methods and
    materials in political science, aimed at the undergraduate or
    beginning graduate student. It explains how to use basic re-
    sources in the field. Annotated listing of books, indexes, ab-
    stracts, bibliographies, etc. (R. R. Bowker Co. , New York
    and London, 1969)

Political Science: A Bibliographical Guide to the Literature
    Robert B. Harmon's guide, which now has three supplements,
    offers extensive lists of works arranged by various sub-field
    and topic classifications. Some annotations. (The Scarecrow
    Press, Inc. , New York and London, 1965- , Supplements:
    1968; 1972; 1974)

HISTORY

Annual Bulletin of Historical Literature (annual) 1911-
        Bibliographic essays on a year's publications of books, ar-
        ranged by subject. Covers prehistory to modern times, with
        a separate section on American history. Short critical and
        descriptive annotations. British emphasis. Main entry index.
        An excellent little series, with each section done by a sep-
        arate author. (The Historical Association, London)

Guide to Historical Literature
        Arranged by subject and country groupings, this briefly an-
        notated bibliography lists works selected by specialists in the
        various areas. History books, as well as bibliographies,
        encyclopedias, dictionaries, and government documents are
        among the types of literature included. (American Historical
        Assoc., Macmillan, New York, 1961)

A Guide to the Study of the United States of America...
        Over 6,450 titles on various aspects of American history and
        culture, arranged in 32 chapters. Entries, which are usually
        annotated, are works published through 1955 or 1958, depend-
        ing on the section. An indispensable resource for students
        of American civilization. (U. S. Library of Congress. Gen-
        eral Reference and Bibliography Division. U. S. Government
        Printing Office, Washington, D. C., 1960)

International Bibliography of Historical Sciences (annual) 1926-
        An international, selective listing of books and articles on
        all aspects of history: social, economic, religious, etc. En-
        tries are arranged by subject. Covers prehistory through
        modern times. Index of names at end of volume. Published
        with the assistance of UNESCO. (Ed. by the International
        Committee of Historical Sciences; publisher varies)

GEOGRAPHY

Aids to Geographical Research: Bibliographies, Periodicals, Atlases,
Gazetteers and Other Reference Books
        Completely revised edition of the 1923 work published by the
        authors. Divided into three sections: general aids, topical
        aids, and regional aids and periodicals. English annotations
        of entries in many languages. Author, subject, title, index.
        Appendix lists professional geographers, libraries and other
        institutions engaged in geographical research. While this
        work is now dated, it is an excellent foundation upon which
        to build present research. (John Kirtland Wright and Eliza-
        beth T. Platt. 2d ed. compl. rev., Published for the Amer-
        ican Geographical Society by Columbia University Press, New
        York, 1947)

Current Geographical Publications: Additions to the Research Cata-

logue of the American Geographical Society 1938- , 10x yr.
>Lists by subject, books, periodical articles, pamphlets, gov-
ernment documents and maps in the American Geographical
Society's collection.   Annual index.   Excellent source for
keeping up with materials in the field of geography.   (American Geographical Society of New York, New York)

General World Atlases in Print
>Instead of singling out specific atlases in the Geography book
section which follows, this handy reference work is com-
mended to readers.   It describes, evaluates and compares
domestic and foreign world atlases, covering such aspects
as age suitability, arrangement, scope, and contents, price,
etc.   Indispensable for gaining an overview of available atlases.   (S. Padraig Walsh, comp.   2nd ed.   R. R. Bowker
Co., New York, 1973)

Geographical Research and Writing (Robert W. Durrenberger)
>An introduction to techniques of research and writing.   Part
I gives background in the field of geography, its orientation
and aims, with a general overview of the mechanics of research.   Part II lists sources of information, including bibliographies and indexes, journals, institutions, etc.   (Thomas
Y. Crowell, New York, 1971)

ANNUAL REVIEWS AND STATE OF THE ART REPORTS

CROSS-DISCIPLINARY

Information Please Almanac, Atlas and Yearbook (annual) 1947-
>Almanacs are a handy source for quick reference on a multi-
tude of topics.   Information Please Almanac, for example,
includes sections on current events, world history, awards,
sports, statistics in a variety of fields, dates of celebrated
persons, and many other areas of general information.   (Dan
Golenpaul, ed. Simon and Schuster, New York)

SOCIOLOGY

The Social Welfare Forum: Official Proceedings of the Annual Forum, 1874+
>The title varies.   Selected papers presented at the annual fo-
rum of the National Conference on Social Welfare, which reflect the major concerns of the times.   (National Conference
on Social Welfare, Columbia University Press, New York and
London, 1874+)

Social Work Yearbook (frequency varies) 1928-1960 (ceased publication)

Represented activities and concerns in the field of social
work. Superseded by Encyclopedia of Social Work. (National Assoc. of Social Workers, New York)

ANTHROPOLOGY

Anthropology Today: An Encyclopedic Inventory
A collection of state-of-the-art papers arising from the International Symposium on Anthropology held in 1952. It includes
such renowned scholars as Pierre Teilhard de Chardin, writing on fossil man; V. Gordon Childe on old world prehistory;
Claude Levi-Strauss on social structure, and many others.
Valuable bibliographies at the conclusion of the essays. (Alfred L. Kroeber, ed. University of Chicago Press, Chicago,
Ill., 1953)

Biennial Review of Anthropology
"It is intended to describe and summarize in a systematic
manner the more noteworthy papers and monographs published
since 1955 in five fields of major current interest: social and
cultural change, physical anthropology, linguistics, social organization, and the psychological dimensions of culture."
(Text of foreword.) Chapters are written by specialists with
bibliographies of literature cited. (Ed. by Bernard J. Siegel,
Stanford University Press, Stanford, Calif., 1959-)

Yearbook of Anthropology
This yearbook, which reflects the field of anthropology in
1955, was intended as the first in a series which never developed. Essays are accompanied by bibliographies, and
there is an international list of doctoral dissertations in anthropology, which was updated by later editions of the periodical Current Anthropology. Since this yearbook is sometimes
difficult to locate, note that some of its essays were reprinted in the work: Current Anthropology: a Supplement to
"Anthropology Today," ed. William L. Thomas. (University
of Chicago Press, Chicago, Ill., 1956) (Wenner-Gren Foundation for Anthropological Research, New York, 1955)

POLITICAL SCIENCE AND HISTORY

America Votes: A Handbook of Contemporary American Election
Statistics. Biennial, 1955/56-
Nationwide statistics on presidential elections since 1948;
state by state statistics for the elections of presidents, governors, senators, and congressmen. Data for the most recent elections extends to county and ward. Political maps
show counties and congressional districts and some wards for
major cities. Best reference source for election statistics.
(Ed. by Richard M. Scammon, Congressional Quarterly, Inc.,
Washington, D. C.)

The Book of the States (biennial) 1935-
    Source of great detail on the activities of the state govern-
    ments. Includes chapters on legislation, administrative organ-
    ization, the judiciary, finance, and major state services, etc.
    Numerous statistical tables. Two supplements list state of-
    ficials and members of the legislature, and administrative
    officials. (Council of State Governments)

The Congressional Quarterly Almanac: a Service for Editors and
Commentators (annual, since 1948)
    Based on the material published in CQ Weekly Reports, this
    almanac surveys the activities of congress for the year. In-
    cludes presidential messages, special reports, legislation
    passed, information on the judiciary, etc. For greater de-
    tail, CQ Weekly Reports should also be consulted. (Congres-
    sional Quarterly News Feature, Washington, D.C., 1945-)

The Europa Year Book (annual)
    This two-volume annual provides excellent coverage of inter-
    national organizations, and countries of Europe (vol. 1),
    Asia, Africa, Australia, and the Americas (vol. 2). In-
    cluded are: statistical surveys, information on the economy,
    politics, government, press, religion, finance, trade, etc.
    of the countries described. Much more comprehensive than
    Statesman's Yearbook. (Europa Publications, London, 1959-)

Facts on File: a Weekly World News Digest with Cumulative Index
1940-
    This loose-leaf service is an essential source for keeping up-
    to-date on news events the world over. Coverage is arranged
    by subject area, and the scope is broad although such spe-
    cialized matters as obituaries are included. Biweekly index,
    cumulating throughout the year. Final annual index, and a
    five year index, starting with the coverage of the year 1946-
    1950. (Facts on File, Inc., New York)

International Year Book and Statesmen's Who's Who (annual) 1953-
    Provides detailed information on international organizations,
    and nations of the world. The third section is a biographical
    directory, international in scope, of figures in government
    and politics. Excellent coverage, particularly of individual
    countries, including extensive statistical data. (Mercury
    House Reference Books, London; publisher varies)

Keesing's Contemporary Archives: Weekly Diary of Important World
Events with Index Kept Up-to-Date 1931-
    The British equivalent of Facts-on-File. Loose-leaf form.
    Strong on world events, with greater detail on the Common-
    wealth and the United Kingdom. Often includes small maps
    and statistics to illustrate points. Publishes the texts of
    documents and speeches. Two years completes a volume.
    Name index, since 1959/60, cumulates annually and biennial-
    ly. (Keesing's Publications, London)

The Municipal Year Book: an Authoritative Resume of Activities
and Statistical Data of American Cities (annual)
> The emphasis has varied over the years, but essentially this
> annual yearbook surveys various aspects of municipal organi-
> zation and personnel in the United States. Statistical informa-
> tion on cities of populations over 10, 000, and some smaller
> cities. (International City Managers' Assoc. , Chicago, Ill. ,
> 1934-)

The Statesman's Year-Book: Statistical and Historical Annual of the
States of the World...
> Invaluable handbook for profiles of the nations of the world
> as well as international organizations such as the United Na-
> tions and NATO. For individual countries, covers aspects
> such as constitution and government, geography, systems of
> finance, justice, education, and many other facts which create
> a concise profile. Special features include some maps and
> comparative statistical tables. An excellent, concise refer-
> ence book. (St. Martin's Press, New York, 1864-)

Statistical Abstract of the United States (annual) 1878-
> "... The standard summary of statistics on the social, politi-
> cal, and economic organization of the United States" (preface).
> Includes both published and unpublished data from governmen-
> tal and private publications. Well documented. The various
> sections are prefaced by essays giving introductory and back-
> ground information. Index and guide to sources. (U. S. Bu-
> reau of the Census, U. S. Government Printing Office, Wash-
> ington, D. C.)

Statistical Yearbook (annual) 1948-
> International in scope. World summary section, followed by
> subject-country tables on numerous topics, including: popula-
> tion, production, energy, trade, transportation, communica-
> tion, wages and prices, and social statistics in the fields of
> education, housing, and "culture. " Tables often cover many
> years figures. Publication is bilingual: French and English.
> (United Nations Statistical Office, New York)

GEOGRAPHY

Geography in the Twentieth Century: A Study of Growth, Fields,
Techniques, Aims and Trends
> Contributors from Britain, Canada, the United States, Poland
> and Czechoslovakia. A three-part study: traces the evolu-
> tion of the field of geography; studies environment as a fac-
> tor; includes essays on special fields within geography. Se-
> lected bibliographies at the end of essays. Chart, maps,
> short glossary. (T. Griffith Taylor, ed. Philosophical Li-
> brary, New York, 1957)

Progress in Geography: International Reviews of Current Research

(annual) 1969–
> This annual is for advanced students of geography. It pub-
> lishes a number of scholarly essays in each volume, meant
> to acquaint the reader with current developments within par-
> ticular areas of the field. Extensive bibliographies. (Ed-
> ward Arnold, London)

BOOKS

SOCIOLOGY (including SOCIAL WORK)

Barker, Roger C. and Schoggen, Phil. Qualities of Community Life.
San Francisco: Jossey-Bass, 1973.

Bartlett, Harriett M. The Common Base of Social Work Practice.
New York: National Association of Social Workers, 1970.

Becker, Howard S. Sociological Work: Method and Substance.
Chicago: Aldine Pub. Co., 1970.

Berdyaev, Nicholas. Solitude and Society. London: G. Bles: The
Centenary Press, 1947 (c. 1938).

Berger, Peter L. Invitation to Sociology: a Humanistic Perspective.
New York: Doubleday, 1963.

Blalock, Hubert M. Social Statistics. New York: McGraw-Hill,
1972.

Blau, Peter M. and Duncan, Otis Dudley. The American Occupational Structure. New York: Wiley, 1967.

Comte, Auguste. A General View of Positivism. Tr. by J. H.
Bridges. Stanford, Calif.: Academic Reprints, 1953(?) (orig.
1848).

Dornbusch, Sandford M. and Schmid, Calvin F. A Primer of Social
Statistics. N.Y.: McGraw-Hill, 1955.

Durkheim, Emile. The Division of Labor in Society. Tr. by
George Simpson. Glencoe, Ill.: Free Press, 1947.

Friedlander, Walter A. Introduction to Social Welfare. N.J.:
Prentice-Hall, 1968.

Goode, William J. and Hatt, Paul K. Methods in Social Research.
N.Y.: McGraw-Hill, 1952.

Harrington, Michael. The Other America: Poverty in the United
States. Revised. N.Y.: Macmillan, 1970.

Hawley, Amos H. Urban Society: An Ecological Approach. N.Y.:
    Ronald Press Co., 1971.

Hofstadter, Richard. Social Darwinism in American Thought. Rev.
    ed. New York: George Braziller, inc., 1959.

Jane Addams: A Centennial Reader. N.Y.: Macmillan, 1960.

Lachenmeyer, Charles W. The Language of Sociology. N.Y.: Co-
    lumbia Univ. Press, 1971.

Marx, Karl. Selected Writings in Sociology and Social Philosophy.
    Tr. by T. B. Bottomore. London: Watts, 1956.

Merton, Robert K. Social Theory and Social Structure. Enl. ed.
    N.Y.: Free Press, 1968.

Mills, C. Wright. White Collar: American Middle Classes. Ox-
    ford: Oxford Univ. Press, 1951.

Montagu, Ashley. On Being Human. N.Y.: Hawthorne Books,
    1966.

Nisbet, Robert A. The Sociological Tradition. N.Y.: Basic Books,
    1966.

Ortega y Gasset, Jose. Man and People. Tr. by Willard R. Trask.
    N.Y.: Norton, 1957.

Parsons, Talcott. The Social System. Glencoe, Ill.: Free Press,
    1951.

_____. Sociological Theory and Modern Society. N.Y.: Free
    Press, 1967.

Simey, T. S. Social Science and Social Purpose. N.Y.: Schocken
    Books, 1969.

Spencer, Herbert. Principles of Sociology. 3 vols. N.Y.: D.
    Appleton & Co., 1898.

Weber, Max. The Protestant Ethic and the Spirit of Capitalism.
    Tr. by Talcott Parsons. London: G. Allen & Unwin, 1930.

ANTHROPOLOGY

Benedict, Ruth. Patterns of Culture. Boston and New York:
    Houghton Mifflin Co., 1934.

Binford, Lewis R. and Binford, S., eds. New Perspectives in Ar-
    chaeology. Chicago: Aldine, 1968.

Boaz, Franz. Primitive Art. Cambridge, Mass.: Harvard Univ. Press, 1927.

Cassirer, Ernst. Language and Myth. Tr. by Susanne K. Langer. N. Y.: Dover Publications, c. 1946.

Childe, V. Gordon. Man Makes Himself. Rev. N. Y.: New American Library, 1962 (c. 1951).

Chomsky, Noam. Language and Mind. Enl. ed. New York: Harcourt Brace Jovanovich, 1972.

Clark, Grahame, and Piggott, Stuart. Prehistoric Societies. N. Y.: Penguin Books, Inc., 1970.

Coon, Carleton S. The Story of Man: From the First Human to Primitive Culture and Beyond. 2nd ed., rev. N. Y.: Knopf, 1962.

Darwin, Charles. The Origin of the Species... Chicago: Encyclopaedia Britannica (Great Books of the Western World Series), 1955 (pub. in 1859).

Dobzhansky, Theodosius. Mankind Evolving: The Evolution of the Human Species. New Haven, Conn.: Yale Univ. Press, 1962.

Evans-Pritchard, Edward Evan. Social Anthropology. Glencoe, Ill.: Free Press, 1952.

Frazer, James G. The Golden Bough: a Study in Magic and Religion. 13 vols. New York: St. Martin's Press, 1936 (original: 1911-1915).

Fried, Morton H. Readings in Anthropology. 2d ed. N. Y.: Crowell, 1968.

Hatch, Elvin. Theories of Man and Culture. N. Y. and London: Columbia Univ. Press, 1973.

Herskovits, Melville J. Cultural Anthropology. N. Y.: Knopf, 1955.

Kluckhohn, Clyde. Mirror for Man: the Relation of Anthropology to Modern Life. N. Y.: Whittlesey, 1949.

Kroeber, Alfred L. The Nature of Culture. Chicago: Univ. of Chicago Press, 1952.

Levi-Strauss, Claude. The Savage Mind. Chicago: Univ. of Chicago Press, 1966.

Linton, Ralph. The Tree of Culture. N. Y.: Knopf, 1955.

Malinowski, Bronislaw. Man, Science and Religion, and Other Es-
    says. New York: Doubleday, 1954 (c. 1948).

Mead, Margaret. The Golden Age of American Anthropology. N. Y.:
    George Braziller, 1960.

_____. Growing Up in New Guinea. N. Y.: W. Morrow, 1930.

Montagu, Ashley. Man: His First Two Million Years: A Brief In-
    troduction to Anthropology. N. Y.: Columbia Univ. Press, 1969.

Murdock, George P. Outline of World Cultures. 4th ed. New
    Haven: Human Relations Area Files (Behavior Science Outline
    Series), 1972.

Oliver, Douglas L. Invitation to Anthropology. N. Y.: Published
    for American Museum of Natural History by Natural History
    Press, 1964.

Penniman, Thomas K. A Hundred Years of Anthropology. 3rd ed.
    N. Y.: Humanities Press, Inc., 1965.

Radcliffe-Brown, Alfred R. Structure and Function in Primitive So-
    ciety. London: Cohen and West, 1952.

POLITICAL SCIENCE

Adcock, Frank E. Roman Political Ideas and Practice. Ann Arbor:
    Univ. of Michigan Press, 1959.

Almond, Gabriel A., and Coleman, James S., eds. The Politics of
    the Developing Areas. N. J.: Princeton Univ. Press, 1960.

Arendt, Hannah. The Origins of Totalitarianism. New ed. Har-
    court Brace Jovanovich, 1973.

Bagehot, Walter. The English Constitution. London: Oxford Univ.
    Press, 1933.

Barkun, Michael. Law Without Sanctions: Order in Primitive So-
    cieties and the World Community. New Haven: Yale Univ.
    Press, 1968.

Beard, Charles A. The Economic Basis of Politics. 3rd ed. rev.
    New York: Knopf, 1945.

Binkley, Wilfred. American Political Parties. 4th ed. rev. N. Y.:
    Knopf, 1963.

Blondel, Jean. An Introduction to Comparative Government. N. Y.:
    Praeger, 1970.

Bone, Richard C. Action and Organization: An Introduction to Contemporary Political Science. New York: Harper and Row, 1972.

Boorstein, Daniel J. The Genius of American Politics. Chicago: Univ. of Chicago Press, 1953.

Cassirer, Ernst. The Myth of State. New Haven: Yale Univ. Press, 1946.

Catlin, George E. Politics and Social Theory and Its Application. Ann Arbor: Univ. of Michigan Press, 1964.

Collingwood, R. G. The New Leviathan: Or, Man, Society, Civilization and Barbarism. Oxford: The Clarendon Press, 1947.

Conn, Paul H. Conflict and Decision Making: An Introduction to Political Science. N. Y.: Harper and Row, 1971.

Dahl, Robert A. Modern Political Analysis. 2nd ed. ref. ed. N. J.: Prentice Hall, 1970.

Deininger, Whitaker T. Problems in Social and Political Thought. N. Y.: Macmillan, 1965.

Deutsch, Karl W. The Analysis of International Relations. N. J.: Prentice Hall, 1968.

Earl, Donald A. The Moral and Political Tradition of Rome. Ithaca, N. Y.: Cornell Univ. Press, 1967.

Easton, David. The Political System: An Inquiry into the State of Political Science. 2nd ed. N. Y.: Knopf, 1971.

Eulau, Heinz. Behavioral Persuasion in Politics. N. Y.: Random House, 1963.

Friedrich, Carl J. Introduction to Political Theory. N. Y.: Harper and Row, 1967.

_____. Pathology of Politics: Violence, Betrayal, Corruption, Secrecy, and Propaganda. N. Y.: Harper and Row, 1972.

Froman, Lewis A., Jr. The Congressional Process: Strategies Rules and Procedures. Boston: Little, 1967.

Grene, David. Greek Political Theory: The Image of Man in Thucydides and Plato. Chicago: Univ. of Chicago Press, 1965.

Hofstadter, Richard. The American Political Tradition. N. Y.: Knopf, 1973.

Jackson, Robert H. The Supreme Court in the American System of Government. Cambridge, Mass.: Harvard Univ. Press, 1955.

Laski, Harold J. Grammar of Politics. 5th ed. N. Y.: Humanities Press, 1967.

Lipset, Seymour M. Political Man: Essays on the Sociology of Democracy. N. Y.: Doubleday and Co., 1959.

Machiavelli, Niccolo. Chief Works, and Others. Tr. by Allan Gilbert. Durham, N. C.: Duke Univ. Press, 1965.

Marx, Karl and Engels, Friedrich. The Communist Manifesto. J. H. Laski, ed. N. Y.: Pantheon Books, Inc., 1967 (pub. 1848).

Murray, Robert H. The History of Political Science from Plato to the Present. 2nd ed. N. Y.: Appleton, 1930.

Palumbo, Dennis J. Statistics in Political and Behavioral Science. N. Y.: Appleton-Century-Crofts, 1969.

Polanyi, Karl. The Great Transformation: The Political and Economic Origins of Our Times. Boston: Beacon Press, 1957.

Popper, Karl R. Open Society and Its Enemies. 2 vols. 5th rev. ed. Princeton, N. J.: Princeton Univ. Press, 1966.

Pritchett, Charles H. The American Constitution. 2nd ed. N. Y.: McGraw-Hill, 1968.

Rossiter, Clinton L. The American Presidency. Rev. ed. N. Y.: Harcourt, Brace, Jovanovich, 1960.

Sabine, George H. A History of Political Thought. 4th ed. N. Y.: Holt, Rinehart and Winston, Inc., 1973.

Shklar, Judith N. After Utopia: The Decline of Political Faith. Princeton: Princeton Univ. Press, 1969.

Strauss, Leo. Liberalism, Ancient and Modern. N. Y.: Basic Books, 1968.

Ullmann, Walter. A History of Political Thought: the Middle Ages. Baltimore: Penguin Books, 1965.

HISTORY

Ashton, Thomas S. The Industrial Revolution: 1760-1830. London and New York: Oxford Univ. Press, 1948.

Barnes, Harry E. A History of Historical Writing. 2nd rev. ed. N. Y.: Dover Publications, 1963.

Boak, Arthur E., and Sinnigen, W. A. A History of Rome to

A. D. 565. 5th ed. N. Y.: Macmillan, 1965.

Brinton, Crane, et al. A History of Civilization. 2 vols. 4th ed.
N. J.: Prentice Hall, 1971.

Burckhardt, Jacob. The Civilization of the Renaissance. 2d ed.
rev. N. Y.: Oxford Univ. Press, 1945.

Bury, John B. A History of Greece to the Death of Alexander the
Great. 3rd ed. New York: St. Martin's Press, 1951.

_____. The Idea of Progress: An Inquiry into Its Origin and
Growth. London: Macmillan, 1924.

Cairns, Grace E. Philosophies of History: Meeting of East and
West in Cycle-Pattern Themes of History. N. Y.: Philosophical
Library, 1962.

Cambridge Ancient History... 12 vols. and 5 vols. plates. Cambridge: Univ. Press; N. Y.: Macmillan, 1923-39.

_____. 3rd ed. London: Cambridge Univ. Press, 1970-

Cambridge Mediaeval History, planned by J. B. Bury... 8 vols.
Cambridge: Univ. Press; N. Y.: Macmillan, 1911-1936.

_____. 2d ed. Cambridge: Univ. Press, 1966-

Collingwood, R. G. The Idea of History. Oxford: Clarendon Press,
1946.

Commager, Henry S. Documents of American History. 9th ed.
N. Y.: Appleton-Century-Crofts, 1973.

Durant, Will, and Durant Ariel. The Story of Civilization. 10 vols.
N. Y.: Simon and Schuster, 1935-1967.

Ekirch, Arthur A. American Intellectual History: The Development
of the Discipline. Washington: American History Assn., 1973.

Gardiner, Alan. Egypt of the Pharaohs: An Introduction. Oxford:
Clarendon Press, 1961.

Gelb, Ignace. A Study of Writing. Rev. ed. Chicago: Univ. of
Chicago Press, 1963.

Gibbon, Edward. Decline and Fall of the Roman Empire. D. M.
Low, ed. New York: Harcourt, Brace, Jovanovich, 1960.
(written: 1776-1788)

Gooch, George P. History and Historians in the Nineteenth Century.
2d ed. London and N. Y.: Longmans, Green, 1952.

Hofstadter, Richard, et al. The United States: The History of a Republic. N. J.: Prentice Hall, 1957.

Huizinga, Johann. The Waning of the Middle Ages. N. Y.: St. Martin's Press, 1924.

Lot, Ferdinand. The End of the Ancient World and the Beginnings of the Middle Ages. N. Y.: Knopf, 1931.

McNeill, William H. The Rise of the West: A History of the Human Community. Chicago: Univ. of Chicago Press, 1963.

Muir, Ramsey. Muir's Historical Atlas: Ancient, Medieval, and Modern. 10th ed. N. Y.: Barnes and Noble, 1964.

Muller, Herbert J. The Loom of History. N. Y.: Harper and Row, 1958.

_____. Uses of the Past: Profiles of Former Societies. New York: Oxford Univ. Press, 1952.

The New Cambridge Modern History. 14 vols. Cambridge: University Press, 1957-70.

Oppenheim, A. Leo. Ancient Mesopotamia: Portrait of a Dead Civilization. Chicago: Univ. of Chicago Press, 1964.

Palmer, Robert R. , and Colton, Joel. A History of the Modern World. 4th ed. N. Y.: Knopf, 1971.

Rostovtzeff, Mikhail. A Social and Economic History of the Hellenistic World. 3 vols. Oxford: Univ. Press, 1941.

Runciman, Steven. Byzantine Civilization. N. Y.: St. Martin's Press, 1933.

Shepherd, William R. Shepherd's Historical Atlas. 9th ed. N. Y.: Barnes and Noble, 1964.

Toynbee, Arnold. A Study of History. 12 vols. London and N. Y.: Oxford Univ. Press, 1955-1961.

Trevelyan, George M. , ed. Illustrated English Social History. 4 vols. London and N. Y.: Longmans, Green, and Co. , 1951-1952.

Trotsky, Leon. The History of the Russian Revolution. Tr. by Max Eastman. Ann Arbor: Univ. of Michigan Press, 1960.

Widgery, Albin G. Interpretations of History: Confucius to Toynbee. London: Allen and Unwin, 1961.

Wilson, Edmund. To the Finland Station. N. Y.: Doubleday, 1953.

GEOGRAPHY

Behavioral and Social Sciences Survey Committee. Geography Panel.
  Geography. Ed. by Edward J. Taaffe. N. J.: Prentice-Hall,
  1970.

Bengston, Nels A. and Van Royen, William. Fundamentals of Economic Geography: An Introduction to the Study of Resources.
  5th ed. N. Y.: Prentice-Hall, 1964.

Bourne, Larry S., ed. Internal Structure of the City: Readings on
  Space and Environment. N. Y.: Oxford Univ. Press, 1971.

Broek, Jan O., and Webb, John W. A Geography of Mankind.
  N. Y.: McGraw-Hill, 1973.

Brown, Ralph H. Historical Geography of the U. S. New York:
  Harcourt, Brace, Jovanovich, 1948.

Butzer, Karl. Environment and Archaeology: An Ecological Approach to Prehistory. 2d ed. Chicago: Aldine, 1971.

Chisholm, Michael. Geography and Economics. N. Y.: Praeger,
  1966.

Cohen, Saul B., ed. Problems and Trends in American Geography.
  N. Y.: Basic Books, 1967.

Critchfield, Howard J. General Climatology. 2d ed. N. J.: Prentice Hall, 1966.

Dohrs, Fred E., and Sommers, Lawrence M., eds. Introduction to
  Geography: Selected Readings. N. Y.: Crowell, 1967.

Everyman's Atlas of Ancient and Classical Geography. Rev. ed.
  London: Dent; New York: Dutton, 1952.

Freeman, Thomas W. A Hundred Years of Geography. Chicago:
  Aldine, 1962.

Hall, Peter. The World Cities. London, New York: McGraw-Hill,
  1966.

James, Preston E. All Possible Worlds: A History of Geographical Ideas. Indianapolis: Bobbs-Merrill, 1972.

King, Leslie J. Statistical Analysis in Geography. N. J.: Prentice-
  Hall, 1969.

Lock, C. B. Muriel. Geography: A Reference Handbook. 2d ed.
  rev. Hamden, Conn.: The Shoe String Press, 1972.

Monkhouse, Francis J. Principles of Physical Geography. 7th ed.

N. Y.:   American Elsevier Pub. Co., 1971.

Robinson, Arthur H., and Sale, Randall D.   Elements of Cartog-
   raphy.   3d ed.   N. Y.:   Wiley, 1969.

Trewartha, Glenn T.   Geography of Populations: World Patterns.
   N. Y.:   Wiley, 1969.

Zelinsky, Wilbur.   The Cultural Geography of the United States.
   N. J.:   Prentice-Hall, 1973.

ENCYCLOPEDIC SUMMARIES

CROSS-DISCIPLINARY

American Men and Women of Science, Vols. 7 and 8:   The Social
and Behavioral Sciences, A-Z (Formerly American Men of Science)
          Vols. 7 and 8 of the set list professional information on over
          34, 000 scholars in the social and behavioral sciences.   In-
          cludes necrology and geographical index.   12th ed.   (Jaques
          Cattell Press/R. R. Bowker Co., New York and London,
          1973)

Concise Dictionary of American Biography
          Summarizes all the articles appearing in the monumental
          Dictionary of American Biography, which notes notable people
          who lived in what is now the United States and died before
          Dec. 31, 1940.   (Charles Scribner's Sons, N. Y., 1964)

A Dictionary of the Social Sciences
          Published through the support of UNESCO, the dictionary "is
          designed to describe and define approximately one thousand
          basic concepts used in the social sciences" (foreword).   270
          social scientists from the United States and the United King-
          dom worked on the signed articles which discuss the usages
          of common and technical terms.   Well documented.   (Gould,
          Julius, and Kalb, eds.   The Free Press of Glencoe, N. Y.,
          1964)

Directory of American Scholars: a Biographical Directory
          Lists biographical and professional information on United
          States scholars in the social sciences and the humanities:
          v. 1:   History; v. 2:   English, Speech, and Drama; v. 3:   For-
          eign Languages, Linguistics, and Philology; v. 4:   Philosophy,
          Religion and Law.   (Jaques Cattell/R. R. Bowker Co., New
          York and London, 5th ed., 1969)

Encyclopaedia of the Social Sciences (1930-1935)
          Sponsored by 10 learned societies, the encyclopedia pioneered
          in setting forth the entire field of the social sciences for

interdisciplinary study. A staff of international scholars con-
tributed the signed articles on topics in the fields of economics, law, politics, anthropology, sociology, social work,
penology and others. Bibliographies accompany articles.
Cross references. Subject Index. This work is not superseded by the International Encyclopedia of the Social Sciences,
which is an entirely new encyclopedia, reflecting the social
sciences in the sixties. (Macmillan, N. Y.)

International Encyclopedia of the Social Sciences (1968)
Signed articles by scholars from over 30 countries on the
theories, concepts, principles and methods of anthropology,
economics, geography, history, law, political science, psychiatry, psychology, sociology and statistics. Emphasis is
on the comparative and analytical rather than the historical
and descriptive. Alphabetical arrangement with cross references and valuable bibliographies at the conclusion of the
articles. Index volume. 600 biographical entries. An excellent, well documented presentation. This encyclopedia
complements the Encyclopaedia of the Social Sciences, which
has more biographical entries and retains its value as a
unique piece of scholarship. No articles have been reprinted
in the International Encyclopedia; it has an entirely new text,
excellent in its own right. (Macmillan, N. Y.)

World Index of Social Science Institutions: Research, Advanced
Training, Documentation and Professional Bodies.
An international directory of organizations, providing such in-
formation as address, date of founding, activities and publica-
tions. The loose-leaf format simplifies up-dating. (UNESCO,
Paris, 1970)

SOCIOLOGY

A Modern Dictionary of Sociology
Defines concepts both from the field of sociology and also
related disciplines. Alternate usages are indicated. Cross
references. (Theodorson, George A. , and Theodorson,
Achilles G. Thomas Y. Crowell, N. Y. , 1969)

Encyclopedia of Social Work
Succeeds The Social Work Year Book. Includes signed articles, accompanied by bibliographies, on the history of social
work, developments in the field, as well as biographies of
leading persons. There is also a very useful statistical section on trends in social welfare and demography. (National
Assoc. of Social Workers, N. Y. , 1965-)

ANTHROPOLOGY

Dictionary of Anthropology

Concise definitions of terms from all areas of anthropology.
Includes short biographies of persons who made contributions
to the field prior to 1970. (Charles Winick. Philosophical
Library, N. Y., 1956)

Encyclopaedia of Religion and Ethics
A monumental work and an acknowledged classic in its field.
Includes articles on world religions and ethical systems, cus-
toms, practices, mythologies, philosophies, etc. Bibliographies accompany the signed articles. (Ed. by James Hast-
ings, with the assistance of John A. Selbie and Louis H.
Gray. Charles Scribner's Sons, N. Y., 1908-1927. 12 vols.
and index.)

Funk and Wagnalls Standard Dictionary of Folklore, Mythology and
Legend
A selection of aspects of many cultures, including articles
on gods, folk heroes, dances, folk songs, riddles, spells,
etc. written by leading scholars. There are longer survey
articles on selected subjects, signed and with accompanying
bibliographies. Contains a wealth of information. 2 vols.
(Maria, Leach, ed. Funk and Wagnalls Co., N. Y., 1949-
50)

Larousse World Mythology
A visually splendid work, which supports essays by leading
scholars with plates of artifacts and art works. Includes
religions and mythologies from a wide range of cultures,
from ancient Egypt to contemporary Africa. Index and bibliography of suggested further readings. (Pierre Grimal,
ed. G. P. Putnam's Sons, N. Y., 1965)

Man, Myth and Magic: An Illustrated Encyclopedia of the Supernatural
While its profuse illustrations may strike the general reader
as somewhat lurid, this encyclopedia boasts an impressive
board of editors and contributors: internationally known
scholars such as Mircea Eliade, E. R. Dodds, Glyn Daniel,
and R. C. Zaehner among them. Articles cover diverse
topics, and include information not readily available in other
reference sources. Students of anthropology and comparative
religions will want to refer to it. 24 vols. (Index included).
(Richard Cavendish, ed. Marshall Cavendish Corp., N. Y.,
1970)

POLITICAL SCIENCE

The American Political Dictionary
Arrangement is by broad topics such as political ideas, the
constitution, civil rights, etc. Within each section, pertinent
terms are defined and agencies, statutes and court cases

listed and explained. Read by section, the work gives the
reader a good-background in a particular subject area. Approached by the index, it can serve as a dictionary. (Jack
C. Plano and Milton Greenberg. 3d ed. Holt, Rinehart and
Winston, Inc., N.Y., 1972)

Dictionary of Political Science
       Identifies and defines persons, places, terms, concepts, or-
       ganizations, acts, etc., related to political science in signed
       articles, written by a staff of close to 200 scholars. (Joseph
       Dunner, ed. Philosophical Library, N.Y., 1964)

A Dictionary of Politics
       International in scope. Defines terms; entries on nations and
       living persons active in international affairs. (Florence El-
       liott and Michael Summerskill. 6th ed. Penguin, Harmonds-
       worth, England, 1969)

Official Congressional Directory (1809-   ) annual
       A concise source to consult for: biographical information on
       Congressmen (arranged by state); details such as mailing ad-
       dresses and terms of service; composition of congressional
       committees and their staffs; maps of congressional districts;
       names of diplomats; biographies of members of the judiciary;
       and a multitude of other details. (U.S. Government Printing
       Office, Washington, D.C.)

White's Political Dictionary
       Although this dictionary is now dated, it remains a standard
       work. Good for definitions of general terms, government
       organizations, treaties, etc. (Wilber Wallace White. World,
       N.Y., 1947)

Who's Who in American Politics
       Biographical and professional information on more than 15,800
       persons in all levels of politics, from national to local. In-
       cludes a geographical index. (Paul A. Theis and Edmund L.
       Henshaw, eds. R. R. Bowker Co., N.Y. and London, 1971.
       3rd ed.)

Worldmark Encyclopedia of the Nations
       "A practical guide to the geographic, historical, political, so-
       cial, and economic status of all nations, their international
       relationships, and the United Nations system" (text). The
       five volumes cover: 1) the United Nations; 2) Africa; 3) the
       Americas; 4) Asia and Australia; and 5) Europe. Country by
       country profiles, covering numerous topics. Some maps;
       statistics. Lengthy bibliographies. 5 vols. (Harper and
       Row, N.Y., 1967)

HISTORY

Dictionary of American History
    More than one thousand historians contributed to this work of
    over 6,000 signed articles on all aspects of American his-
    tory: social, cultural, political, economic, etc. No biog-
    raphies. Cross references. Volumes 1-5 extend to 1940.
    Volume 6 covers 1940-1960 and revises dated articles from
    the original set. Alphabetical arrangement. (James Truslow
    Adams, ed. 2d ed. rev. Scribner, N.Y., 1942-61. 6 vols.
    and index)

Encyclopedia of American History
    Arranged chronologically and topically, coverage extends from
    earliest times through the sixties. Its three parts contain:
    principally military and political events arranged in chrono-
    logical sequence; specific topics, treated chronologically, such
    as American expansion, population, the economy, thought and
    culture; profiles of 400 notable Americans. Includes statisti-
    cal tables, maps and charts. A useful reference work.
    (Richard B. Morris and Henry S. Commager, eds. Harper,
    N.Y., 1970)

An Encyclopedia of World History: Ancient, Medieval, and Modern,
Chronologically Arranged
    Arranged in chronological sequence, Langer's narrative hand-
    book spans historical events, from ancient to modern. There
    are maps and genealogical tables, as well as handy listings
    of Popes, Holy Roman Emperors, etc. Useful as a quick
    guide for orienting the reader within a particular period. Ap-
    pendices and index. Excellent handbook. (William L. Langer,
    ed. and compiler. 4th ed. rev. and enl. Houghton Mifflin
    Co., Boston, 1968)

The Oxford Classical Dictionary
    This scholarly dictionary's emphasis is on aspects of Greek
    and Roman culture: religion, philosophy, antiquities, biog-
    raphy, etc. The signed entries usually include bibliography,
    and there are longer survey articles throughout the text. An
    excellent reference work. (N.G.L. Hammond and H. H.
    Scullard, eds. 2d ed. Clarendon Press, Oxford, 1970)

GEOGRAPHY

A Dictionary of Geography
    Includes about 4,000 terms; selection is based on usage.
    Cross references. Diagrams, analytical list of entries by
    topic. A concise, useful reference work. (Francis J. Monk-
    house. 2d ed. Edward Arnold, London; Aldine, Chicago,
    1970)

Webster's New Geographical Dictionary
        Includes over 47,000 entries and 217 maps. International in
        scope.   Information given varies with type of entry.   Among
        aspects covered: spelling, pronunciation, population, loca-
        tion, size, economy and history.   Cross references.   The
        United States and Canada are most fully represented, with
        all incorporated places having a population over 2,500 listed,
        but coverage of other countries is good considering the size
        of the work.   An interesting feature is the inclusion of short
        historical notes on famous cities, such as Thebes and Mem-
        phis in Egypt, which are now archaeological sites.   A useful,
        portable gazetteer.   (G. & C. Merriam Co., Springfield,
        Mass., 1972)

Search Procedure Form	GENERAL SOCIAL SCIENCES
NAME OF USER	**DATE OF INQUIRY**

REDEFINED QUESTION STATEMENT

KEYWORDS

WORK IN PROGRESS

☐   Contemporary Authors

UNPUBLISHED STUDIES

Cross-Disciplinary
☐   Dissertation Abstracts International
☐   Guide to Lists of Master's Theses
☐   Masters Abstracts
Sociology
☐   Social Service Review
☐   Sociology Dissertations in American Universities, 1893-1966
Anthropology
☐   Yearbook of Anthropology
Political Science

☐   American Political Science Review
History
☐   Dissertations in History: An Index to Dissertations Completed in History Departments of United States and Canadian Universities, 1873-1960
☐   List of Doctoral Dissertations in History. . .
Geography
☐   A bibliography of Dissertations in Geography: 1901-1969: American and Canadian Universities

PERIODICALS

Sociology
☐   Aging
☐   American Behavioral Scientist
☐   American Journal of Sociology
☐   American Sociological Review
☐   American Sociologist
☐   Current Sociology
☐   International Journal of Comparative Sociology
☐   Journal of Marriage and the Family
☐   Journal of Social Issues
☐   Public Administration Review
☐   Public Welfare
☐   Race Today
☐   Social Casework
☐   Social Problems
☐   Social Research
☐   Social Security Bulletin
☐   Social Service Review
☐   Social Work
☐   Society
☐   Sociometry
☐   Urban Affairs Quarterly
☐   Welfare Fighter
☐   Welfare in Review
Anthropology
☐   American Anthropologist
☐   American Antiquity
☐   American Journal of Archaeology
☐   American Schools of Oriental Research
☐   Anthropological Journal of Canada
☐   Anthropological Quarterly
☐   Anthropos
☐   Antiquity
☐   Archaeology
☐   Current Anthropology

☐   Current History
☐   Dept. of State Bulletin
☐   Foreign Affairs
☐   International Affairs
☐   International Development Review
☐   Journal of Politics
☐   Orbis
☐   Political Science Quarterly
☐   Public Administration Review
☐   Public Opinion Quarterly
☐   Review of Politics
☐   State Government
☐   Urban Affairs Quarterly
☐   Weekly Compilation of Presidential Documents
☐   World Politics
History
☐   American Chronical
☐   American Heritage
☐   American Historical Review
☐   American Quarterly
☐   Catholic Historical Review
☐   Comparative Studies in Society and History
☐   English Historical Review
☐   Historian, A Journal of History
☐   History Today
☐   Horizon
☐   Journal of African History
☐   Journal of American Studies
☐   Journal of Contemporary History
☐   Journal of Modern History
☐   Journal of Negro History
☐   Journal of Social History
☐   Journal of the History of Ideas
☐   Mankind: the Magazine of Popular History

☐ Expedition - The Magazine of Archaeology/Anthropology
☐ Journal of American Folklore
☐ Journal of Near Eastern Studies

Political Science
☐ American City
☐ American County Government
☐ American Political Science Review
☐ Atlas
☐ Canadian Journal of Political Science
☐ Comparative Politics

Geography
☐ Association of American Geographers, Annals
☐ Canadian Geographical Journal
☐ Economic Geography
☐ Explorers Journal
☐ Focus
☐ Geographical Journal
☐ Geographical Review
☐ Journal of Geography
☐ National Geographic Magazine

REPORTS AND MONOGRAPHS

Sociology
☐ Sociological Series

Anthropology
☐ Memoirs
☐ Contributions to Anthropology, 1910-

Political Science
☐ Monograph Series, 1933+
☐ CQ Weekly Reports

☐ The Congressional Quarterly Almanac
☐ Harvard Political Studies 1930+

History
☐ Publications, 1932+
☐ Smith College Studies in History, 1915+

Geography
☐ Research Series 1921 -
☐ Northwestern University Studies in Geography 1952+

INDEXES AND ABSTRACTING SERVICES

Cross-Disciplinary
☐ The Gallup Opinion Index: Political, Social and Economic Trends
☐ Index to Periodical Articles By and About Negroes
☐ Index to Selected Periodical Received in the Hallie Q. Brown Library
☐ Index to Periodicals Articles by and About Negroes
☐ Monthly Catalog of United States Government Publications, 1895+
☐ The New York Times Index
☐ Public Affairs Information Service Bulletin
☐ Social Sciences and Humanities Index

Sociology
☐ Abstracts for Social Workers
☐ Crime and Delinquency Abstracts
☐ Population Index
☐ Sociological Abstracts

Anthropology
☐ Abstracts in Anthropology
☐ Abstracts of Folklore Studies
☐ Art Index
☐ Motif-Index of Folk Literature: A Classification of Narrative Elements in Folktales, Ballads, Myths, Fables, and Mediaeval Romances, Exempla, Fabliaux, Jest-Books and Local Legends

Political Science
☐ Arms Control and Disarmament: A Quarterly Bibliography with Abstracts and Annotations
☐ International Political Science Abstracts
☐ Poverty and Human Resources Abstracts

History
☐ America: History and Life: A Guide to Periodical Literature
☐ Historical Abstracts: Bibliography of the World's Periodical Literature

Geography
☐ Geo Abstracts

BIBLIOGRAPHIC LISTS AND ESSAYS

Cross-Disciplinary
☐ The ABS Guide to Recent Publications in the Social and Behavioral Sciences
☐ A London Bibliography of the Social Sciences. . .
☐ A Reader's Guide to the Social Sciences
☐ Sources of Information in the Social Sciences
☐ A Classified Bibliography for the Field of Social Work
☐ International Bibliography of the Social Sciences: International Bibliography of Sociology

Anthropology
☐ A Bibliography of North American Folklore and Folksong
☐ International Bibliography of the Social Sciences: International Bibliography of Social and Cultural Anthropology

Political Science
☐ The Foreign Affairs 50-year Bibliography: New Evaluations of Significant Books on International Relations 1920-1970
☐ International Bibliography of the Social Sciences: International Bibliography of Political Science 1953 -

☐ The Literature of Political Science: A Guide for Students, Librarians, and Teachers
☐ Political Science: A Bibliographical Guide to the Literature

History
☐ Annual Bulletin of Historical Literature
☐ Guide to Historical Literature
☐ A Guide to the Study of the United States of America. . .
☐ International Bibliography of Historical Sciences

Geography
☐ Aids to Geographical Research: Bibliographies, Periodicals, Atlases, Gazetteers and Other Reference Books
☐ Current Geographical Publications: Additions to the Research Catalogue of the American Geographical Society
☐ General World Atlases in Print
☐ Geographical Research and Writing

ANNUAL REVIEWS AND STATE-OF-THE-ART REPORTS

Cross-Disciplinary
☐ Information Please Almanac, Atlas and Yearbook

Sociology
☐ The Social Welfare Forum: Official Proceedings of the Annual Forum
☐ Social Work Yearbook

Anthropology
☐ Anthropology Today: An Encyclopedic Inventory
☐ Biennial Review of Anthropology
☐ Yearbook of Anthropology

Political Science and History
☐ America Votes: A Handbook of Contemporary American Election Statistics
☐ The Book of the States
☐ The Congressional Quarterly Almanac: a Service for Editors and Commentators

☐ The Europa Year Book
☐ Facts on File: a Weekly World News Digest with Cumulative Index
☐ International Year Book and Statesmen's Who's Who
☐ Keesing's Contemporary Archives: Weekly Diary of Important World Events with Index Kept up-to-date 1931
☐ The Municipal Year Book: an Authoritative Resume of Activities and Statistical Data of American Cities
☐ The Statesman's Year-Book: Statistical and Historical Annual of the States of the World. . .
☐ Statistical Abstract of the United States
☐ Statistical Yearbook

Geography
☐ Geography in the Twentieth Century: A Study of Growth, Fields, Techniques, Aims and Trends
☐ Progress in Geography: International Reviews of Current Research

ENCYCLOPEDIC SUMMARIES

Cross-Disciplinary
☐ American Men and Women of Science, The Social and Behavioral Sciences, A-Z
☐ Concise Dictionary of American Biography
☐ A Dictionary of the Social Sciences
☐ Directory of American Scholars: A Biographical Directory
☐ Encyclopedia of the Social Sciences
☐ International Encyclopedia of the Social Sciences
☐ World Index of Social Science, Institutions: Research, Advanced Training, Documentation and Professional Bodies

Sociology
☐ A Modern Dictionary of Sociology
☐ Encyclopedia of Social Work

Anthropology
☐ Dictionary of Anthropology
☐ Encyclopedia of Religion and Ethnics
☐ Funk and Wagnalls Standard Dictionary of Folklore, Mythology and Legend
☐ Larousse World Mythology
☐ Man, Myth, and Magic: An Illustrated Encyclopedia of the Supernatural

Political Science
☐ The American Political Dictionary
☐ Dictionary of Political Science
☐ A Dictionary of Politics
☐ Official Congressional Directory
☐ White's Political Dictionary
☐ Who's Who in American Politics
☐ Worldmark Encyclopedia of the Nations

History
☐ Dictionary of American History
☐ Encyclopedia of American History
☐ An Encyclopedia of World History: Ancient, Medieval, and Modern, Chronologically Arranged
☐ The Oxford Classical Dictionary

Geography
☐ A Dictionary of Geography
☐ Webster's New Geographical Dictionary

COMMENTS:

SEARCHER'S SIGNATURE

DATE COMPLETED

Discipline Resource Package

PSYCHOLOGY

Jovian P. Lang
St. John's University

Psychology is that branch of the social sciences which deals with man as an individual and as a member of groups. It is a bio-social science using theoretical, experimental and observational tech-niques to study the nature, mind, and behavior of individual man and the activities of groups of men.

WORK IN PROGRESS

Contemporary Authors

A comprehensive source for biographical data on contemporary authors, many of which may not yet appear in traditional bio-graphical sources. Entries are short, with personal, career, and work-in-progress information. A list of writings and sources of biographical and critical data are given when pos-sible. The set is now in its 48th volume but many of the earlier volumes have been cumulated. Each volume is a sep-arate alphabet but a cumulative name index is provided at the end of volume 48. (Gale Research Co., Detroit)

UNPUBLISHED STUDIES

Dissertation Abstracts International

The most complete source for abstracts of doctoral disserta-tions written in the United States. Most U.S. universities contribute to this system operated by a private corporation. Unfortunately, several important universities do not partici-pate. Microfilm or paper copies of the dissertations are available for purchase. Until recently, the indexing has been spotty and of poor quality. Fortunately, a much better (and very expensive) 37-volume cumulative index is now available. (University Microfilms, Ann Arbor, Mich.)

Masters Abstracts

This is a selective, classified and annotated list of master's theses produced by many, but by no means all, U.S. colleges and universities. As with dissertations, microfilm or paper copies of the theses are available for purchase from the publisher of the Abstracts. Due to its selectivity, it is much easier to use than <u>Dissertation Abstracts International</u>. <u>MA</u> is presently being published quarterly. (University Microfilms, Ann Arbor, Mich.)

PERIODICALS

American Imago; a Psychoanalytic Journal for Culture, Science, and the Arts (quarterly)
American Journal of Psychiatry (monthly)
American Journal of Psychology (quarterly)
American Journal of Psychotherapy (quarterly)
Behavior Therapy (quarterly)
Biological Psychiatry (quarterly)
British Journal of Psychiatry (monthly)
Cognitive Psychology (quarterly)
Contemporary Psychology; a Journal of Reviews (monthly)
Educational and Psychological Measurement (quarterly)
Group Psychotherapy and Psychodrama (quarterly)
Journal of Applied Behavior Analysis (quarterly)
Journal of Applied Psychology (bi-monthly)
Journal of Counseling Psychology (monthly)
Journal of Personality and Social Psychology (monthly)
Journal of Social Issues (quarterly)
Mental Hygiene (quarterly)
Mental Retardation (bi-monthly)
Personality, an International Journal (quarterly)
Psychoanalytic Quarterly
Psychology; a Journal of Human Behavior (quarterly)
Psychology Today (monthly)
Psychotherapy (quarterly)
Rehabilitation Record (bi-monthly)
You (monthly)

INDEXES AND ABSTRACTING SERVICES

<u>Child Development Abstracts and Bibliography</u> (3x yr.)
    Materials related to maturation (birth to adulthood) are included; including educational materials, psychological, medical, etc. (University of Chicago Press, Chicago, Ill.)

<u>Mental Health Book Review Index</u>
    Refers to signed book reviews, if they appeared in three or more journals of the over 200 periodicals indexed each year in the fields of psychiatry, psychoanalysis, and psychology. (Library, Queens College, Flushing, N.Y. 11367)

<u>Psychological Abstracts</u>
    Signed abstracts of each new book and article are grouped by

subjects covering several related fields, but with an author
index in each number.   Each volume has an author-subject
index.   Published monthly with 6-month cumulative indexes.
(American Psychological Association, Washington, D.C.)

BIBLIOGRAPHICAL LISTS AND ESSAYS

Bibliography of Philosophy, Psychology, and Cognate Subjects
        Out of date, but this most important bibliography in English
        is divided into three parts: 1.. General; 2.   History, in-
        cluding individual philosophers arranged alphabetically; 3. Log-
        ic, ethics, psychology, aesthetics, systematic philosophy and
        the philosophy of religion.   (Peter Smith, N.Y.)

Harvard List of Books in Psychology
        Over 700 books are annotated by psychologists at Harvard
        University because of their value and importance in psychology
        today.   (Harvard University Press, Cambridge, Mass.)

ANNUAL REPORTS AND STATE OF THE ART REPORTS

Annual Review of Psychology
        Contemporary psychology, with an emphasis on interpretation
        and evaluation, is reviewed each year by prominent psycholo-
        gists.   After four or five years certain areas are reinter-
        preted.   (Annual Reviews, Stanford, CA.)

BOOKS

Allport, Gordon W.   The Nature of Prejudice.   Cambridge, Mass.:
        Addison, 1954.

_____.   Pattern in Growth and Personality.   N.Y.:   Holt, 1961.

Boring, Edwin G.   A History of Experimental Psychology, 2nd ed.
        N.Y.:   Appleton, 1957.

Bruner, Jerome S., et al.   A Study of Thinking.   N.Y.:   Wiley,
        1956.

Brunswik, Egon.   The Conceptual Framework of Psychology.   Chi-
        cago: University of Chicago Press, 1952.

Cronbach, Lee J.   Educational Psychology.   N.Y.:   Harcourt, 1954.

_____.   Essentials of Psychological Testing, 2nd ed.   N.Y.:
        Harper, 1960

Dreikurs, Rudolf. Fundamentals of Adlerian Psychology. N. Y.:
    Greenberg, 1950.

Erikson, Erik H. Childhood and Society. N. Y.: Norton, 1950.

Fisher, Ronald A. The Design of Experiments, 7th ed. N. Y.:
    Hafner, 1960.

Freud, Sigmund. A General Introduction to Psychoanalysis. N. Y.:
    Boni and Liveright, 1920.

_____. The Interpretation of Dreams. N. Y.: Basic Books,
    1955 (c1900)

Fromm, Erich. Escape from Freedom. N. Y.: Farrar, 1941.

Fryer, Douglas H. and Henry, Edwin R., eds. Handbook of Applied
    Psychology. N. Y.: Rinehart, 1950.

Gagne, Robert. Conditions of Learning, 2nd ed. N. Y.: Holt, 1970.

Garfield, Sol L. Introductory Clinical Psychology. N. Y.: Macmil-
    lan, 1957.

Gilmer, Beverly von H., et al. Industrial Psychology. N. Y.: Mc-
    Graw-Hill, 1961.

Guilford, Joy P. Psychometric Methods, 2nd ed. N. Y.: McGraw-
    Hill, 1954.

Guthrie, Edwin R. The Psychology of Learning, rev. ed. N. Y.:
    Harper, 1952.

Hall, Calvin S. and Lindzey, Gardner. Theories of Personality.
    N. Y.: Wiley, 1957.

Harris, Thomas A. I'm Okay--You're Okay: A Practical Guide to
    Transactional Analysis. N. Y.: Harper & Row, 1969.

Hayakawa, Samuel I. Symbol, Status, and Personality. N. Y.: Har-
    court Brace & Jovanovich, 1963.

Hilgard, Ernest R. Introduction to Psychology, 2nd ed. N. Y.:
    Harcourt, 1957.

James, William. The Principles of Psychology. N. Y.: Holt, 1890.

Jung, Carl G. Contributions to Analytic Psychology. N. Y.: Har-
    court, 1928.

Katz, Daniel, et al. Public Opinion and Propaganda; a Book of
    Readings. N. Y.: Dryden, 1954.

Koffka, Kurt. The Growth of the Mind: an Introduction to Child
    Psychology, 2nd ed. London: Routledge, 1928.

_____. Principles of Gestalt Psychology. N. Y.: Harcourt,
    1935.

Maslow, Abraham H. and Mittelmann, Bela. Principles of Abnor-
    mal Psychology: the Dynamics of Psychic Illness, Rev. ed.
    N. Y.: Harper, 1951.

May, Rollo. Psychology and the Human Dilemma. Princeton, N. J.:
    Van Nostrand, 1967.

Miller, George A. Language and Communication. N. Y.: McGraw-
    Hill, 1951.

Murphy, Gardner. Historical Introduction to Modern Psychology,
    rev. ed. N. Y.: Harcourt, 1951.

Osgood, Charles E., et al. The Measurement of Meaning. Urbana,
    Ill.: University of Illinois Press, 1957.

Pavlov, Ivan P. Conditioned Reflexes; an Investigation of the Psy-
    chological Activity of the Cerebral Cortex. London: Oxford Uni-
    versity Press, 1927.

Piaget, Jean. Logic and Psychology. N. Y.: Basic Books, 1957.

Rogers, Carl R. Client-Centered Therapy; its Current Practice,
    Implications, and Theory. Boston: Houghton, 1951.

Rorschach, Hermann. Psychodiagnostics; a Diagnostic Test Based
    on Perception. N. Y.: Grune, 1942.

Shannon, Claud E. and Weaver, Warren. The Mathematical Theory
    of Communication. Urbana, Ill.: University of Illinois Press,
    1949.

Skinner, Burrhus F. The Behavior of Organisms; an Experimental
    Analysis. N. Y.: Appleton, 1938.

_____. Science and Human Behavior. N. Y.: Macmillan, 1953.

Terman, Louis M. and Merrill, Maud A. The Stanford-Binet Intelli-
    gence Scale; Manual for the Third Revision. Boston: Houghton,
    1960.

Underwood, Benton J. Experimental Psychology; an Introduction.
    N. Y.: Appleton, 1949.

Wechsler, David. The Measurement and Appraisal of Adult Intelli-
    gence, 4th ed. Baltimore: Williams and Wilkins, 1958.

ENCYCLOPEDIC SUMMARIES

American Psychological Association. Biographical Directory
  Typical directory information on education, experience, spe-
  cialty, publications, etc., with a geographical index. (Bowker,
  N. Y.)

Comprehensive Dictionary of Psychological and Psychoanalytical
Terms (English)
  The best English dictionary containing numerous terms and
  how they are used by psychologists. It is edited by Horace
  English. (Longmans, N. Y.).

Dictionary of Philosophy and Psychology (Baldwin)
  At one time the only authoritative work available in English
  and still useful except for modern developments. Concise,
  not exhaustive, with signed articles and numerous bibliographies. Slights Greek and scholastic philosophy. Includes
  entries in German, French, and Italian equivalents of English
  terms. (Peter Smith, N. Y.)

Encyclopedia of Human Behavior (Goldenson)
  Terms, theories, treatment, techniques and biographical data
  concerning psychology, psychiatry and mental health are concisely presented, even giving illustrative cases. Indexed and
  cross referenced. (Doubleday, Garden City, N. Y.)

Encyclopedia of Psychology (Eysenck) 3 vols.
  It succeeds in keeping interested persons aware of the international flavor of modern psychology. The longer articles
  with their bibliographies are its strong point, except that the
  citations are limited to the contributor's linguistic ability.
  Although there are some new definitions, most scholars will
  be better satisfied with English and English's Comprehensive
  Dictionary (q. v.). However, since it is published in six
  languages with over three hundred international contributors,
  it hopes to standardize terms and information. (Herder and
  Herder, N. Y.)

Handbook of Abnormal Psychology (Eysenck)
  Wide and eclectic coverage well-organized to reach an integration of experimental abnormal psychology to help the
  movement toward a solution of problems in the field of mental
  health. Not restricted to theoretical interests, it proposes
  objective measurement of meaningful behavioral dimensions.
  (Basic Books, N. Y.)

Handbook of Experimental Psychology (Stevens)
  A technical survey to systematize, digest and appraise the
  state of experimental psychology of mid-century emphasizes
  biological foundations and aspects of psychology. "A dis-

tinguished achievement in scientific commentary. " (Wiley,
N. Y.)

Handbook of General Experimental Psychology (Murchison)
Various authors present critical reviews of psychological experimentation in specialized fields; of value despite its date,
1934.   (Clark University Press, Worcester, Mass.)

Handbook of Psychological Literature (Louttit)
A competent description of the basic tools, e. g., general
reference books, periodicals, series and indexing services;
how to use the library effectively; bibliography of journals;
special collections in the U. S. and Great Britain.   (Principia
Press, Bloomington, Ind.)

Handbook of Social Psychology (Lindzey)
In a rapidly growing field, every effort was made to present
all aspects of major areas of concern to social psychology,
by calling upon contributors of diverse professional compe-
tence and background, even some non-psychologists.   Undergraduates to trained psychologists will appreciate the changes
and advances reflected by the increased activity in research
and application, divided by volumes into: 1) systematic positions, 2) research methods, 3) the individual in a social context, 4) group psychology, and 5) applied social psychology.
(Addison-Wesley, Reading, Mass.)

Mental Measurements Yearbook (Buros)
1.   Commercially available educational, psychological and
vocational tests with reviews.   2.   Authorities upholding different viewpoints write reviews of books on testing, arranged
by subject.   (Gryphon, Highland Park, N. J.)

Personality Tests and Reviews (Buros)
Besides including original test reviews, excerpts from other
reviews, and references on the construction, use and validity
of specific personality tests in the first six Mental Measurements Yearbooks, new material of a similar nature on these
tests and later tests are included.   There is a comprehensive
bibliography of personality tests.   Includes a scanning index.
(Gryphon, Highland Park, N. J.)

Professional Problems in Psychology (Daniel & Louttit)
Scientific reports, professionalism and literature search are
treated for the student with emphasis on materials and skills.
Appendices of reference books, periodicals, sources for texts,
apparatus, etc., and a glossary are valuable.   (Prentice-
Hall, N. Y.)

Tests in Print (Buros)
This comprehensive bibliography of tests, which can be used
in education, psychology and industry, is an index and supple-

ment to the Mental Measurements Yearbooks.   Name and title indexes, a publishers' directory, and even out-of-print tests are included.   (Gryphon, Highland Park, N. J.)

Search Procedure Form	PSYCHOLOGY
NAME OF USER	DATE OF INQUIRY

REDEFINED QUESTION STATEMENT

KEYWORDS

WORK IN PROGRESS

☐   Contemporary Authors

UNPUBLISHED STUDIES

☐   Dissertation Abstract International
☐   Masters Abstracts

PERIODICALS

☐   American Imago; a Psychoanalytic Journal for Culture, Science, and the Arts
☐   American Journal of Psychiatry
☐   American Journal of Psychology
☐   American Journal of Psychotherapy
☐   Behavior Therapy
☐   Biological Psychiatry
☐   British Journal of Psychiatry
☐   Cognitive Psychology
☐   Contemporary Psychology, a Journal of Reviews
☐   Educational and Psychological Measurement
☐   Group Psychotherapy and Psychodrama
☐   Journal of Applied Behavior Analysis
☐   Journal of Applied Psychology
☐   Journal of Counseling Psychology
☐   Journal of Personality and Social Psychology
☐   Journal of Social Issues
☐   Mental Hygiene
☐   Mental Retardation
☐   Personality an International Journal
☐   Psychoanalytic Quarterly
☐   Psychology; a Journal of Human Behavior
☐   Psychology Today
☐   Psychotherapy
☐   Rehabilitation Record
☐   You

INDEXES AND ABSTRACTING SERVICES

☐   Child Development Abstracts and Bibliography
☐   Mental Health Book Review Index
☐   Psychological Abstracts

BIBLIOGRAPHIC LISTS AND ESSAYS

☐   Bibliography of Philosophy, Psychology, and Cognate Subjects
☐   Harvard List of Books in Psychology

ANNUAL REVIEW AND STATE-OF-THE-ART REPORTS

☐   Annual Review of Psychology

ENCYCLOPEDIC SUMMARIES

☐   American Psychological Association, Biographical Directory
☐   Comprehensive Dictionary of Psychological and Psychoanalytical
      Terms
☐   Dictionary of Philosophy and Psychology
☐   Encyclopedia of Human Behavior
☐   Encyclopedia of Psychology
☐   Handbook of Abnormal Psychology
☐   Handbook of Experimental Psychology
☐   Handbook of General Experimental Psychology
☐   Handbook of Psychological Literature
☐   Handbook of Social Psychology
☐   Mental Measurements Yearbooks
☐   Personality Tests and Reviews
☐   Professional Problems in Psychology
☐   Tests in Print

COMMENTS:

SEARCHER'S SIGNATURE	DATE COMPLETED

Discipline Resource Package

BUSINESS AND ECONOMICS

Thomas W. Mulford
Detroit Public Library

Together the terms Business and Economics encompass the study and practice of production, distribution, and consumption of goods and services designed to satisfy the material needs of society. Economics emphasizes the theoretical approach to the practical problems of the business world.

WORK IN PROGRESS

Contemporary Authors

A comprehensive source for biographical data on contemporary authors, many of which may not yet appear in traditional biographical sources. Entries are short, with personal, career, and work-in-progress information. A list of writings and sources of biographical and critical data are given when possible. The set is now in its 48th volume but many of the earlier volumes have been cumulated. Each volume is a separate alphabet but a cumulative name index is provided at the end of volume 48. (Gale Research Co., Detroit)

UNPUBLISHED STUDIES

Dissertation Abstracts International

The most complete source for abstracts of doctoral dissertations written in the United States. Most U.S. universities contribute to this system operated by a private corporation. Unfortunately, several important universities do not participate. Microfilm or paper copies of the dissertations are available for purchase. Until recently, the indexing has been spotty and of poor quality. Fortunately, a much better (and very expensive) 37-volume cumulative index is now available. (University Microfilms, Ann Arbor, Mich.)

Masters Abstracts

This is a selective, classified and annotated list of master's theses produced by many, but by no means all, U.S. colleges and universities. As with dissertations, microfilm or paper copies of the theses are available for purchase from the

publisher of the Abstracts. Due to its selectivity, it is much
easier to use than Dissertation Abstracts International. MA
is presently being published quarterly. (University Microfilms, Ann Arbor, Mich.)

PERIODICALS

Loose-leaf Services:

Bureau of National Affairs, Inc:
  Labor Relations Reporter

Commerce Clearing House:
  Accounting Articles
  Trade Regulation Reporter

Moody's Investor Service:
  Banks and Finance
  Bond Survey
  Handbook of Common Stocks
  Industrials
  Over the Counter Industrials
  Public Utilities
  Stock Survey
  Transportation

Prentice-Hall Services:
  Federal Tax Service
  State and Local Tax Service

Standard and Poor's Service:
  Standard Corporation Records
  Industry Surveys
  Outlook
  Trade and Securities Statistics

Magazines and Journals:

Accounting (monthly)
Administrative Science Quarterly
Advertising Age (weekly)
American Banker (5x wk.)
American Economic Review (5x yr.)
American Import and Export Bulletin (monthly)
Applied Economics (quarterly)
Barclays Overseas Review (monthly)
Black Enterprise (monthly)
Business Abroad (monthly)
Business Asia (weekly)
Business Conditions Digest (monthly)

Business Europe (weekly)
Business Horizons (bi-monthly)
Business Latin America (weekly)
Business Quarterly
Business Week
Commerce Today (bi-weekly)
Commodities, the Magazine of Futures Trading (monthly)
Conference Board Journal (monthly)
Cost and Management (bi-monthly)
Current Wage Developments (monthly)
Duns (monthly)
Econometrica (bi-monthly)
Economic Indicators (monthly)
Economic Review (irregular)
Economist (weekly)
Employment and Earnings (monthly)
Federal Reserve Bulletin (monthly)
Finance, the Magazine of Money (monthly)
Forbes (semi-monthly)
Fortune (14x yr.)
Harvard Business Review (bi-monthly)
Industry Week
International Economic Review (3x yr.)
Journal of Common Market Studies (quarterly)
Journal of Developing Areas (quarterly)
Journal of Economic History (quarterly)
Journal of International Economics (quarterly)
Journal of Marketing (quarterly)
Journal of Political Economy (bi-monthly)
Journal of the American Statistical Association (quarterly)
Kiplinger Weekly Newsletter
Manpower (monthly)
Mergers and Acquisitions (bi-monthly)
Modern Office Procedures (monthly)
Monthly Labor Review (monthly)
National Tax Journal (quarterly)
Nations Business (monthly)
OECD Main Economic Indicators (monthly)
Public Relations Journal (monthly)
Quarterly Journal of Economics (quarterly)
Sales Management (bi-monthly)
Survey of Current Business (monthly)
Tax Advisor (monthly)
Treasury Bulletin (monthly)
Wall Street Journal (daily)

REPORTS AND MONOGRAPHS

Current Industrial Reports
          Published weekly, monthly, quarterly, and annually, it con-
sists of statistical tables covering production, shipments, and

inventories for over 5,000 products manufactured in the
United States. It is designed to update the Census of Manufacturers between editions. Production statistics are also
grouped by States. (U.S. Bureau of the Census, Washington,
D.C.)

Overseas Business Reports
Covering separate business analyses and market reports for
each of many foreign countries, it summarizes business
practices in countries where U.S. companies may be doing
business. These pamphlets relating to sales, starting new
businesses, trade regulations, or market profiles are updated
every few years. They also may contain bibliographies on,
information sources about, or institutions in the country discussed for further reference. Published by the U.S. Dept.
of Commerce. (Government Printing Office, Washington,
D.C.)

INDEXES AND ABSTRACTING SERVICES

Accountants Index
Formerly published every two years and now every year, it
is the most comprehensive one-volume index to periodicals
and books covering accounting subjects. Names of authors,
titles, and subject topics are arranged together alphabetically.
Professional pamphlets, government documents, and over 400
periodical titles are indexed. Also included is a directory
list of publishers and their addresses for the material indexed
from the United States and other countries. (American Institute of Certified Public Accountants, New York, N.Y.)

Accounting Articles
A looseleaf service which is updated monthly, it contains abstracts of periodical articles, books, and pamphlets of interest to accountants. The abstracts are arranged by accounting topics and subjects. It has three sections to keep
its coverage current. Back-issue binders cover accounting
literature in 4-year intervals. Alphabetical sections by author
and subject aid in locating the section numbers of the material, which is also indexed by author and topic. (Commerce
Clearing House, New York, N.Y.)

Business Education Index
An annual index to articles on business education (including
typing and shorthand) compiled from about 30 periodicals are
arranged under nearly 80 subject headings. The index is
compiled by the Gregg Division of the McGraw-Hill Book Co.,
working in cooperation with the honorary fraternity in business education, Delta Pi Epsilon. (McGraw-Hill, New York,
N.Y.)

Business Methods Index
        The predecessor to Management Index, it has been discon-
tinued for several years. Starting in 1960, it arranged articles, books, pamphlets, and documents under business subject headings; each entry was numbered and then listed alphabetically after each subject heading. (Keith Business Library,
Ottawa, Canada)

Business Periodicals Index
        One of the major indexes to business periodicals, it was
formed in 1958 when its publisher split an original index into
two sections separating business and science subjects. Titles
to articles from about 150 different periodicals in the United
States are listed alphabetically after extensive headings and
subheadings on business topics and names. Each entry includes the periodical title, an abbreviation of its source, its
volume and page numbers, and the date of issue. When
available, authors of articles are included. The subject
heading "Book Reviews" has been used in recent years. Full
titles to the periodicals indexed, their publishers, and addresses are listed in each annual cumulation. (H. W. Wilson,
New York, N. Y.)

Dictionary of Occupational Titles
        Volume 1 consists of a dictionary of titles of occupations in-
cluding brief definitions, cross references, and six-digit
classification code numbers for each occupation title. Volume
2 groups related occupational fields together by nine different
worker groups and traits. There is a glossary of terms section. Personnel offices and employment services use both
volumes to categorize civilian job skills. (U. S. Dept. of
Labor, Washington, D. C., 1965)

Economic Abstracts
        Published semi-monthly with annual cumulations, it lists ab-
stracts of periodical articles appearing in more important publications from many different countries. Articles covering
economics, finance, labor, management, trade, foreign aid,
and other topics are frequently abstracted in English and
given enough information (like authors and titles) to make the
abstracts suitable for use as catalog cards on file in university libraries in the Netherlands and Belgium. (Library of
the Economic Information Service, The Hague, Netherlands)

F & S Index of Corporations
        Nearly 600 periodical titles, business-oriented newspapers,
financial reports, and services are indexed for business and
trade information in annual cumulative hardbound editions and
quarterly, monthly, and weekly supplements. In one section,
titles, dates, and page numbers of articles are grouped according to Standard Industrial Classification (SIC) product
numbers and additional code numbers for economic, government, business, and labor topics. These may be accessed

by an alphabetic list of subjects corresponding to the SIC numbers.   Another section groups articles covering company information by major SIC product groups.   A third white-page
section lists, alphabetically by company, articles describing
company news.   These unique index arrangements make this
an important source for current market information. (Predicasts, Cleveland, Ohio)

F & S International Index
        In annual cumulative editions with quarterly and monthly sup-
plements, one section indexes periodical articles about foreign
companies alphabetically by company name.   Another section
groups titles of articles on foreign industry by major product
group according to Standard Industrial Classification (SIC)
numbers.   An alphabetic subject guide indexes these product
number groups.   A third section arranges articles on foreign
industries by country of origin.   The many sources indexed
include periodicals, important newspapers, financial reports,
and newsletters written in English.   The SIC numbers have
been enriched to include an emphasis on governmental, economic, and labor-related topics. (Predicasts, Cleveland,
Ohio)

Index of Economic Articles
        Sponsored by the American Economic Association, it indexes
books and periodicals on economics written in English.   Articles and book titles are arranged by decimal classification
numbers and then arranged by author.   There is an author
index, and a list of books indexed and annotated.   Having the
same publisher as the American Economic Review, it includes
book reviews and appears as an annual after a time lag of
several years. (Richard D. Irwin, Inc., Homewood, Ill.)

Management Index
        Its publisher suspended publication in September, 1971.   Dur-
ing the 1960's it indexed from 200 to 400 periodical titles on
a selective basis with large topical groupings.   American,
Canadian, and British books, pamphlets, and periodical articles were indexed monthly so that names and keywords of
titles were listed alphabetically after each subject.   An annual issue at the end of each year indexed the subject section page numbers for the articles indexed monthly. (Keith
Business Library, Ottawa, Canada)

Monthly Catalog of U. S. Government Publications
        The most comprehensive catalog of U.S. government publica-
tions of the Superintendent of Documents, the National Technical Information Service, and other government agencies.
Published monthly, it has an annual author and subject index
in every December issue.   Each monthly issue groups entries
by titles after their issuing division, as well as by accession
number for convenient indexing.   Included are sales prices,
stock numbers, and classification numbers to aid the

purchaser.   Also included are Library of Congress card numbers and depository library notations.   Each issue has an
alphabetical subject index to its contents in the back; these
subjects are cross-referenced by key title words, authors
names, and serial titles.   (U. S. Government Printing Office,
Washington, D. C.)

Public Affairs Information Service Bulletin

For over 60 years, PAIS has selectively indexed a wide
variety of periodical articles, books, pamphlets, government
reports, and other publications printed in English from many
countries on such topics as social studies, economics, international relations, and business conditions.   It is published
weekly, cumulated five times a year, and then bound into annual editions.   Article titles and accompanying bibliographic
data (like dates, pages, and volumes) are listed alphabetically
after subject headings.   Subject headings consist of an alphabetical list of topics and many subtopics, which include country and personal names.   (New York Public Library, New
York, N. Y.)

Thomas Register of Products and Services

Since 1911, Thomas has been published annually in multiple
volumes that list United States company names, products,
services, and brand names.   In six volumes arranged by
product category, each company name is followed by its address, product description, and size rating after being grouped
by state and city.   Volume 7 is an alphabetical listing of each
company name and address.   Volume 8 has a useful alphabetical listing by brand name and company owning it and an
alphabetical listing of the product categories and page numbers used in the first 6 volumes.   The last few volumes
serve as an alphabetical product catalog for some of the companies listed in other sections.   Along with MacRae's Blue
Book and the Conover-Mast Purchasing Directory, it is a key
source for locating the plants and products of many small
manufacturers in the United States.   (Thomas Pub. Co. , New
York, N. Y.)

Topicator

A monthly index and an annual cumulative index to nearly 20
periodicals covering the advertising and broadcasting fields.
Article titles are grouped by about 90 major subject headings
and other subheadings in large topics.   Periodical sources,
their dates, and page numbers are included with the titles.
(Thompson Bureau, Littleton, Colorado)

Wall Street Journal Index

Articles, from the final Eastern edition of the Wall Street
Journal, are indexed in two sections.   The first section is
an alphabetical listing by company name of news items appearing about the company in daily issues of the journal.   The
second section has an alphabetic listing of broad subject

headings that cover general business topics.   Published since
the late 1950's in monthly paperbound issues and annual cumulative hardbound ones, it also contains for each month the
daily closings for the various Dow Jones averages.   Although
the user of this index is aided by the lengthy titles, pages,
and column numbers for articles, the user should also be
aware that discrepancies may occur because of many editions
published and extra news insertions often made only for the
index.   (Dow Jones Books, Princeton, N. J.)

BIBLIOGRAPHIC LISTS AND ESSAYS

ANACOM Resources for the Professional Manager in Print
    This title cumulates the monthly publisher's catalog used by
    the American Management Association (Management Book-
    shelf).   It is an annotated catalog of books published by a
    division of the association called ANACOM.   Titles of books,
    periodicals, and other material are listed in separate sec-
    tions alphabetically by title.   Authors, prices, order num-
    bers, and a few blank order forms are included so that as-
    sociation members may purchase items listed in this annual
    publication.   Titles are grouped by business topic in the back
    pages and this annual booklet is supplemented by monthly
    pamphlets.   (American Management Assn. , New York, N. Y.)

Business and Technology Sources
    This bi-monthly pamphlet serves as a topical bibliography of
    periodical articles and government documents.   Entries in-
    clude titles, authors, dates, publisher, and call number at
    the Cleveland Public Library.   Prices are not included.
    (Cleveland Public Library, Cleveland, Ohio)

Business Literature
    An annotated bi-monthly bibliography, it covers books, peri-
    odical articles, reference works, and directories under broad
    topics like "Consumerism. "   It is arranged alphabetically by
    topics and subtopics.   Because the authors, titles, dates,
    pages, prices, and publishers are included, it is a handy
    guide for ordering publications.   (Newark Public Library,
    Newark, N. J.)

Business Service Checklist
    A weekly pamphlet that serves as a convenient purchase guide
    for U. S. Dept. of Commerce publications.   On its back page
    is a list of the most current 12 key business indicators pub-
    lished by the government.   Its a useful source for obtaining
    the lastest Census Bureau publications.   Occasional annota-
    tions.   (U. S. Dept. of Commerce, Washington, D. C.)

International Bibliography of the Social Sciences--Economics
    One of four sections of a series of publications on social

sciences sponsored by UNESCO, and the International Economic Association for this section.   Nearly 2,000 periodicals of
international economic interest are indexed and their entries
arranged by a subject/decimal code.   Authors and subjects
are indexed.   Periodicals indexed and subjects used are
listed.   A long time-lag occurs between publication date of
this and the dates covered in the periodicals.   (UNESCO,
New York, N. Y.)

ANNUAL REVIEWS AND STATE OF THE ART REPORTS

Budget in Brief
A concise annual survey of the main points in the President's
proposed budget for the United States for the coming year.
Three-color charts, statistical tables covering recent years,
and a brief glossary of terms help to clarify economic subjects.   Chapters may provide a budget overview, describe
the budget process, portray peace and defense plans, or consider the nation's physical resources.   (U. S. Office of Management and Budget, Washington, D. C.)

Business Statistics
Published biennially, it presents cumulated historical data appearing in the "S" pages of the monthly Survey of Current
Business.   It has statistical tables covering product, trade,
business indicator, labor, finance, commodity, and other
data.   An index in the back facilitates locating the desired
statistical series.   (U. S. Dept. of Commerce, Washington,
D. C.)

Census of Business (U. S.)
Published in four volumes every five years, it covers statistics on firms engaged in retail trade, wholesale trade, and
selected services of all 50 states, Guam, and the Virgin Is-
lands.   In a separate Census of Business, Puerto Rico is
covered.   In the 1967 edition, volume 1 presents data about
various types of retail businesses for the U. S. , the states,
and standard metropolitan statistical areas.   Volume 2 covers
retail trade area statistics, such as the number of establishments and employment.   Volume 3 lists statistics about
wholesale trade establishments, and volume 4 treats wholesale trade area statistics.   (U. S. Bureau of the Census,
Washington, D. C.)

Census of Manufacturers (U. S.)
It covers types of firms engaged in manufacturing as defined
by the latest Standard Industrial Classification Manual and is
published every five years.   Volume 1 contains statistics
summarizing data about U. S. firms, volume 2 has statistics
arranged by type of industry, volume 3 covers manufacturing
by state, volume 4 contains data about the location of manu-

facturing plants, and volume 5 has production indexes. Data
for manufacturing groups and specific SIC numbers are indexed alphabetically in volume 2. Appendices to the bound
volumes explain terms, standard metropolitan statistical areas,
and descriptions. (U. S. Bureau of the Census, Washington,
D. C.)

Commodity Yearbook

Published every July, it provides charts and statistical tables
for about 100 commodities, depicting their production, imports, and average prices in major U. S. and world markets
for a number of years in the past, to date. It also discusses
the immediate past and future situation for each commodity.
The charts, tables, and discussions are listed by each of the
commodities which are arranged alphabetically throughout the
book. About a half-dozen articles by commodity analysts
consider significant aspects of commodity trading. (Commodity Research Bureau, New York, N. Y.)

Economic Almanac

At this writing the latest edition is dated 1967-68. It is a
compact handbook on business and economic statistics for
businessmen. An index lists subjects, countries, and subheadings together alphabetically. A glossary explains common economic terms. (The Conference Board, New York,
N. Y.)

Economic Report of the President

Prepared by the United States President's Council of Economic
Advisers annually, this report groups extensive statistical
tables on the U. S. economy after describing such topics as
the international economy, energy, inflation control, economic
policies of the administration, and economic developments
over the past year. Its explanation of governmental economic
policies and its current statistics on the economy make this
a convenient source of economic information. (Government
Printing Office, Washington, D. C.)

Guide to Consumer Markets

This combines statistical tables on the United States consumer
market and more than 100 charts to illustrate trends over recent years in population, employment, income, expenditures,
production, distribution, and prices. Published annually.
There is a glossary of economic terms used and a general
index to the tabular and graphic material illustrated. (The
Conference Board, New York, N. Y.)

Insurance Almanac

An annual publication by the publisher of the Weekly Underwriter magazine, it contains 14 sections which are indexed
by a general company index. Some of the sections furnish
names and addresses of insurance groups, stock property
insurance companies, mutual insurance companies, insurance

exchanges, personal accident/health insurance companies, and
life insurance companies (all in the United States). Insurance
associations in the United States and Canada, their addresses,
and officers are listed. A very general listing of some insurance agents and brokers in principle cities is included.
(Underwriter Printing and Pub. Co., New York, N.Y.)

Picks Currency Yearbook

The currencies from over 100 different countries are described in this annual publication. Ten-year currency records, exchange rates with the United States, black market
rates, and currency in circulation are included for each currency. Recent histories and restrictions on currencies are
described. Special features include a money glossary, a
special section on gold, government debt per capita, currency areas, and a central bank directory. An index lists the
pages for the currency names and countries of origin. (Pick
Pub. Corp., New York, N.Y.)

Statistical Abstract of the United States

This is an annual summary and guide to other U.S. government publications that present statistical data in table and
chart form. It serves as a convenient and concise source
for social, political, and economic data concerning the United
States. An alphabetic subject index is included. One of the
most useful volumes available for statistical information on
all kinds of business and economic topics. (Government Printing Office, Washington, D.C.)

Statistics of Income, Individual Income Tax Returns

The Internal Revenue Service computes averages based on
samples from recent individual income tax returns and provides many kinds of statistical data like adjusted gross in-
comes, taxpayers over 65, sources of income, and statuses
of taxpayers. There are also historical summaries, some
three-color charts, and market data that would apply to taxpayers in each state. (Government Printing Office, Washington, D.C.)

Statistics of Income: Corporate Income Tax Returns

The Internal Revenue Service had compiled average statistics
from tax returns on corporation assets, liabilities, receipts,
tax credits, and distribution to stockholders, for example,
and has broken them down by size of business. There is an
alphabetic subject index to all tables and historical summaries. Of interest to small businesses is a section on active
small business corporation returns. Data from this section
may be used to determine ratios and percentages for com-
parisons with those of individual concerns. (Government
Printing Office, Washington, D.C.)

U.S. Tax Cases

A publication presenting the full text of all court decisions

involving federal tax decisions.   Published both as a looseleaf
service and as a semi-annual cumulative bound edition.   In
the back of each index is a clear topical index with both main
topics and subheadings referring to paragraph numbers within
each decision.   In the front is an alphabetical listing of each
case by both plaintiffs' and defendants' names.   Cross-index
tables refer from the National Reporter System (see Discipline
Resource Package on "Law") citations to opinions in U. S.
Tax Cases.   (Commerce Clearing House, New York, N. Y.)

Yearbook of Labor Statistics
      It summarizes labor statistics from about 180 countries in
English, French, and Spanish.   It relies on statistical services from the United Nations and individual countries.   Most
of the yearbook consists of tables based on indexes covering
statistics for the preceding ten years.   Chapters cover such
topics as employment, unemployment, wages, consumer
prices, and productivity.   A statistical summary of data by
country serves as an index.   (International Labour Office,
Geneva, Switzerland)

Yearbook of International Trade Statistics
      Published since the early 1950's by the United Nations, it
covers annual statistics for over 135 countries each year for
six-year periods.   All values are in U. S. dollars for trade
by principal producing countries and the last assignment of
their goods.   Imports by commodities and exports are listed
by a Standard International Trade Classification and by country.   Quarterly data may be found each quarter in the Monthly Bulletin of Statistics.   (United Nations, New York, N. Y.)

BOOKS

Bancroft, Gertrude.   The American Labor Force: Its Growth
   and Changing Composition.   N. Y. : Wiley, 1958.

Bentham, Jeremy.   Jeremy Bentham's Economic Writings.   Ed. by
   W. Stark.   London: Allen, 1954.

Black, John D.   Economics for Agriculture.   Cambridge, Mass. :
   Harvard University Press, 1959.

Blough, Roy.   The Federal Taxing Process.   N. Y. :   Prentice-Hall,
   1952.

Bucher, Karl.   Industrial Evolution.   N. Y. :   Holt, 1901.

Clark, John M.   Social Control of Business.   2nd ed.   N. Y. :   Mc-
   Graw-Hill, 1939.

Dalton, Hugh, et. al.   Unbalanced Budgets.   London: Routledge, 1934.

Dorfman, Joseph. The Economic Mind in American Civilization. N. Y.:
Viking, 1959.

Douglass, Paul H. The Theory of Wages. N. Y.: Macmillan, 1934.

Ferber, Robert and Wales, Hugh G., eds. Motivation and Market
Behavior. Homewood, Ill.: Irwin, 1958.

Frankel, Sally H. The Economic Impact on Under-developed Societies. Cambridge, Mass.: Harvard University Press, 1953.

Fraser, Lindley M. Economic Thought and Language. London:
Black, 1937.

Galbraith, John K. Affluent Society. 2nd ed. Boston: Houghton
Mifflin, 1969.

Haberler, Gottfried. The Theory of International Trade. N. Y.:
Macmillan, 1937.

Hansen, Alvin H. Fiscal Policy and Business Cycles. N. Y.:
Norton, 1941.

Heckscher, Eli F. Mercantilism. N. Y.: Macmillan, 1955.

Isard, Walter. Methods of Regional Analysis. N. Y.: Wiley, 1960.

Keynes, John M. The General Theory of Employment, Interest,
and Money. London: Macmillan, 1936.

_____. Monetary Reform. N. Y.: Harcourt, 1924.

Lange, Oskar and Taylor, Fred M. On the Economic Theory of
Socialism. Minneapolis, Minn.: Univ. of Minnesota Press,
1938.

Letische, John M. Balance of Payments and Economic Growth.
N. Y.: Harper, 1959.

March, James G. and Simon, Herbert A. Organizations. N. Y.
Wiley, 1958.

Menderhausen, Horst. The Economics of War. N. Y.: Prentice-
Hall, 1940.

Mill, John Stuart. Principals of Political Economy. London:
Longmans, 1909.

Reder, Melvin W. Studies in the Theory of Warfare Economics.
N. Y.: Columbia Univ. Press, 1947.

Robbins, Lionel. An Essay on the Nature and Significance of Economic Science. London: Macmillan, 1935.

Rostow, Walt W. The Stages of Economic Growth. Cambridge,
    Eng.: University Press, 1960.

Samuelson, Paul. Economics. 5th ed. N.Y.: McGraw-Hill, 1961.

Sayers, Richard S. Modern Banking, 5th ed. Oxford, Eng.:
    Clarendon Press, 1960.

Simon, Herbert A. The New Science of Management Decisions.
    N.Y.: Harper, 1960.

Smith, Adam. An Inquiry Into the Nature and Causes of the Wealth
    of Nations. N.Y.: Modern Library, 1937 (c1776).

Spiegel, Henry W., ed. The Development of Economic Thought:
    Great Economics in Perspective. N.Y.: Wiley, 1952.

Studenski, Paul. A Study of the Income of Nations: Theory Meas-
    urement and Analysis, Past and Present. N.Y.: New York Uni-
    versity Press, 1958.

Ulman, Lloyd. The Rise of the National Trade Union. Cambridge,
    Mass.: Harvard University Press, 1955.

Weisskopf, Walter A. The Psychology of Economics, 2nd ed. Chi-
    cago: University of Chicago Press, 1957.

ENCYCLOPEDIC SUMMARIES

Accountant's Encyclopedia
        Ten sections, each covering different areas of accounting
    like setting fees, accounting systems, and practical reviews
    make this a handy guide for professional accountants, stu-
    dents, and businessmen. An extensive index in the back
    pages and contents pages before each section facilitates use
    of this publication. Its contributors have included extensive
    charts and solutions to accounting problems. Infrequently re-
    vised. (Prentice-Hall, New York, N.Y.)

Accountant's Handbook
        Written with the aid of over 40 contributors, most of whom
    are CPA's, it covers the field of accounting in 28 chapters.
    Contents are listed in the front, and before each section, for
    such topics as "cash," "liabilities," "consolidated state-
    ments," and "partnership accounting." Topics and terms
    are indexed. A 15-page list of sources is included. (Ronald
    Press, New York, N.Y.)

Business Executive's Handbook
        A guide to businessmen's practical questions about direct
    mailing, advertising, letter writing, insurance, accounting,

business math, sales, and office management in 12 sections.
A glossary of abbreviations, a master subject index, and
many lists are aids to finding information in it.   Infrequent
revisions result in dated material.   (Prentice-Hall, New York,
N. Y. ,   1953.)

Chemical Business Handbook
Compiled by over 100 contributors, it is intended to help
technical professionals to broaden their understanding of business areas that may be outside their own specialties.   It is
designed as a textbook with 20 sections, some of which cover
business math, patent law, finance, sales, law and public relations.   Sections on marketing contain data and indexes that
cover many years stop in the early 1950's and are therefore
dated.   (McGraw-Hill, New York, N. Y. ,   1954)

Dictionary of American Firms Operating in Foreign Countries
This is volume 2 of a ten-volume set of directories and handbooks dealing with international trade and revised every few
years.   It covers about 3, 200 American corporations which
control or operate more than 15, 000 foreign companies.   It
has three sections, the first of which is an alphabetical list
of the United States firms, their addresses in the U. S. , key
officers, principle product or service, and the foreign nations
in which they operate.   A second section is a geographical
list of these operations and their addresses in foreign countries, and section 3 classifies both U. S. firms and their
foreign operations by their product or service.   Noncommer-
cial enterprises and foreign-controlled corporations are not
included.   (Simon and Schuster, New York, N. Y.)

Dictionary of Business and Finance
Alphabetically arranged for the main terms, with occasional
subheadings for general terms such as "bonds. "   Brief definitions and cross references are included.   All fields of economics and business are within its scope.   It is designed for
the experienced businessman needing precise information as
well as the student.   Useful tables cover such topics as
"bond interest, " "equivalents, " and "compound interest. "
Comp. by Donald Clark and Bert Gottfried.   (Crowell Pub.
Co. , New York, N. Y. , 1957)

Dictionary of Economic Terms
This dictionary is intended for economists and students and
emphasizes applied economics.   Paragraph-length definitions
accompany most terms.   Terms used in context are cross-
referenced.   British economic institutions and approaches to
economics are emphasized.   A few charts and tables are included.   Ed. by Alan Gilpin.   (Philosophical Library, New
York, N. Y. , 1970)

Dictionary of Economics, 5th ed.
Frequently updated, this dictionary is in its 5th edition in

20 years. It attempts to keep up with new developments in
economics covering analytical, quantitative, and institutional
approaches to economics. In addition to the alphabetical
listing of economic terms, terms defined in text are cross
referenced. Also described are governmental economic acts,
economic institutions, and national monetary units (in an appendix). A descriptive classification of defined terms, national monetary units, and gross national products are placed
in the appendix. Ed. by Harold Sloan. (Barnes and Noble,
New York, N. Y. , 1970)

Encyclopedia of Accounting Systems
       Although it was written in 1956, this five-volume set is still
a convenient source for concise summaries of accounting
systems in over 65 lines of business. Accounting specialists
who were expert within each business area, have followed a
uniform outline that gives the characteristics of each industry
described, its unique set of records, its organization, and
special accounting short-cuts used. Industries that are controlled by a few extremely large corporations are not covered
and special modifications necessary for small business have
been included. Each volume has a detailed index and volume
5 has a master index to all of the volumes to aid in locating
the different types of accounting systems described. (Prentice-
Hall, Englewood Cliffs, N. J. , 1956)

Encyclopedia of Banking and Finance
       Terms are arranged alphabetically and may receive long and
detailed coverage, occasionally up to several pages. Published once or twice every ten years, it includes definitions
of nearly 4, 000 legal, banking, financial, stock market, and
economic terms. Statistical tables, lists, cross references,
and bibliographies are included. (Bankers Publishing Co. ,
Boston, Mass.)

Encyclopedia of Business Information Sources
       This two-volume work is a complete revision of the Execu-
tives Guide to Information Sources (Gale, 1965). It was designed to meet the needs of executives in management positions as well as for scholarly research. Volume one lists
sources on general subjects and volume two controls geo-
graphically-oriented items. Each volume has a classified
arrangement with detailed table of contents in the front.
Cross references are included in the main section. Ed. by
Paul Wasserman. (Gale Research Co. , Detroit, 1970)

Financial Handbook
       About 30 contributors have synthesized the literature describ-
ing both the theory and practice of finance and investment.
Each of 27 sections has its own index and the entire handbook has an index arranged alphabetically by topics and sub-
topics. Key words and terms are printed in bold face type
throughout the text. Some of the sections cover financial

mathematics, profit-sharing plans, corporate stock, and banking in detail. It is revised occasionally. (Ronald Press, New York, N. Y.)

Handbook of Business Administration

Containing 17 sections dealing with the general subject of management, it has been compiled by over 150 contributors from the ranks of universities and corporations. It is aimed at both managers and students of management. Its chief asset is a detailed index of over 50 pages that includes the names of authors of management literature as well as business topics. The index, the italicized lists, and a selective bibliography after each section facilitate finding facts about the field of management. Extensive charts, tables, and outlines make this a convenient first place to check. (McGraw-Hill, New York, N. Y., 1967)

Handbook of Modern Marketing

Each chapter contains the name of its contributing author and a selective bibliography. It is designed for researchers and executives wanting a quick review of different marketing areas for goods and services rather than wholesaling and retailing. Major market areas for government, industry, and the consumer, a section on the application of sciences to marketing, and a summary of laws affecting marketing are included. A topical index and tables facilitate finding general information. (McGraw-Hill, New York, N. Y., 1970)

Jane's Major Companies of Europe

This annual contains one- to two-page financial profiles for about 1,000 major European companies. Included in the profiles are addresses, phone numbers, lists of main officers, subsidiaries, balance sheet figures, and brief stock statistics. These European corporations are classified into six categories: banking services, light industry, engineering, building, metals, and minerals. The names of the companies are indexed alphabetically, and alphabetically by country. There is a comparative glossary of financial terms in ten languages. (McGraw-Hill, New York, N. Y.)

McGraw-Hill Dictionary of Modern Economics

This volume includes lengthy paragraph definitions of about 1,400 economic or marketing terms; 225 economic and marketing organizations are listed in a separate section. Controversial topics are represented with more than one viewpoint and many charts, tables and diagrams are included. An outstanding aid to following up the definitions to terms is the bibliographic references to sources including specific page numbers for additional reading on each topic. Ed. by Douglas Greenwald. (McGraw-Hill, New York, 1965)

Marketing Handbook

The 30 sections of this book cover marketing and sales

topics.   A great variety of areas such as sales promotion, advertising organization, advertising media, mathematics, and sales training are included.   Each section has its own index and a master index refers to topics arranged into paragraph groupings.   Revised infrequently.   (Ronald Press, New York, N. Y. , 1965)

National Product Accounts of the U. S.:   1929-1965
       Published as a special supplement to the monthly Survey of Current Business to mark its 50th anniversary, it contains over 40 sizable reviews and articles.   An index in the back lists the authors and topics of each article.   Prominent business leaders and economists praise and criticize the survey from both retrospective and prospective viewpoints.   Staff members of the Office of Business Economics review programs they have worked on for the survey.   One useful discussion concerns statistical programs, such as econometric research, carried out by the government.   (Government Printing Office, Washington, D. C.)

New Dictionary of Economics
       More than 1, 500 economic terms frequently found in college textbooks are defined in brief paragraphs.   Terms are marked to indicate their use as cross references used in the text.   Nuances of terms are provided and British viewpoints and economic institutions are represented.   Ed. by Philip Taylor.   (Augustus M. Kelley Pub. , New York, N. Y. , 1966)

Personal Income by States Since 1929
       A special supplement to the Survey of Current Business it consists of statistical tables that provide estimates on U. S. wage and salary disbursements and property income.   The first part discusses trends and illustrates them with tables and charts.   A middle section explains statistical procedures used by the Office of Business Economics group that compiled the study.   (Government Printing Office, Washington, D. C. , 1956)

Poor's Register of Corporations, Directors, and Executives
       An annual, alphabetical listing by name of over 34, 000 companies in the United States.   Included with the name of each company are its address, phone number, top officers, number of employees, and annual sales volume.   There is a section indexing companies by their Standard Industrial Classification number.   Another section contains a brief biographical summary and list of corporate affiliations for more than 260, 000 officials employed by the corporations listed.   Revisions are made in supplements published three times a year.   This directory is supplemented by an annual geographical index which groups corporations alphabetically by the state and city of their headquarter offices.   (Standard and Poor's Corp. , New York, N. Y.)

Rand, McNally Commercial Atlas and Marketing Guide
>An annual compendium of maps, charts, and statistical tables
that concentrate on the states and provinces of the United
States and Canada. Other maps cover major American urban
areas and foreign countries. A condensed index inside the
front cover facilitates locating page numbers for the maps of
states, provinces, and countries. An extensive index in the
back lists names of cities and locations. Alphabetic lists of
cities, their locations on the maps, and their population accompany each separate map section for the states and provinces. Other data for states and their countries including
trade, manufacturing, and other statistics are listed. Many
other charts, tables, maps, and lists are included in this
large one-volume atlas. Cities in the U.S. are ranked by
population. Retail sales, trading areas, and manufacturers
are mapped. Railroads, universities, airlines, and military
installations are included. (Rand-McNally, Chicago)

Standard Directory of Advertisers
>Information about approximately 17,000 corporations in the
United States are listed by product groups arranged according
to two-digit Standard Industrial Classification code groups.
Each company entry includes its name, address, telephone
number, top executives and marketing managers, principle
products, trademarks, and advertising agency. Additional
data included are sales, advertising expenditures, and advertising media used. A convenient index by company name is
located in the front of the directory. A separate section contains a directory of trademarks and the companies owning
them. It is published annually each spring and is supplemented monthly. Other affiliated directories published are a
Directory of Advertising Agencies, and a booklet listing corporations geographically by state and city. (National Directory Pub. Co., New York, N.Y.)

U.S. Income and Output
>A 1969 publication covering the United States economy in
1963 from an econometric viewpoint. Published as a special
supplement to the Survey of Current Business, it lists input
and output statistics for about 370 different industries. Volume 1 provides input and output data by buying and reselling;
volume 2 covers transactions based on producer prices, and
the last includes statistics for total production by industry.
To determine output, one must read the data by rows, and
to determine the input, one must read the columns. (Government Printing Office, Washington, D.C., 1969)

Who's Who in Finance and Industry
>This directory systematically lists the executives of the larg-
est 1,000 corporations in the world. Over 20,000 executives
were asked to fill out biographical profiles covering such
facts as their home addresses, positions held, educational
background, and immediate relatives. In addition to the

section arranged alphabetically by the executives' names,
there is a section arranged by principal businesses with lists
of their executives.   (Marquis Who's Who, Inc., Chicago,
Ill.)

Search Procedure Form	BUSINESS AND ECONOMICS

NAME OF USER | **DATE OF INQUIRY**

REDEFINED QUESTION STATEMENT

KEYWORDS

WORK IN PROGRESS

☐ Contemporary Authors

UNPUBLISHED STUDIES

☐ Dissertation Abstracts International
☐ Masters Abstracts

PERIODICALS

Loose-Leaf Services:
Bureau of National Affairs Inc.:
☐ Labor Relations Reporter
Commerce Clearning House:
☐ Accounting Articles
☐ Trade Regulation Reporter
Moody's Investor Service:
☐ Banks and Finance
☐ Bond Survey
☐ Handbook of Common Stocks
☐ Industrials
☐ Over the Counter Industrials

☐ Public Utilities
☐ Stock Survey
☐ Transportation
Prentice-Hall Services:
☐ Federal Tax Service
☐ State and Local Tax Service
Standard and Poor's Service:
☐ Standard Corporation Records
☐ Industry Surveys
☐ Outlook
☐ Trade and Securities Statistics

MAGAZINES AND JOURNALS

☐ Accounting
☐ Administrative Science Quarterly
☐ Advertising Age
☐ American Banker
☐ American Economic Review
☐ American Import and Export Bulletin
☐ Applied Economics
☐ Barclays Overseas Review
☐ Black Enterprise
☐ Business Abroad
☐ Business Asia
☐ Business Conditions Digest
☐ Business Europe
☐ Business Horizons
☐ Business Latin America
☐ Business Quarterly
☐ Business Week
☐ Commerce Today
☐ Commodities, the Magazine of Futures Trading
☐ Conference Board Journal
☐ Cost and Management
☐ Current Wage Developments
☐ Duns
☐ Economic Indicators
☐ Economic Review
☐ Econometrica
☐ Economist
☐ Employment and Earnings

☐ Federal Reserve Bulletin
☐ Finance, the Magazine of Money
☐ Forbes
☐ Fortune
☐ Harvard Business Review
☐ Industry Week
☐ International Economic Review
☐ Journal of Common Market Studies
☐ Journal of Developing Areas
☐ Journal of Economic History
☐ Journal of International Economics
☐ Journal of Marketing
☐ Journal of Political Economy
☐ Journal of the American Statistical Association
☐ Kiplinger Weekly Newsletter
☐ Manpower
☐ Mergers and Acquisitions
☐ Modern Office Procedures
☐ Monthly Labor Review
☐ National Tax Journal
☐ Nations Business
☐ OECD Main Economic Indicators
☐ Public Relations Journal
☐ Quarterly Journal of Economics
☐ Sales Management
☐ Survey of Current Business
☐ Tax Adviser
☐ Treasury Bulletin
☐ Wall Street Journal

REPORTS AND MONOGRAPHS

☐   Current Industrial Reports
☐   Overseas Business Reports

INDEXES AND ABSTRACTING SERVICES

☐   Accountants Index
☐   Accounting Articles
☐   Business Education Index
☐   Business Methods Index
☐   Business Periodicals Index
☐   Dictionary of Occupational Titles
☐   Economic Abstracts
☐   F & S Index of Corporations

☐   F & S International Index
☐   Index of Economic Articles
☐   Management Index
☐   Monthly Catalog of U.S. Government Publications
☐   Public Affairs Information Service Bulletin
☐   Thomas Register of Products and Services
☐   Topicator
☐   Wall Street Journal Index

BIBLIOGRAPHIC LISTS AND ESSAYS

☐   Business and Technology Sources
☐   Business Literature
☐   Business Service Checklist
☐   International Bibliography of the Social Sciences Economics
☐   ANACOM Resources for the Professional Manager in Print

ANNUAL REVIEWS AND STATE-OF-THE-ART REPORTS

☐   Budget in Brief
☐   Business Statistics
☐   Census of Business (U.S.)
☐   Census of Manufacturers (U.S.)
☐   Commodity Yearbook
☐   Economic Almanac
☐   Economic Report of the President
☐   Guide to Consumer Markets

☐   Insurance Almanac
☐   Picks Currency Yearbook
☐   Statistical Abstract of the United States
☐   Statistics of Income, Individual Income Tax Returns
☐   Statistics of Income: Corporate Income Tax Returns
☐   U.S. Tax Cases
☐   Yearbook of Labor Statistics
☐   Yearbook of International Trade Statistics

ENCYCLOPEDIC SUMMARIES

☐   Accountant's Encyclopedia
☐   Accountant's Handbook
☐   Business Executive's Handbook
☐   Chemical Business Handbook
☐   Dictionary of Business and Finance
☐   Dictionary of Economics
☐   Dictionary of Economic Terms
☐   Dictionary of American Firms Operating in Foreign Countries
☐   Encyclopedia of Accounting Systems
☐   Encyclopedia of Banking and Finance
☐   Encyclopedia of Business Information Sources
☐   Financial Handbook
☐   Handbook of Business Administration

☐   Handbook of Modern Marketing
☐   Jane's Major Companies of Europe
☐   McGraw-Hill Dictionary of Modern Economics
☐   Marketing Handbook
☐   National Product Accounts of the U.S.: 1929-1965
☐   New Dictionary of Economics
☐   Personal Income by States Since 1929
☐   Poor's Register of Corporations, Directors, and Executives
☐   Rand, McNally Commercial Atlas and Marketing Guide
☐   Standard Directory of Advertisers
☐   U.S. Income and Output
☐   Who's Who in Finance and Industry

COMMENTS:

SEARCHER'S SIGNATURE   **DATE COMPLETED**

Discipline Resource Package

EDUCATION

James M. Doyle
Macomb County Community College

Education is one of the major social sciences that the writers of this book chose to handle separately. For our purposes, education encompasses elementary, secondary, university, and adult education as it is generally known in the U.S.

Although meant for the untrained searcher, this list of resources will cover both practitioner (teacher)-oriented materials and those resources keyed to administrators and researchers. It will reflect both traditional materials and those resources created by the educational explosion of the 1960's.

WORK IN PROGRESS

Contemporary Authors (semi-annual)
> Designed to give an up-to-date source of information about authors working in all fields, including education. One section of each biography lists the author's "work in progress." (Gale Research Co., Detroit)

Pacesetters in Innovation (annual)
> Annual index to the specialized microfiche collection of the Educational Resources Information Center (ERIC). This collection includes project descriptions and microfiche copies of the reports of innovative projects funded by Title IV of the Elementary and Secondary Education Act. Institution and subject indexes are provided. (Government Printing Office, Washington, D.C.)

Research in Education (monthly)
> The monthly abstracting journal that indexes the documents fed into the Educational Resources Information Center's microfiche collection by ERIC's 16 clearinghouses. The publication also has a "projects" section which supplies abstracts of educational projects just funded by the U.S. Office of Education. (Government Printing Office, Washington, D.C.)

UNPUBLISHED STUDIES

DATRIX

DATRIX (Direct Access to Reference Information--a Xerox Service) is a method whereby one can, for a fee, search the complete file of doctoral dissertations maintained by University Microfilms in Ann Arbor, Michigan. Users should request a keyword list and a search form which allows one to structure the subject search of the computer, thus gaining efficient access to the largest body of unpublished studies in the U. S. (University Microfilms, Ann Arbor, Michigan)

Dissertation Abstracts International (monthly)

A monthly abstracting service which controls the doctoral dissertations stored by University Microfilms. Most of the universities in the U. S. send their dissertations to University Microfilms. The publication presents lengthy abstracts but, until recently, the indexing system left something to be desired (see also DATRIX, above). (University Microfilms, Ann Arbor, Michigan)

Masters Abstracts (quarterly)

A selected list of abstracts of master's essays from various universities which are microfilmed by University Microfilms. Classified arrangement but no indexes. (University Microfilms, Ann Arbor, Michigan)

PERIODICALS

American Documentation (quarterly)
American Education (monthly; bi-m - D to Jl)
American Educational Research Journal (quarterly)
American Libraries (monthly)
Audiovisual Instruction (monthly - S to Jl)
Automated Education Handbook (monthly)
Bulletin - National Association of Secondary School Principals
Child Development (quarterly)
Children (bi-monthly, S to Jl)
College and University Reports (weekly)
Comparative Education Review (3x yr.)
Congressional Quarterly Service (weekly)
Croft Newsletter Services
Education
Education Court Digest (monthly)
Education Recaps (monthly)
Educational Administration Quarterly (quarterly)
Educational Leadership (monthly, O-My)
Educational Product Report (9x yr.)
Educational Technology (bi-monthly)
Government Contracts Guide

Guide to Federal Assistance for Education (monthly)
Harvard Educational Review (quarterly)
Joint Council on Educational Telecommunications DATA Base Service
Journal of Applied Psychology (bi-monthly)
Journal of Educational Psychology (bi-monthly, O-Ag)
Journal of Educational Research (10x yr.)
Journal of Research and Development in Education (quarterly)
Journal of Teacher Education (quarterly)
National Elementary Principal (6x yr.)
Phi Delta Kappan (monthly, S to Je)
Psychological Review (bi-monthly)
Report on the Education of the Disadvantaged (bi-monthly)
Review of Educational Research (5x yr.)
Saturday Review (bi-weekly)
School and Society (bi-weekly)
Social Education (monthly, O-My)
Teachers College Record (monthly, O-My)
Theory into Practice (5x yr.)
Today's Education; the Journal of the NEA (monthly)
Urban Education (quarterly)

REPORTS AND MONOGRAPHS

Abstracts of Papers
    Annual compilations of the abstracts of papers given at the
    annual meetings of the American Educational Research Asso-
    ciation.   The abstracts are lengthy and scholarly.   (AERA,
    1201 16th St., N.W., Washington, D.C.)

Cooperative Research Monograph Series
    An irregular series of monographs that represent the findings
    of research projects funded by the U.S. Office of Education.
    They include both individual and project research.   (Govern-
    ment Printing Office, Washington, D.C.)

ERIC Document Collections
    The Educational Resources Information Center (ERIC) which
    is the dissemination arm of the U.S. Office of Education,
    publishes the reports collected by its 16 clearinghouses in the
    form of microfiche and sells them individually or in collec-
    tions.   The documents are abstracted and indexed in accom-
    panying indexing services.   There are two self-contained col-
    lections: one on the Disadvantaged and one on Higher Educa-
    tion.   Pacesetters, which is the proposals of Title III, ESEA
    projects, is supplemented annually.   A special Manpower col-
    lection comes out biannually.   The main collection, from the
    16 clearinghouses, is monthly.   Its index is the monthly ab-
    stracting service Resources in Education (see "Indexing and Ab-
    stracting Services").
        For information about ERIC and its services, contact
    ERIC, Bureau of Research, USOE, Washington, D.C.   The

indexes are available from the Government Printing Office, Washington, D. C. (The microfiche may be ordered directly from the ERIC Document Reproduction Service.)

NEA Research Reports
Irregularly published detailed research reports of studies conducted by the Research Division of the National Education Association. (NEA, 1201 16th St., N. W., Washington, D. C.)

What Research Says to the Teacher
An irregularly issued series of pamphlets dealing with special interest areas of education. Attempts to keep the practitioner up with current research results in the area in question. (National Education Association, 1201 16th St., N. W., Washington, D. C.)

INDEXES AND ABSTRACTING SERVICES

Abstracts of Instructional Materials in Vocational and Technical Education (AIM)
A quarterly abstracting service which indexes and abstracts items collected by the ERIC Clearinghouse for Vocational and Technical Education which relate to instruction. (The Clearinghouse, Ohio State University, Columbus, Ohio)

Abstracts of Research and Related Materials in Vocational and Technical Education (ARM)
Issued four times a year by the ERIC Clearinghouse for Vocational and Technical Education, this abstracting journal controls items collected by the Clearinghouse which relate to research. (The Clearinghouse, Ohio State University, Columbus, Ohio)

British Education Index (3x yr.)
A subject index to over 50 British journals and magazines related to education. An author index is included. (The Library Association, London, England)

Child Development Abstracts and Bibliography (3x yr.)
Materials related to maturation (birth to adulthood) are abstracted, including educational materials, psychological, medical, etc. (University of Chicago Press, Chicago, Ill.)

CIRF Abstracts (quarterly)
International in scope, this abstracting service controls literature in the area of vocational training and related areas. (International Labor Office, Geneva, Switzerland)

College Student Personnel Abstracts (quarterly)
The abstracts contained in this publication are concerned with college students and their problems. Other college

topics are not included.   (College Student Personnel Institute, Claremont, Calif.)

Current Contents - Education (weekly)
This periodical reproduces tables of contents of hundreds of educational magazines and journals.   Subscribers to Current Contents may then select titles and purchase photocopies of the articles.   (Institute for Scientific Information, 325 Chestnut, Philadelphia, Pa. , 19106)

Current Index to Journals in Education (monthly)
Designed as a companion publication to Research in Education, this publication indexes the articles of about 200 educational research-oriented periodicals, including items located by the ERIC clearinghouses.   There is a strong representation of education-related literature.   (CCM Information Services, 866 Third Ave. , New York, N.Y.)

Education Index (monthly)
A continuing subject index to several hundred periodicals, both research and practitioner-oriented.   Author indexing was discontinued in 1960 but restored in 1969.   (H.W. Wilson Co. , Bronx, N.Y.)

Educational Administration Abstracts (quarterly)
Classified according to the major sub-fields of educational administration, this abstracting medium selects articles from over a hundred educational journals related to administration. Published by the University Council for Educational Administration.   (Interstate Printers and Publishers, 19-27 N. Jackson, Danville, Ill. , 61832)

Exceptional Child Education Abstracts (quarterly)
Besides abstracting articles from over 200 journals, summaries are also given for books, convention proceedings, curriculum guides, monographs, research reports, administrative guides, bibliographies, etc. , with the primary focus on the education of the handicapped or gifted including teaching methods, motivation, class placement, cognitive and psychological process, testing, curriculum, child development, and topics of related interests.   (Council for Exceptional Children, Jefferson Plaza, Suite 900, 1411 South Jefferson Davis Highway, Arlington, Va. 22202)

Perceptual Cognitive Development (bi-monthly)
This indexing service indexes articles, books, book chapters, reports, monographs, and similar items concerning perceptual, cognitive, and creative development of children.   (Galton Institute, Box 35336, Preuss Station, Los Angeles, Calif. 90035)

Resources in Education (monthly)
Monthly abstracting service of the Educational Resources

Information Center (ERIC), U. S. Office of Education. It abstracts and indexes those materials identified by ERIC's 16 subject-oriented clearinghouses. ERIC sells the complete documents thus indexed on microfiche. (See "ERIC Document Collections" under REPORTS AND MONOGRAPHS)

State Educational Journal Index (semi-annual)
Twice yearly index to the journals of the state education associations, most of which are not indexed elsewhere. (State Education Journal Index, P. O. Box 1030, Fort Collins, Colo. 80522)

Subject Index to Children's Magazines (monthly)
Subject arranged list of magazines of interest to children. Full subscription information is provided. (The Index, 2223 Chamberlain Ave., Madison, Wisconsin 53705)

BIBLIOGRAPHIC LISTS AND ESSAYS

"Outstanding Education Books of 19- ," Today's Education, the Journal of the NEA (annual, Mar.-Apr. issue)
An annual annotated bibliography reviewing the educational publications of the year and selecting the outstanding books of the period. (NEA, 1201 16th St., N.W., Washington, D.C.)

Research Studies in Education. Bloomington, Ind.: Phi Delta Kappa.
A regularly updated subject and author list of doctoral dissertations, reports, and field studies. One volume includes a research methods bibliography.

Sources in Educational Research. By Theodore Manheim, et al. Detroit: Wayne State University Press, 1969.
A comprehensive descriptive listing of research sources in education. Chapter one covers general works and succeeding chapters are discipline arranged.

The Teachers Library: How to Organize it and What to Include (1968)
In addition to explaining the organization of a professional teachers' library, this volume supplies a basic book list, arranged by format, for the compilation of same. (National Education Association, 1201 16th St., N.W., Washington, D.C.)

Textbooks in Print (annual)
An author and title index to commercially published elementary and secondary textbooks and related teaching materials. (R. R. Bowker Co., New York, N.Y.)

ANNUAL REVIEWS AND STATE OF THE ART REPORTS

Annual Phi Delta Kappa Symposium on Educational Research
>   This annual compilation of papers on current educational re-
>   search topics is the result of Phi Delta Kappa's annual sym-
>   posium co-sponsored by various universities. (PDK, Bloom-
>   ington, Ind.)

Association for Supervision and Curriculum Development Yearbook
>   The ASCD's yearbook is focused on a different topic in educa-
>   tional administration or curriculum each year. It constitutes
>   a state-of-the-art in that field. (ASCD, 1201 16th St., N.W.,
>   Washington, D.C.)

Biennial Survey of Education
>   A compilation of U.S. school statistics, such as enrollment,
>   number of instructional personnel, funding data, etc. Covers
>   public and private, K through college. (Government Printing
>   Office, Washington, D.C.)

Bowker Annual
>   An almanac-type work that supplies library statistics and
>   annual review articles about important topics in the field of
>   library science. Statistics, awards, association activities,
>   etc., are also included. (R. R. Bowker Co., New York,
>   N.Y.)

International Yearbook of Education
>   This is a compilation of the annual reports of the education
>   officials of nations participating in the International Conference
>   on Public Education each year in Geneva. Each report covers
>   all aspects of education in the nation in question and an over-
>   all comparative study is written of all reports. (UNESCO,
>   Paris)

National Council for the Social Studies Yearbook
>   Each year this department of the National Education Associa-
>   tion publishes a yearbook which summarizes the recent re-
>   search and literature on a particular topic relevant to the
>   scope of the NCSS. (NCSS, 1201 16th St., N.W., Washington,
>   D.C.)

National Society for the Study of Education Yearbook
>   Compilation of scholarly papers on various topics currently
>   important to education and its related fields. Two volumes
>   are issued on different topics each year. (SSE Yearbook,
>   University of Chicago Press, Chicago, Ill.)

Review of Research in Education
>   A recently inaugurated (volume one is dated 1973) annual de-
>   signed to synthesize "critical inquiry" in education and related
>   fields when it applies to education. Here, critical inquiry

"includes but is not exclusively empirical research. " Volume
one's four major divisions are Learning and instruction;
School organization, effectiveness, and change; History of
education; and Research methodology.   The nine subdivisions
constitute lengthy bibliographic essays.   Most end with lengthy
bibliographies.   It's adequately indexed by name and subject.
It was created by the American Educational Research Association.   (F. E. Peacock Pub., Itasca, Illinois)

BOOKS

Adams, Henry.   The Education of Henry Adams.   N. Y.:   Modern
    Library, 1931 (c1918)

American Education Research Association.   Handbook of Research
    on Teaching.   Chicago: Rand McNally, 1963.

Association for Supervision and Curriculum Development, NEA.   In-
    dividualizing Instruction; 1964 Yearbook.   Washington, D. C.:
    ASCD, 1964.

Bloom, Benjamin S., ed.   Taxonomy of Educational Objectives, the
    Classification of Educational Goals, Handbook I: Cognitive Do-
    main.   N. Y.:   McKay, 1956.

Braddock, Richard, et al.   Research in Written Composition.   Cham-
    paign, Ill.:   National Council of Teachers of English, 1963.

Briggs, Leslie J., et al.   Instructional Media: a Procedure for
    the Design of Multi-Media Instruction... (Monograph No. 2) Pitts-
    burgh, Pa.:   American Institutes for Research, 1967.

Bruner, Jerome S.   The Process of Education.   Cambridge, Mass.:
    Harvard University, 1960.

Chall, Jeanne S.   Learning to Read: The Great Debate.   N. Y.:
    McGraw, 1967.

Coleman, James S.   Equality of Educational Opportunity.   Washing-
    ton, D. C.:   U. S. Office of Education, 1966.

Combs, Arthur W., ed.   Perceiving, Behaving, Becoming.   Wash-
    ington, D. C.:   Association for Supervision and Curriculum De-
    velopment, NEA, 1962.

Cornfield, Ruth R.   Foreign Language Instruction, Dimensions and
    Horizons.   N. Y.:   Appleton, 1966.

Cruickshank, William M. and Johnson, G. Orville, eds.   Education
    of Exceptional Children and Youth, 2nd ed.   Englewood Cliffs,
    N. J.:   Prentice-Hall, 1967.

Dewey, John. Democracy and Education: an Introduction to the Philosophy of Education. N. Y.: Macmillan, 1916.

Erickson, Carlton W. H. Administering Audiovisual Services. N. Y.: Macmillan, 1965.

Fenton, Edwin. Teaching the New Social Studies in Secondary Schools: An Inductive Approach. N. Y.: Holt, 1966.

Frierson, Edward C. and Barbe, Walter B., eds. Educating Children with Learning Disabilities: Selected Readings. N. Y.: Appleton, 1967.

Gagne, Robert M. Conditions of Learning. N. Y.: Holt, 1965.

Glaser, Robert, ed. Teaching Machines and Programmed Learning, II: Data and Directions. Washington, D. C.: Department of Audiovisual Instruction, NEA, 1965.

Goodman, Paul. Growing Up Absurd: Problems of Youth in the Organized System. N. Y.: Random, 1960.

Hack, Walter G., et al. Educational Administration: Selected Readings. Boston: Allyn and Bacon, 1965.

Halpin, Andrew W. Theory and Research in Administration. N. Y.: Macmillan, 1966.

Haviland, Virginia. Children's Literature, a Guide to Reference Sources. Washington, D. C.: U. S. Government Printing Office, 1966.

Herndon, James. The Way It Spozed to Be. N. Y.: Simon, 1968.

Hill, Joseph and Kerber, August. Models, Methods, and Analytical Procedures in Education Research. Detroit: Wayne State University Press, 1967.

Holt, John. How Children Learn. N. Y.: Pitman, 1967.

Kemp, Jerrold. Instructional Design: A Plan for Unit and Course Development. Belmont, Calif.: Fearon, 1971.

Krathwohl, David R., et al. Taxonomy of Educational Objectives, the Classification of Educational Goals, Handbook II, Affective Domain. N. Y.: McKay, 1964.

Lieberman, Myron. Education as a Profession. Englewood Cliffs, N. J.: Prentice-Hall, 1956.

Loughary, John W., ed. Counseling--A Growing Profession. Washington, D. C.: American Personnel and Guidance Association, 1965.

Mager, Robert. Preparing Instructional Objectives. Palo Alto, Calif.: Fearon, 1962.

National Society for the Study of Education. Programed Instruction 66th Yearbook, Part II. Phil C. Lange, editor. Chicago: University of Chicago, 1967.

Neill, Alexander S. Summerhill; a Radical Approach to Child Rearing. N. Y.: Hart, 1960.

Passow, A. Harry, et al. Education of the Disadvantaged: A Book of Readings. N. Y.: Holt, 1967.

Rogers, Carl. On Becoming a Person; A Therapist's View of Psychotherapy. Boston: Houghton, 1961.

Rogers, Everett. Diffusion of Innovation. N. Y.: Free Press of Glencoe, 1962.

Rousseau, Jean Jacques. Emile. N. Y.: Dutton, 1911 (c1762).

Shores, Louis. Instructional Materials. N. Y.: Ronald, 1960.

Silberman, Charles E. Crisis in the Classroom, the Remaking of American Education. N. Y.: Random, 1970.

Skinner, B. F. and Holland, James G. Analysis of Behavior: A Program for Self Instruction. N. Y.: McGraw, 1961.

Taba, Hilda and Elkins, Deborah. Teaching Strategies for the Culturally Disadvantaged. Chicago: Rand McNally, 1966.

Thorndyke, Edward L. The Principals of Teaching, Based on Psychology. N. Y.: Seiler, 1906.

ENCYCLOPEDIC SUMMARIES

Dictionary of Education
        The newly released (1973) edition is the best specialized dictionary available for the educational researcher and graduate student. Comp. by C. Good. (McGraw-Hill, New York, N. Y.)

Encyclopaedia Britannica
        International in scope, this scholarly encyclopedia has major articles on education and most of its fields. Excellent source

for historical surveys and basic philosophical statements, although the unusual arrangement of the new edition decreases its effectiveness as a research tool. (Encyclopaedia Britannica, Chicago, Illinois)

Encyclopedia of Education
Comprehensive and scholarly encyclopedia on education. Excellent source of bibliographies and up-to-date articles on all aspects of education. (Macmillan Co., N. Y., N. Y.)

Encyclopedia of Educational Research (decennial)
The basic encyclopedic work in the field of education; has scholarly articles on all relevant topics in education and lengthy bibliographies. Published every ten years, it is updated by the Review of Educational Research (see "Periodicals" above). Sponsored by the American Educational Research Association. (Macmillan, New York, N. Y.)

Encyclopedia of Library and Information Science
The coverage is broad and international in scope with long, scholarly articles written by recognized authorities. The encyclopedia fills a need in the fields of library and information science. (Marcel Dekker, Inc., New York, N. Y.)

Who's Who in American Education
The first volume of a projected three-volume set covers eminent professors, principal school officials, librarians, and others who are still living. (Who's Who in American Education, Inc., Hattiesburg, Miss.)

Search Procedure Form	EDUCATION

NAME OF USER | **DATE OF INQUIRY**

REDEFINED QUESTION STATEMENT

KEYWORDS

WORK IN PROGRESS

- ☐ Contemporary Authors
- ☐ Pacesetters in Innovation

- ☐ Research in Education

UNPUBLISHED STUDIES

- ☐ DATRIX
- ☐ Dissertation Abstracts International

- ☐ Masters Abstracts

PERIODICALS

- ☐ American Documentation
- ☐ American Education
- ☐ American Educational Research Journal
- ☐ American Libraries
- ☐ Audiovisual Instruction
- ☐ Automated Education Handbook
- ☐ Bulletin - National Association of Secondary School Principals
- ☐ Child Development
- ☐ Children
- ☐ College and University Reports
- ☐ Comparative Education Review
- ☐ Congressional Quarterly Service
- ☐ Croft Newsletter Services
- ☐ Education
- ☐ Education Court Digest
- ☐ Education Recaps
- ☐ Educational Administration Quarterly
- ☐ Educational Leadership
- ☐ Educational Technology
- ☐ Educational Product Report
- ☐ Government Contracts Guide

- ☐ Guide to Federal Assistance for Education
- ☐ Harvard Educational Review
- ☐ Joint Council on Educational Telecommunications DATA Base Service
- ☐ Journal of Applied Psychology
- ☐ Journal of Educational Psychology
- ☐ Journal of Educational Research
- ☐ Journal of Research and Development in Education
- ☐ Journal of Teacher Education
- ☐ National Elementary Principal
- ☐ Phi Delta Kappan
- ☐ Psychological Review
- ☐ Report on the Education of the Disadvantaged
- ☐ Review of Educational Research
- ☐ Saturday Review
- ☐ School and Society
- ☐ Social Education
- ☐ Teachers College Record
- ☐ Theory into Practice
- ☐ Today's Education: the Journal of the NEA
- ☐ Urban Education

REPORTS AND MONOGRAPHS

- ☐ Abstracts of Papers
- ☐ Cooperative Research Monograph Series
- ☐ ERIC Document Collections

- ☐ NEA Research Reports
- ☐ What Research Says to the Teacher

INDEXES AND ABSTRACTING SERVICES

- ☐ Abstracts of Instructional Materials in Vocational and Technical Education (AIM)
- ☐ Abstracts of Research and Related Materials in Vocational and Technical Education (ARM)
- ☐ British Education Index
- ☐ Child Development Abstracts and Bibliography
- ☐ CIRF Abstracts
- ☐ College Student Personal Abstracts
- ☐ Current Contents - Education
- ☐ Current Index to Journals in Education

- ☐ Education Index
- ☐ Educational Administration Abstracts
- ☐ Exceptional Child Education Abstracts
- ☐ Perceptual Cognitive Development
- ☐ Research in Education
- ☐ State Educational Journal Index
- ☐ Subject Index to Children's Magazines

BIBLIOGRAPHIC LISTS AND ESSAYS

- ☐ "Outstanding Education Books of 19" Today's Education, the Journal of the NEA
- ☐ Research Studies in Education
- ☐ Sources in Educational Research
- ☐ The Teachers Library: How to Organize it and What to Include
- ☐ Textbooks in Print

ANNUAL REVIEWS AND STATE OF THE ART REPORTS

- ☐ Annual Phi Delta Kappa Symposium on Educational Research
- ☐ Association for Supervision and Curriculum Development Yearbook
- ☐ Biennial Survey of Education
- ☐ Bowker Annual
- ☐ International Yearbook of Education
- ☐ National Council for the Social Studies Yearbook
- ☐ National Society for the Study of Education Yearbook
- ☐ Review of Educational Research
- ☐ Review of Research in Education

BOOKS (List appropriate subject headings as well as author and title for books selected. See Discipline Resource Package for list of basic titles.)

ENCYCLOPEDIC SUMMARIES

- ☐ Dictionary of Education
- ☐ Encyclopedia Britannica
- ☐ Encyclopedia of Education
- ☐ Encyclopedia of Educational Research
- ☐ Encyclopedia of Library and Information Science
- ☐ Who's Who in American Education

COMMENTS:

| SEARCHER'S SIGNATURE | DATE COMPLETED |

Discipline Resource Package

LAW

Kent D. Talbot
University of Texas - Austin

Law refers to that discipline which encompasses the principals and regulations established by society to govern itself whether by custom, legislation, or court decision. This Discipline Resource Package is limited to materials concerning U. S. law.

Legal resources are designed to give the searcher access to information on:

> Common Law
> Court decisions (precedents)
> Statutes and Legislative history
> Administrative regulations
> Research literature (journal articles, scholarly commentaries, and reformulations of the law)
> Election and other statistics

The publication of legal research tools in the U. S. is dominated by one publisher, West Publishing Co. Most of the serial publications mentioned below are West publications.

West's Key Number System facilitates the use of their Key Number Digests and many of their other publications as well. A classification scheme was created and each topic and subtopic in it is assigned a "key number." As cases are digested in the Key Number Digests, "headnotes" are written summarizing each significant point of law in the decision and the appropriate key number is assigned to each headnote.

The value of the Key Number System is that once you locate the key number for the Topic you're interested in, you can quickly locate any similar decisions in the other Key Number Digests as well.

WORK IN PROGRESS

Contemporary Authors
A comprehensive source for biographical data on contemporary authors, many of which may not yet appear in traditional biographical sources. Entries are short, with personal, career,

and work-in-progress information. A list of writings and sources of biographical and critical data are given when possible. The set is now in its 48th volume but many of the earlier volumes have been cumulated. Each volume is a separate alphabet but a cumulative name index is provided at the end of volume 48. (Gale Research Co., Detroit)

UNPUBLISHED STUDIES

Dissertation Abstracts International
>The most complete source for abstracts of doctoral dissertations written in the United States. Most U. S. universities contribute to this system operated by a private corporation. Unfortunately, several important universities do not participate. Microfilm or paper copies of the dissertations are available for purchase. Until recently, the indexing has been spotty and of poor quality. Fortunately, a much better (and very expensive) 37-volume cumulative index is now available. (University Microfilms, Ann Arbor, Mich.)

Masters Abstracts
>This is a selective, classified and annotated list of master's theses produced by many, but by no means all, U. S. colleges and universities. As with dissertations, microfilm or paper copies of the theses are available for purchase from the publisher of the Abstracts. Due to its selectivity, it is much easier to use than Dissertation Abstracts International. MA is presently being published quarterly. (University Microfilms, Ann Arbor, Mich.)

PERIODICALS

American Bar Association Journal (monthly)
American Business Law Journal (3x yr.)
American Journal of International Law (quarterly)
American Journal of Legal History (quarterly)
Antitrust Law and Economics Review (quarterly)
Arms Control and Disarmament (quarterly)
Columbia Law Review (monthly)
Congressional Record (daily)
Copyright Bulletin (quarterly)
Criminal Law Bulletin (10x yr.)
Criminologist (quarterly)
FBI Law Enforcement Bulletin (monthly)
Federal Probation (quarterly)
Federal Register (5x yr.)
Food and Agricultural Legislation (bi-monthly)
Harvard Law Review (8x yr.)
Journal of Criminal Law, Criminology, and Police Science (quarterly)

Journal of Urban Law (quarterly)
Juvenile Court Digest (bi-monthly)
Law and Contemporary Problems (quarterly)
Law and Society Review (quarterly)
Military Law Review (quarterly)
New York University Journal of International Law and Politics (3x yr.)
Trial (bi-monthly).
Weekly Compilation of Presidential Documents

REPORTS AND MONOGRAPHS

National Reporter System

REGIONAL:

Atlantic Reporter, 1st series (1885-1938), 2d series (1938--date)
        Contains the decisions of the appellate courts of Connecticut,
        Delaware, District of Columbia, Maine, Maryland, New Hamp-
        shire, New Jersey, Pennsylvania, Rhode Island, and Vermont.
        Supplemented by paperbound advance sheets that are later re-
        placed by bound volumes. (West Pub. Co., St. Paul, Minn.)

Northeastern Reporter, 1st series (1885-1936), 2d series (1936--
date)
        Contains select decisions of the appellate courts of Illinois,
        Indiana, Massachusetts, New York, Ohio. Supplemented by
        paperbound advance sheets. (West Pub. Co., St. Paul,
        Minn.)

Northwestern Reporter, 1st series (1879-1940), 2d series (1940--
date)
        Contains select appellate court decisions from Iowa, Michigan,
        Minnesota, Nebraska, North Dakota, South Dakota, and Wis-
        consin. Paperbound advance sheets supplement the bound
        volumes. (West Pub. Co., St. Paul, Minn.)

Pacific Reporter, 1st series (1883-1931), 2d series (1931--date)
        Contains select appellate decisions of Alaska, Arizona, Cali-
        fornia, Colorado, Hawaii, Idaho, Kansas, Montana, Nevada,
        New Mexico, Oklahoma, Oregon, Utah, Washington, and
        Wyoming. Weekly paperbound advance sheets precede the is-
        suance of the bound volumes. (West Pub. Co., St. Paul,
        Minn.)

Southeastern Reporter, 1st series (1887-1939), 2d series (1939--
date)
        Contains select appellate decisions of Georgia, North Carolina,
        South Carolina, Virginia, and West Virginia. Bound volumes
        supplemented by weekly paperbound advance sheets. (West
        Pub. Co., St. Paul, Minn.)

Southwestern Reporter, 1st series (1887-1928), 2d series (1928--date)
> Contains select decisions of the appellate courts of Arkansas, Kentucky, Missouri, Tennessee, and Texas. Supplemented weekly by paperbound advance sheets. (West Pub. Co., St. Paul, Minn.)

Southern Reporter, 1st series (1887-1940), 2d series (1940--date)
> Contains select appellate court decisions of Alabama, Florida, Louisiana, and Mississippi. Weekly paperbound advance supplements. (West Pub. Co., St. Paul, Minn.)

SPECIAL:

American Law Reports, 1st series (1919-1948), 2d series (1948-1965), 3rd series (1965--date)
> Selected decisions from all jurisdictions are copiously annotated. (West Pub. Co., St. Paul, Minn.)

Federal Reporter, 1st series (1880-1924), 2d series (1924--date)
> Contains selected decisions of the U.S. Courts of Appeals and up to v. 60 of the 2d series contains selected Federal District Court Decisions. Paperbound supplements. (West Pub. Co., St. Paul, Minn.)

Federal Rules Decisions, (1941--date)
> Contains District and Appellate decisions affecting the Federal Rules of procedure. Also contains reports of conferences on the Rules and proposed rule changes. Paperbound supplements. (West Pub. Co., St. Paul, Minn.)

Federal Supplement, (1932--date)
> Contains select decisions of Federal District (trial) Courts. Paperbound supplements cumulate into bound volumes. (West Pub. Co., St. Paul, Minn.)

United States Supreme Court Reporter
> It begins its coverage with v. 106 of the official reports. Paperbound supplements are used until the bound volume appears. It reports the decisions and orders of the U.S. Supreme Court and adds headnotes that are keyed or key numbered to other West Pub. Co. Reporters and Digests. (West Pub. Co., St. Paul, Minn.)

United States Supreme Court Reports
> The official reporting of the decisions and orders of this court. Paperbound supplements. The decisions are arranged chronologically, with an alphabetical table of cases in each volume. (Government Printing Office, Washington, D.C.)

INDEXES AND ABSTRACTING SERVICES

Congressional Index
        An annual looseleaf service in two volumes supplemented by
new pages weekly. It traces the progress of legislation in
both houses of the U.S. Congress. It does not contain the
texts of bills; its purpose is to identify pending and enacted
legislation for the current session of Congress. (Commerce
Clearing House, New York, N.Y.)

Congressional Information Service Index
        Recently started index of Congressional documents; it can be
approached by author, title, or subject. An extremely useful
shortcut method in identifying specific publications. Remember that it covers Congress only, and not other branches of
government. The documents are available as a collection of
microfiche from the publisher. (Congressional Information
Service, Washington, D.C.)

Congressional Quarterly Weekly Reports
        A weekly summary of the progress of legislation, and cover-
age and reprints of newsworthy statements related to all
branches of government. A good source of Congressional
voting records. Monthly index. Each year, the weeklies
are summarized in a bound Almanac. (C.Q., Inc., Washington, D.C.)

Digest of Public General Bills and Resolutions
        A subject, number, and sponsor index to all bills for the
current session of the U.S. Congress. The Digest provides
a summary of the particular legislation, in contrast to the
Congressional Index that reports progress only. Published
monthly. (Government Printing Office, Washington, D.C.)

General Digest, 1966 to date
        Part of a larger digest system divided into decades (Decen-
nials) covering all reported Federal, State, decisions back
to 1897. Prior to 1897, the Century Digest digests cases
back to 1658. (West Pub. Co., St. Paul, Minn.

Index to Legal Periodicals
        A subject and author index to the articles in over 300 legal
periodicals. Published 11 times per year. (H. W. Wilson,
Bronx, N.Y.)

Modern Federal Practice Digest
        Key-numbered digest following subject arrangement for all
reported Federal cases since 1939. (West Pub. Co., St.
Paul, Minn.)

Monthly Catalog of U.S. Government Publications
        Published by the federal government and listing all publica-

tions except administrative or confidential items.   Monthly
subject index; December index cumulates the year.   Use for
exact bibliographic identification of the multitude of government publications.   (Government Printing Office, Washington,
D. C.)

National Journal
    Similar to the Congressional Quarterly but it attempts to
    provide in-depth reports on topics of current interest in the
    field of national politics.   It's published weekly.   (Govern-
    ment Research Co., Washington, D. C.)

Restatement in the Courts
    The generic title for a series of publications that are similar
    to Shepard's Citations in the sense that they collect the cita-
    tions to court decisions that have construed the various Re-
    statements of the Law, which was a partially successful at-
    tempt to state the common law in textual form.   The wide
    number of jurisdictions within the United States have paid var-
    ying degrees of attention to the Restatements.   (West Pub.
    Co., St. Paul, Minn.)

Shepard's Citations
    The generic name of a series of citators that correspond to
    the regional as well as state and federal reporters.   Used as
    a source to see if a decision has been modified or overruled
    by later court action.   Follow instructions carefully; it is
    mandatory that every case relied upon be "Shepardized" in
    order to be assured of its authority.   (Shepard's Citations,
    Inc., Colorado Springs, Colo.)

U.S. Code, Congressional, and Administrative News
    Since 1946, a source for part of the legislative history of
    each significant Federal law as well as a current source for
    the text of law itself.   Indexed by subject, Bill number, and
    Public Act Number.   2 bound volumes per year.   Supple-
    mented frequently by paperbound pamphlets.   (West Pub. Co.,
    St. Paul, Minn.)

United States Supreme Court Digest
    A West key-number digest of opinions from 1754 to date.
    Supplemented by pocket-parts in the back of each bound vol-
    ume.   (West Pub. Co., St. Paul, Minn.)

U.S. Treaties and Other International Agreements
    A chronological listing of the texts of these documents; a re-
    cent (1973) index published by Kavass and Sprudzs makes bib-
    liographic access to this compilation a reality.

Words and Phrases
    A multi-volume compendium of judicially construed definitions
    of terms.   It is not key-numbered according to the West sys-
    tem.   Supplemented by pocket parts in the back of each

volume and the frequent reissuance of bound volumes. Arranged alphabetically, it may be the only current legal dictionary of any value. Its drawback is its bulk. (West Pub.
Co., St. Paul, Minn.)

BIBLIOGRAPHIC LISTS AND ESSAYS

Catalogue of the Law College at New York University
    The only major annotated legal bibliography offering commen-
    tary as well as subject and author indexing. Over 20 years
    old, it is a one-of-a-kind necessity for any law library.

Current Legal Bibliography
    A subject listing of monographs, multi-volume works, and
    articles within law journals that have been added to the
    Harvard Law School Collection. Monthly paperback, cumu-
    lated annually. (Harvard Law School Library, Cambridge,
    Mass.)

Current Publications in Legal and Related Fields
    A monthly checklist of new titles in law. Good for book
    selection, it is published nine times per year by the Ameri-
    can Association of Law Libraries. (Fred B. Rothman & Co.,
    Hackensack, N.J.)

Law Books in Print
    Only recently started, it is published in two volumes with
    paper supplements. It is arranged by author, title, subject,
    series, and publisher. (Glenville Pub., Dobbs Ferry, N.Y.)

Law Books Recommended for Libraries
    Published in 1967 and supplemented by inserts in six binders.
    It contains a subject-organized list of over 50,000 law related
    monographs and bibliographic data for each. Published by
    the Association of American Law Schools. (Fred B. Rothman
    Pub., South Hackensack, N.J., 1967-70)

ANNUAL REVIEWS AND STATE OF THE ART REPORTS

America Votes
    A geo-statistical listing of recent election results. The bien-
    nial volumes (each general election year) begin in 1952.
    (C.Q., Inc., Washington, D.C.)

Current American Government
    A semi-annual summary in news report format on legislative,
    executive, and legal actions. Indexed by sponsor of legisla-
    tion, or name of news happening. It is a good, accurate
    summary of current events in the political sphere. Excellent

for small libraries and individuals who can't afford the C. Q.
Weekly Reports. (C. Q., Inc., Washington, D. C.)

Municipal Yearbook
It reports recent trends in local legislation and some statistics relevant to this legislation. Indexed by subject. (International City Management Assn., Washington, D. C.)

BOOKS

Anderson, James N. D. (editor) Changing Law in Developing Countries. New York: Praeger, 1963.

Berger, Monroe. Equality by Statute: Legal Controls Over Group
Discrimination. N. Y.: Columbia Univ. Press, 1952.

Berman, Harold J. Justice in the U. S. S. R.: An Interpretation of
Soviet Law. Rev. & enl. ed. Cambridge, Mass.: Harvard
Univ. Press, 1950.

Blaustein, Albert P.; and Porter, Charles O. The American Lawyer: A Summary of the Survey of the Legal Profession. Chicago:
Univ. of Chicago Press, 1954.

Carlin, Jerome E. Lawyers' Ethics: A Survey of the New York
City Bar. N. Y.: Russell Sage Foundation, 1966.

_____. Lawyers on Their Own: a Study of Individual Practi-
tioners in Chicago. New Brunswick, N. J.: Rutgers Univ. Press,
1962.

Cohen, Morris R. Reason and Law: Studies in Juristic Philosophy.
Glencoe, Ill.: Free Press, 1950.

Davis, R. James, et al. Society and the Law: New Meanings for
an Old Profession. N. Y.: Free Press, 1962.

Dicey, Albert V. Lectures on the Relation Between Law and Public
Opinion in England, During the Nineteenth Century. 2d ed. N. Y.:
Macmillan, 1905.

Eels, Richard. The Government of Corporations. N. Y.: Free
Press, 1962.

Eulau, Heinz; and Sprague, John D. Lawyers in Politics: a Study
in Professional Convergence. Indianapolis, Ind.: Bobbs-Merrill,
1964.

Friedman, Lawrence M. Contract Law in America: a Social and
Economic Case Study. Madison: Univ. of Wisconsin Press,
1965.

Friedman, Wolfgang. Legal Theory. 4th ed. London: Stevens, 1944.

Fuller, Lon L. The Morality of Law. New Haven: Yale Univ. Press, 1964.

Hart, H. L. A. The Concept of Law. Oxford: Clarendon, 1961.

Hoebel, E. Adamson. The Law of Primitive Man: A Study in Comparative Legal Dynamics. Cambridge, Mass.: Harvard Univ. Press, 1954.

Hurst, James W. The Growth of American Law: the Law Makers. Boston: Little, 1950.

_____. Law and Social Process in United States History. Ann Arbor: Univ. of Michigan Law School, 1960.

Jackson, Richard M. The Machinery of Justice in England. 4th ed. Cambridge Univ. Press, 1940.

Kalven, Harry; and Zeisel, Hans. The American Jury. Boston: Little, 1966.

Kirchheimer, Otto. Political Justice: the Use of Legal Procedure for Political Ends. Princeton, N. J.: Princeton Univ. Press, 1961.

Lindesmith, Alfred R. The Addict and the Law. Bloomington: Indiana Univ. Press, 1965.

Llewellyn, Karl N. The Common Law Tradition: Deciding Appeals. Boston: Little, 1960.

_____. Jurisprudence: Realism in Theory and Practice. Chicago: Univ. of Chicago Press, 1962.

Maine, Henry J. S. Ancient Law: its Connection with the Early History of Society, and its Relations to Modern Ideas. Rev. ed. N. Y.: Dutton, 1861.

Malinowski, Bronislaw. Crime and Custom in Savage Society. London: Routledge, 1926.

Marx, Karl, and Engels, Friedrich. Selected Works. Moscow: Foreign Languages Publishing House, 1848-1898.

Plucknett, Theodore F. T. A Concise History of the Common Law. 5th ed. London: Butterworth, 1929.

Pound, Roscoe. Jurisprudence. 5 vols. St. Paul, Minn.: West, 1959.

_____. The Lawyer from Antiquity to Modern Times: With Particular Reference to the Development of Bar Associations in the United States. St. Paul, Minn.: West, 1953.

Radin, Max. Law as Logic and Experience. New Haven: Yale Univ. Press, 1940.

Schubert, Glendon. Quantitative Analysis of Judicial Behavior. Glencoe, Ill.: Free Press, 1960.

Schur, Edwin M. Crimes Without Victims. Englewood Cliffs, N. J.: Prentice-Hall, 1965.

Skolnick, Jerome H. Justice Without Trial. N. Y.: Wiley, 1966.

Stone, Julius. The Province and Function of Law: Law as Logic, Justice, and Social Control; a Study in Jurisprudence. Cambridge, Mass.: Harvard Univ. Press, 1946.

Vinogradoff, Paul. Outlines of Historical Jurisprudence. 2 vols. Oxford Univ. Press, 1920-1922.

Weber, Max. The Theory of Social and Economic Organization. Edited by Talcott Parsons. Glencoe, Ill.: Free Press, 1922.

Wigmore, John H. A Panorama of the World's Legal Systems. 3 vols. Washington: Washington Law Book, 1928.

ENCYCLOPEDIC SUMMARIES

American Jurisprudence, 2d.
> A subject attempt to summarize the existing law in all of the U. S. It's not key-numbered, but it does contain case citations. It is supplemented by annual pocket-parts and new volumes. The encyclopedic approach suffers from an inability to cover all statutory materials. (Lawyers Cooperative Pub. Co., Rochester, N. Y.)

Black's Law Dictionary
> A dated one-volume dictionary of legal terms, both in English and Latin, that has no counterpart. Needs updating; for this, one must resort to the multi-volume Words and Phrases. (West Pub. Co., St. Paul, Minn.)

Code of Federal Regulations
> The official source of regulations arranged under subject "titles" similar to the U. S. Code. Paper volumes in need of drastic revision are published annually in paperback. Supplemented almost daily by the Federal Register. (Government Printing Office, Washington, D. C.)

Corpus Juris Secundum
          Published by West, but not key-numbered, this subject-ar-
     ranged summary suffers the same fate as all encyclopedias:
     that the law, especially statutory, is too specific and com-
     plex for this treatment. Supplemented by annual pocket parts
     and frequently revised volumes. (West Pub. Co., St. Paul,
     Minn.)

Federal Register
          An almost daily chronology of new Federal administrative
     regulations and some that are proposed. It supplements the
     Code of Federal Regulations. (Government Printing Office,
     Washington, D. C.)

United States Code, 1970 (supp. 1972)
          Collects and arranges laws of the Federal government under
     numbered subject divisions called "Titles. " It frequently lags
     behind legislation. It has a subject index. (Government
     Printing Office, Washington, D. C.)

United States Code Annotated
          This set takes Congressional enactments and arranges them
     under subject headings. It is supplemented by annual pocket
     parts and paperback supplements. Case annotations to each
     section of legislation are included. It often has a historical
     note for antecedent legislation. An extensive subject index
     and popular name table make this a useful source of Federal
     law and a good access tool to cases, even though it is not
     key numbered. (West Pub. Co., St. Paul, Minn.)

United States Statutes at Large
          Bound volumes of legislation passed by the U. S. Congress and
     enacted into law. It is the official text of the law, but because
     cause it is arranged chronologically and much Federal legisla-
     tion is a product of amendment, it is very difficult to use,
     unless the specific text of a specific act is all you want.
     Each volume contains a subject index. (Government Printing
     Office, Washington, D. C.)

Search Procedure Form	LAW

NAME OF USER	DATE OF INQUIRY

REDEFINED QUESTION STATEMENT

KEYWORDS

WORK IN PROGRESS

- ☐ Contemporary Authors

UNPUBLISHED STUDIES

- ☐ Dissertation Abstracts International
- ☐ Masters Abstracts

PERIODICALS

- ☐ American Bar Association Journal
- ☐ American Business Law Journal
- ☐ American Journal of International Law
- ☐ American Journal of Legal History
- ☐ Antitrust Law and Economics Review
- ☐ Arms Control and Disarmament
- ☐ Columbia Law Review
- ☐ Congressional Record
- ☐ Copyright Bulletin
- ☐ Criminal Law Bulletin
- ☐ Criminologist
- ☐ FBI Law Enforcement Bulletin
- ☐ Federal Probation
- ☐ Federal Register
- ☐ Food and Agricultural Legislation
- ☐ Harvard Law Review
- ☐ Journal of Criminal Law, Criminology, and Polic Science
- ☐ Journal of Urban Law
- ☐ Juvenile Court Digest
- ☐ Law and Contemporary Problems
- ☐ Law and Society Review
- ☐ Military Law Review
- ☐ New York University Journal of International Law and Politics
- ☐ Trail
- ☐ Weekly Compilation of Presidential Documents

REPORTS AND MONOGRAPHS

NATIONAL REPORTER SYSTEM REGIONAL:

- ☐ Atlantic Reporter, 1 st series (1885-1938), 2d series (1938-date)
- ☐ Northeastern Reporter, 1st series (1885-1936), 2d series (1940-date)
- ☐ Northwestern Reporter, 1st series (1879-1940), 2d series 1940-date)
- ☐ Pacific Reporter, 1st series (1883-1931), 2d series (1931-date)
- ☐ Southeastern Reporter, 1st series (1887-1939), 2d series (1939-date) •
- ☐ Southwestern Reporter, 1st series (1887-1928), 2d series (1928-date)

- ☐ Southern Reporter, 1st series (1887-1940), 2d series (1940-date)

SPECIAL:

- ☐ Federal Reporter, 1st series (1880-1924), 2d series (1924-date)
- ☐ Federal Rules Decisions, (1941-date)
- ☐ Federal Supplement, (1931-date)
- ☐ United States Supreme Court Reporter
- ☐ United States Supreme Court Reports
- ☐ American Law Reports, 1st series (1919-1948), 2d series (1948-1965), 3rd series (1965-date)

INDEXES AND ABSTRACTING SERVICES

- ☐ Congressional Index
- ☐ Congressional Information Service Index
- ☐ Congressional Quarterly Weekly Reports
- ☐ Digest of Public General Bills and Resolutions
- ☐ Index to Legal Periodicals
- ☐ General Digest, 1966 to date
- ☐ Modern Federal Practice Digest
- ☐ United States Supreme Court Digest

- ☐ Monthly Catalog of U.S. Government Publications
- ☐ National Journal
- ☐ Shepard's Citations
- ☐ U.S. Code, Congressional, and Administrative News
- ☐ U.S. Treaties and Other International Agreements
- ☐ Words and Phrases
- ☐ Restatement in the Courts

BIBLIOGRAPHIC LISTS AND ESSAYS

- ☐ Current Legal Bibliography
- ☐ Catalogue of the Law College at New York University
- ☐ Current Publications in Legal and Related Fields
- ☐ Law Books in Print
- ☐ Law Books Recommended for Libraries

ANNUAL REVIEWS AND STATE-OF-THE-ART REPORTS

- ☐ America Votes
- ☐ Current American Government
- ☐ Municipal Yearbook

ENCYCLOPEDIC SUMMARIES

- ☐ American Jurisprudence, 2d.
- ☐ Corpus Juris Secundum
- ☐ United States Code, 1970 (supp. ·1972)
- ☐ United States Code Annotated
- ☐ United States Statutes at Large
- ☐ Black's Law Dictionary
- ☐ Code of Federal Regulations
- ☐ Federal Register

COMMENTS:

SEARCHER'S SIGNATURE   **DATE COMPLETED**

Discipline Resource Package

PHILOSOPHY AND RELIGION

Jovian P. Lang
St. John's University

Philosophy encompasses a broad, interdisciplinary field that searches for wisdom or truth through logical reasoning rather than factual observation. It includes such specialities as metaphysics, logic, epistemology, ethics, and aesthetics, having for its object the study of all things from every aspect to determine the causes and laws of reality.

Religion seems to lend itself to an even greater array of possible definitions than Philosophy. Webster, for instance, describes it as "a personal awareness or conviction of the existence of a supreme being or of supernatural powers or influences controlling one's own, humanity's, or all nature's destiny."

Due to the considerable overlap of these two fields, the authors have decided to combine them into one Discipline Resource Package. Such concepts as morality, logic, metaphysics, and ethics may be approached from either a religious or a philosophical point of view, and often the same reference resources are used in literature searching. Concerning religion in some instances a title in the package may reflect one denomination's view. There could be a comparable source by another denomination that may be more satisfactory to the user.

WORK IN PROGRESS

Contemporary Authors

A comprehensive source for biographical data on contemporary authors, many of which may not yet appear in traditional biographical sources. Entries are short, with personal, career, and work-in-progress information. A list of writings and sources of biographical and critical data are given when possible. The set is now in its 48th volume but many of the earlier volumes have been cumulated. Each volume is a separate alphabet but a cumulative name index is provided at the end of volume 48. (Gale Research Co., Detroit)

UNPUBLISHED STUDIES

Dissertation Abstracts International
> The most complete source for abstracts of doctoral disserta-
> tions written in the United States. Most U. S. universities
> contribute to this system operated by a private corporation.
> Unfortunately, several important universities do not partici-
> pate. Microfilm or paper copies of the dissertations are
> available for purchase. Until recently, the indexing has been
> spotty and of poor quality. Fortunately, a much better (and
> very expensive) 37-volume cumulative index is now available.
> (University Microfilms, Ann Arbor, Mich.)

Masters Abstracts
> This is a selective, classified and annotated list of master's
> theses produced by many, but by no means all, U.S. colleges
> and universities. As with dissertations, microfilm or paper
> copies of the theses are available for purchase from the pub-
> lisher of the Abstracts. Due to its selectivity, it is much
> easier to use than Dissertation Abstracts International. MA
> is presently being published quarterly. (University Micro-
> films, Ann Arbor, Mich.)

PERIODICALS

America (weekly)
American Judaism (quarterly)
American Philosophy Quarterly
Analysis (bi-monthly)
Bible Today (bi-monthly)
British Journal of Aesthetics (quarterly)
Chicago Studies (quarterly)
Christian Century (weekly)
Christianity and Crisis (fortnightly)
Commentary (monthly)
Commonweal (weekly)
Criterion (bi-monthly)
Diogenes: an International Review of Philosophy and Humanistic
    Studies (quarterly)
Ecumenist (bi-monthly)
Ethics; an International Journal of Social, Political, and Legal Phi-
    losophy (quarterly)
Harvard Theological Review (quarterly)
IPQ; International Philosophical Quarterly
Journal of Philosophy (semi-monthly)
Journal of Religion (quarterly)
Journal of Symbolic Logic (quarterly)
Journal of the History of Philosophy (quarterly)
Katallagete; Be Reconciled (3x year)
Mind; a Quarterly Review of Psychology and Philosophy
Mind and World (quarterly)

National Catholic Reporter (weekly)
Philosophical Quarterly
Philosophical Review (quarterly)
Philosophical Studies (6x year)
Philosophy (quarterly)
Philosophy and Public Affairs (quarterly)
Philosophy Today (quarterly)
Religion Teacher (monthly, Sept.-May)
Review of Metaphysics (quarterly)
Theological Studies (quarterly)
Theology Digest (quarterly)
Theology Today (quarterly)

INDEXES AND ABSTRACTING SERVICES

Catholic Periodical and Literature Index (quarterly)
Besides indexing over 200 periodicals from many countries, books are also abstracted (as in the former Guide to Catholic Literature). Since the subject coverage is universal and not limited to theological concerns, even non-Catholic libraries will find it a good general index. (Catholic Library Association, Haverford, Pa.)

Index to Jewish Periodicals (quarterly)
Selected American and Anglo-Jewish periodicals of scholarly and general interest are indexed by subject and author. Book reviews are included. Annual cumulations. (16620 Lomond Blvd., Cleveland, Ohio)

Index to Religious Periodical Literature; an author and subject index to periodical literature (annual)
International in scope and Protestant in viewpoint, it indexes a few Catholic and Jewish periodicals. List of book reviews with an author index is included. (American Theological Library Association, Chicago.)

New Testament Abstracts (3x yr.)
Articles that appear in Catholic, Protestant, and Jewish periodicals in many languages are abstracted in English. Index of authors and of Scripture texts in each volume. (Theological Faculty of Weston College, Weston, Mass.)

Philosopher's Index (quarterly)
A subject and author index (KWIC approach) to all major American and British philosophical periodicals, with selective indexing from journals in other languages and from related interdisciplinary publications. (Bowling Green University, Bowling Green, Ohio.)

Religious and Theological Abstracts (quarterly)
Brief abstracts from a selected list of Christian, Jewish and

Muslim religious journals in various languages are nonsec-
tarian. Each volume contains author, subject and biblical
indexes. (301 S. College St., Myerstown, Pa. 17067)

BIBLIOGRAPHIC LISTS AND ESSAYS

Bibliographie de la Philosophie (10 vols.)
Periodical articles, doctoral dissertations and books are covered in this international bibliography, which is superseded
by a quarterly with the same name, the English Bibliography
of Philosophy. In the quarterly, books only are abstracted,
ordinarily in the language of the original. (International Institute of Philosophy, Vrin, Paris)

Bibliography of Philosophy, Psychology, and Cognate Subjects (Rand)
Out of date, but this most important bibliography in English
is divided into three parts: 1. General; 2. History, including individual philosophers arranged alphabetically; 3. Logic,
ethics, psychology, aesthetics, systematic philosophy and the
philosophy of religion. (Peter Smith, N. Y.)

Catholic Bookman's Guide
Comparable in scope to the Reader's Adviser; besides the
judicious choice of titles and incisive critiques for material
in all disciplines where a Christian outlook is desired, the
areas of philosophy and religion are particularly helpful.
(Hawthorn, Englewood Cliffs, N. J.)

Critical Bibliography of Religion in America (Burr)
A running commentary accompanies this classified arrangement of a comprehensive bibliography divided into Bibliographical guides, the Development of American religion, Religion and society, Religion in the arts and literature, and
finally, theology, philosophy, intellectual history and science.
Author index only. (Princeton Univ. Press, Princeton, N. J.)

Hundred Years in Philosophy (Passmore)
This survey studies the immediate background of today's
philosophy and cogently proves our indebtedness to European
philosophers of the past century. Includes a large bibliography of the authors cited, plus extensive footnotes to pertinent literature. (Macmillan, N. Y.)

International Bibliography of the History of Religions (Annual)
A classified arrangement of books and articles which appear
each year on the history of various religions of the world.
Author indexes started in 1958. (E. J. Brill, Leiden)

Philosophical Books (3x yr.)
British journal, reviewing usually from an analytical point of
view, is selective, preferring titles of interest to philosophers

who back the periodical <u>Analysis.</u> (Leicester Univ. Press)

Readers Guide to Books in Philosophy
  Dealing mainly with British and some American philosophers
  after 1900, this annotated bibliography is systematically arranged. (County Libraries Section, Library Association,
  London.)

Répertoire Bibliographique de la Philosophie (quarterly)
  Books and articles on philosophy from various countries appear in this comprehensive bibliography in classified order
  with annual author indexes. The November issue lists book
  reviews. (Ed. de l'Inst. Supérieur de Philosophie, Louvain)

ANNUAL REVIEWS AND STATE OF THE ART REPORTS

Catholic Almanac (formerly National Catholic Almanac) (annual)
  Aside from the expected handbook material, the church cal-
  endar, terms, statistics, and directory information, it includes news events by the month, synopses of special reports
  or the complete text of many important documents. Therefore preserve all earlier yearbooks. Also supplies material
  on non-Catholic faiths, ecumenism, etc. (Our Sunday Visitor,
  Huntington, Ind.)

Theological Investigations (Rahner)
  At a time of upsurge in theological development, the foremost
  Catholic theologian thinks through theology in the hope that
  young theologians will see how they can and must advance,
  while remaining true to laws and traditions. Volume 1 treats
  of God, Christ, Mary and Grace; vol. 2 researches Man in
  the Church; vol. 3 reflects on the Theology of Spiritual Life.
  Vols. 4 and 5 are later writings to be interspersed among the
  first three volumes. (Helicon Press, Baltimore)

Yearbook of American Churches
  Covers information on the organizations and activities of all
  faiths, with emphasis on Protestantism. (National Council
  of the Churches of Christ in the U.S.A., N.Y.)

Yearbook of Liturgical Studies (1960-1967)
  Scientific liturgical scholarship produces mature reflective research for the serious reader and scholar to keep abreast of
  developments. Precis, and sometimes critiques, of salient
  books and articles appear in the survey of liturgical literature
  of the preceding year which follows in a classified listing.
  (Liturgical Press, Collegeville, MN.)

BOOKS

Alexander, Samuel. Space, Time and Deity. London, 1920.

Austin, J. L. "Ifs and Cans," in Philosophical Papers. Oxford, 1961, pp 179-180.

Ayer, A. J. Language, Truth and Logic. London, 1936.

Bradley, F. H. Appearance and Reality. London, 1893.

Broad, C. D. "Speculative and Critical Philosophy," in J. H. Muirhead, ed., Contemporary British Philosophy, First Series. London, 1924.

Buber, Martin. Eclipse of God: Studies in the Relations between Religion and God. N. Y.: Harper & Row, 1957.

Bultmann, Rudolf & five critics. Kerygma and Myth: a Theological Debate. N. Y.: Harper & Row, 1961.

Cicero, Marcus Tullius. De Finibus ("Concerning Ends"). Translated by H. Rackham. Loeb Classical Library, no. 40. Cambridge, Mass., 1914. III, 2, 4.

Collingwood, R. G. Speculum Mentis. Oxford, 1924.

Copleston, Frederick. Contemporary Philosophy. Rev. ed. Paramus, N. J.: Paulist-Newman, 1972.

_____. History of Philosophy. 8 vols. Paramus, N. J.: Paulist-Newman, 1946-1966.

Croce, Benedetto. Filosofia coma scienza dello spirito, 5 vols. Bari, Italy, 1909-1917. Translated by D. Ainslie as Philosophy of the Spirit. London, 1909-1921.

Descartes, Rene. Philosophical Works, 2 vols. Translated by E. S. Haldane and G. R. T. Ross, Cambridge, 1911. Vol. 1 includes Meditationes de Prima Philsophiae (1641) and the Preface to the French translation of Principia Philosophiae (1650).

Dewey, John. Reconstruction in Philosophy. New York, 1920.

Ducasse, C. J. Philosophy as a Science. New York, 1941. Contains the best general discussion of the word "philosophy."

Frankl, Viktor. Logotherapy. N. Y.: Simon & Schuster, 1970.

Gilby, Thomas. Barbara Celerent; a Description of Scholastic Dialectic. Toronto: Longmans, 1949.

Goddard, Leonard. Philosophical Thinking. Armidale, New South Wales, 1962. Inaugural lecture.

Hamilton, William. Lectures on Metaphysics and Logic. 4 vols. Edinburgh, 1859-1860.

Hare, R. M. Freedom and Reason. Oxford, 1963.

Harnack, Adolf. What is Christianity? N. Y.: Harper & Row, 1958.

Hegel, G. W. F. Encyclopädie der Philosophischen Wissenschaft. Heidelberg, 1817. Part III. Translated by William Wallace as Hegel's Philosophy of Mind.

Heidegger, Martin. Discourse on Thinking. N. Y.: Harper & Row, 1966.

_____. Was ist das--die Philosophie? Pfullingen, 1956. Translated by W. Kluback and J. T. Wilde as What is Philosophy? London, 1958.

Hobbes, Thomas. De Corpore. London, 1655. Translated as Concerning Body. London, 1656.

Hoffer, Eric. First Things, Last Things. N. Y.: Harper & Row, 1971.

Hudson, Winthrop S. Religion in America; an Historical Account of the Development of American Religious Life. 2d ed. N. Y.: Scribners, 1973.

Hume, David. A Treatise of Human Nature. London, 1739.

Husserl, Edmund. Logische Untersuchungen. 2 vols. Halle, 1900-1901.

James, William. Some Problems in Philosophy. New York, 1911.

Lotze, (Rudolf) Hermann. Metaphysik. Leipzig, 1841. Translated and edited by Bernard Bosanquet as Metaphysic, 2 vols. Oxford, 1884.

Mill, J. S. Auguste Comte and Positivism. London, 1865.

Moore, G. E. Some Main Problems of Philosophy. London, 1953.

Mounier, Emmanuel. Personalism. University of Notre Dame Press, 1970.

New Catechism. N. Y.: Herder & Herder, 1969.

Passmore, J. A. "The Place of Argument in Metaphysics," in

W. E. Kennick and Morris Lazerowitz, eds., Metaphysics. Englewood Cliffs, N. J.: Prentice-Hall, 1966.

Popper, K. R. Conjectures and Refutations. New York, 1962.

Quasten, Johannes. Patrology. 3 vols. Paramus, N. J.: Paulist-Newman, 1950-1960.

Raeymaker, Louis, ed. Introduction à la philosophie. Louvain, 1938.

Russell, Bertrand. Our Knowledge of the External World. London, 1914.

Sidgwick, Henry. Philosophy, Its Scope and Relations. London, 1902.

Spencer, Herbert. First Principles. London, 1862.

Spinoza, Benedict. Ethica, in Opera Posthuma. Amsterdam, 1677. Translated by W. H. White and A. H. Stirling as Ethics. Oxford, 1927.

Strawson, P. F. Individuals. London, 1959.

Teilhard de Chardin, Pierre. The Divine Milieu. N. Y.: Harper & Row, 1960.

_____. The Phenomenon of Man. N. Y.: Harper & Row, 1959.

Tillich, Paul. What is Religion? N. Y.: Harper & Row, 1973.

Ueberweg, Friedrich. Grundriss der Geschichte der Philosophie. 3 vols. Berlin, 1862-1866. Translated by G. S. Morris as The History of Philosophy. London, 1871. Contains a discussion of the word "philosophy."

Walsh, W. H. Metaphysics. London, 1963. Contains one of the best general discussions of the word "philosophy."

Ward, Hiley. Documents of Dialogue. Englewood Cliffs, N. J.: Prentice-Hall, 1966.

Ward, James. Naturalism and Agnosticism. London, 1899.

Whitehead, A. N. Process and Reality. Cambridge, 1929.

Wittgenstein, Ludwig. Philosophical Investigations. Translated by G. E. M. Anscombe. Oxford, 1953.

_____ Tractatus Logico-philosophicus. Translated by D. F. Pears and B. F. McGuinness. London, 1961.

ENCYCLOPEDIC SUMMARIES

Anchor Bible (in progress)
> Similar to the Interpreter's Bible, but consists of a new
> translation with extensive commentaries, the work of Jewish,
> Protestant and Catholic scholars. (Doubleday, Garden City,
> N. Y.)

Atlas of the Early Christian World (Van der Meer)
> Illustrations of the sculpture, architecture, mosaics, Chris-
> tian cities, etc. of the first six centuries, accompanied by
> comments on their geographical and historical background.
> Maps show various parts of the Roman Empire in great de-
> tail, even plans of regions, important cities, churches, dio-
> ceses, and monuments. (Thomas Nelson, London)

Directory of American Philosophers (biennial)
> Lists philosophers from philosophical societies and staffs of
> academic departments of philosophy (except some 300 who
> fail to answer). Extends coverage to Canada; includes bib-
> liography of recent books, fellowship and employment oppor-
> tunities available, and information on philosophical societies.
> (Dept. of Philosophy, University of New Mexico, Albuquer-
> que)

Dictionary of Hymnology Setting Forth the Origin and History of
Christian Hymns of All Ages and Nations.   Rev. ed.
> Signed articles, with bibliographies, on hymnology, hymn
> writers, and individual hymns, with important subjects dealt
> with profusely. Indexes of authors, translators, and first
> lines in various languages. (Dover, N. Y.)

Dictionary of Philosophy and Psychology (Baldwin)
> At one time the only authoritative work available in English
> and still useful except for modern developments. Concise,
> not exhaustive, with signed articles and numerous bibliog-
> raphies. Cites Greek and scholastic philosophy. Includes
> entries in German, French and Italian equivalents of English
> terms. (Peter Smith, N. Y.)

Dictionary of the Bible (MacKenzie)
> Dictionary format of brief entries, with etymology, for the
> general reader. However, several pages are given to some
> articles. Few cross-references and only a general bibliog-
> raphy. Depth, breadth, and accuracy in the objective analy-
> sis of all aspects of the Bible appear in•this scientific scru-
> tiny. The up-to-date scholarly approach and tolerance in
> disputed questions wins respect from Protestant peers.
> (Bruce, Milwaukee)

Dictionary of the History of Ideas; Studies of Selected Pivotal Ideas.
(Wiener)

In our world of growing specialization and alienation, this 4-
vol. collection of signed essays endeavors to present the unity
of human thought and its cultural impact on the world by trac-
ing ideas from ancient times through succeeding periods, by
showing how the ideas evolved in their leading proponents'
minds and by studying a given period or century along cross-
cultural lines. (Scribners, N. Y.)

Encyclopaedia Judaica
An important work on Judeo-Christian heritage by 1, 800 con-
tributors synthesizes twentieth century Jewish scholarship,
not to supersede earlier works, but to supplement them.
Volume one, besides the index, is a ready reference tool.
An annual yearbook is planned. (Macmillan, N. Y.)

Encyclopaedia of Philosophy
Objective handling of all aspects of philosophy, including
serious subjects tangentially connected to it, insures prime
importance to this synthesis of 20th century philosophy.
There is a welcome stress on present day philosophical
trends.   Signed articles with bibliographies.   Ample subject
index.   (Macmillan, N. Y.)

Encyclopaedia of Religion and Ethics
Very comprehensive on all religions; treats of beliefs, cus-
toms, ethical movements and systems, moral practices,
philosophical ideas, and subjects in all interdisciplinary fields,
including persons and places. (Scribner's, N. Y.)

Exhaustive Concordance of the Bible (Strong)
Each word of the King James version appears in this con-
cordance, together with a comparative concordance of the
Authorized and Revised versions.   Includes a dictionary of
Hebrew and Greek words used in the original.   For the Douay
version use Thompson and Stock; for the Apocrypha use
Cruden; Concordance for the New American Bible is in prog-
ress.   (Abingdon-Cokesbury, N. Y.)

The Great Ideas, a Syntopicon of Great Books of the Western World
This work uncovers the unity and continuity of Western civilization by guiding a person in reading the world's common
themes and problems, whether speculative or practical, until
it becomes a unified whole.   Not only is it a reference book
of ideas, but a book to read, since it has an essay on each
of the 102 great ideas.   The syntopical approach to reading
great books proffers persons a liberal education.   Whether
one studies the history of ideas, a single author, or a particular period, the syntopicon becomes an instrument of discovery and research.   (Encyclopaedia Britannica, Chicago)

Handbook of Denominations in the United States (5th ed.)
Updating and revision attains objectivity in presenting concise
information on the organization, doctrine, history and present

status of more than 250 religions in the U.S.   Includes addresses of denominational headquarters, glossary, index of
proper names, and a classified bibliography.   (Abingdon,
Nashville, TN.)

Interpreter's Bible (12 vols.)
General articles with an introduction (biblical sense or usage),
exegesis and exposition for each book of the Bible.   (Abingdon-Cokesbury, Nashville, TN.)

Interpreter's Dictionary of the Bible
Planned for the general reader, student, teacher, preacher
and scholar and solidly dependent on recent research and
archaeological discoveries, this illustrated and scholarly dictionary is indispensable for biblical study today.   Refers to
King James version and Revised Standard version, to the
Dean Sea Scrolls, Pseudepigrapha, the apocrypha, etc., and
has maps, bibliographies and signed articles.   (Abingdon-
Cokesbury, N. Y.)

Jerome Biblical Commentary
Up-to-date commentary on the entire Bible by Roman Catholic scholars, with bibliographies, cross references and a
general index.   (Prentice-Hall, Englewood Cliffs, N. J.)

Larousse World Mythology
Several scholars summarize the evolution and substance of
the mythologies of various geographical areas so as to present a pre-history of society as it is spiritually founded in
myth, at least as currently theorized and understood.   Pos-
sibly controversial, this updated work becomes an enrichment
and reference source with illustrations and suggested further
readings.   (Putnam's Sons, N. Y.)

Lives of the Saints (Butler) 4th rev. ed.
For ordinary purposes this is probably the most popular collection, arranged by months according to the saints' feast
days.   The one-volume brief biographical A Dictionary of
Saints, compiled by Donald Attwater, is also an index to the
set.   (Kenedy, N. Y.)

New Catholic Encyclopedia (15 vols.)
International in scope, but with emphasis on the Catholic
Church in the United States, English speaking countries and
Latin America, this new work treats the present state of reform, reflecting the outlook and interests of the latter half
of the twentieth century.   Biography excluded.   Good illustrations, maps and bibliographies.   Earlier encyclopedia still
valuable for different bibliographies, entries that do not appear in the new work, and for more extensive treatment of
certain topics.   (McGraw-Hill, N. Y.)

Official Catholic Directory (annual)

Detailed information in directory and statistical format of institutions, e.g., churches, schools, missions, and of the organization, clergy, religious orders, etc., of the Catholic
Church in English-speaking countries. Similar directories
exist for other denominations. (Kenedy, N.Y.)

Religious Issues in American History
Religious history in America has experienced clashes and
confrontations; the issues behind these are discussed in this
source-book. (Harper-Row, N.Y.)

Sacramentum Mundi: Encyclopedia of Theology (6 vols.)
Current development of the understanding of faith based on
modern postconciliar theological investigation of central
themes of theological disciplines. (Herder & Herder, N.Y.)

Sacramentum Verbi: an Encyclopedia of Biblical Theology (Bauer)
Outstanding biblical theologians of the world contribute to this
up-to-date and comprehensive encyclopedia, which is an aid
to the professional and general reader. Pastoral and academic concerns are satisfied. Signed articles, extensive bibliographies and indexes to articles and biblical references
lend authority and usefulness. (Herder & Herder, N.Y.)

Theological Dictionary (Rahner & Vorgrimler)
Brief fresh expositions of important ideas in modern Catholic
dogmatic theology, written with consideration of difficulties
felt by non-Catholic Christians. (Herder & Herder, N.Y.)

Theological Dictionary of the New Testament. 9 vols. (Kittel)
The eighth volume reaches to the letter Y in this exposition
of theologically significant words in the New Testament which
is still in progress. (Eerdmans, Grand Rapids, MI.)

Westminster Historical Atlas to the Bible
Besides clear and well drawn maps and many illustrations,
this well researched atlas contains historical information and
archaeological discussions, hence the need for three indexes
to the text, to the maps topographically in accord with the
Bible, and to Arabic names of biblical places in Palestine and
Syria. (Westminster, Philadelphia)

Search Procedure Form	PHILOSOPHY AND RELIGION

NAME OF USER 　　　　　　　　　　　　　　　　　　　**DATE OF INQUIRY**

REDEFINED QUESTION STATEMENT

KEYWORDS

WORK IN PROGRESS

☐　Contemporary Authors

UNPUBLISHED STUDIES

☐　Dissertation Abstracts International
☐　Masters Abstracts

PERIODICALS

☐　America
☐　American Judaism
☐　American Philosophy Quarterly
☐　Analysis
☐　Bible Today
☐　British Journal of Aesthetics
☐　Chicago Studies
☐　Christian Century
☐　Christianity and Crisis
☐　Commentary
☐　Commonweal
☐　Criterion
☐　Diogenes: an International Review of Philosophy and Humanistic Studies
☐　Ecumenist
☐　Ethnics; an International Journal of Social, Political, and Legal Philosophy
☐　Harvard Theological Review
☐　IPQ; International Philosophical Quarterly
☐　Journal of Philosophy
☐　Journal of Religion
☐　Journal of Symbolic Logic

☐　Journal of the History of Philosophy
☐　Katallagete; Be Reconciled
☐　Mind; a Quarterly Review of Psychology and Philosophy
☐　Mind and World
☐　National Catholic Reporter
☐　Philosophical Quarterly
☐　Philosophical Review
☐　Philosophical Studies
☐　Philosophy
☐　Philosophy and Public Affairs
☐　Philosophy Today
☐　Religion Teacher
☐　Review of Metaphysics
☐　Theological Studies
☐　Theology Digest
☐　Theology Today

INDEXES AND ABSTRACTING SERVICES

☐　Catholic Periodical and Literature Index
☐　Index to Jewish Periodicals
☐　Index to Religious Periodical Literature
☐　New Testament Abstracts
☐　Philosopher's Index
☐　Religious and Theological Abstracts

BIBLIOGRAPHIC LISTS AND ESSAYS

☐　Bibliographie de la Philosophie
☐　Bibliography of Philosophy, Psychology, and Cognate Subjects
☐　Catholic Bookman's Guide
☐　Critical Bibliography of Religion in America
☐　Hundred Years in Philosophy

☐　International Bibliography of the History of Religions
☐　Philosophical Books
☐　Readers Guide to Books in Philosophy
☐　Repertoire Bibliographique de la Philosophie

ANNUAL REVIEWS AND STATE-OF-THE-ART REPORTS

- ☐ Catholic Almanac
- ☐ Theological Investigations
- ☐ Yearbook of American Churches
- ☐ Yearbook of Liturgical Studies

ENCYCLOPEDIC SUMMARIES

- ☐ Anchor Bible
- ☐ Atlas of the Early Christian World
- ☐ Directory of American Philosophers
- ☐ Dictionary of Hymnology Setting Forth the Origin and History of Christian Hymns of All Ages and Nations
- ☐ Dictionary of Philosophy and Psychology
- ☐ Dictionary of the Bible
- ☐ Dictionary of the History of Ideas
- ☐ Encyclopaedia Judaica
- ☐ Encyclopaedia of Philosophy
- ☐ Encyclopaedia of Religion and Ethnics
- ☐ Exhaustive Concordance of the Bible
- ☐ Exhaustive Concordance of the Bible
- ☐ The Great Ideas, a syntopicon of Great Books of the Western World
- ☐ Handbook of Denominations in the United States
- ☐ Interpreter's Bible
- ☐ Interpreter's Dictionary of the Bible
- ☐ Jerome Biblical Commentary
- ☐ Larousse World Mythology
- ☐ Lives of the Saints
- ☐ New Catholic Encyclopedia
- ☐ Official Catholic Directory
- ☐ Religious Issues in American History
- ☐ Sacramentum Mundi: Encyclopedia of Theology
- ☐ Sacramentum Verbi: an Encyclopedia of Biblical Theology
- ☐ Theological Dictionary
- ☐ Theological Dictionary of the New Testament
- ☐ Westminster Historical Atlas to the Bible

COMMENTS:

SEARCHER'S SIGNATURE | **DATE COMPLETED**

Discipline Resource Package

LANGUAGE AND LITERATURE

Rose Mary Magrill
University of Michigan

Literature refers to writing in which ideas of universal interest are incorporated into recognized forms such as poetry, fiction, biography, essays, etc. Literature, therefore, is an art form. Linguistics is the science devoted to the study of language.

WORK IN PROGRESS

American Literature (quarterly)
>Each issue lists "Research in Progress," which includes announced dissertation topics and other projects. (Duke University Press, Durham, North Carolina)

American Quarterly
>One issue a year contains a list of American studies dissertations in progress and completed during the past year. Topics withdrawn are also noted. (University of Pennsylvania, Philadelphia, Pa.)

Contemporary Authors
>A comprehensive source for biographical data on contemporary authors, many of which may not yet appear in traditional biographical sources. Entries are short, with personal, career, and work-in-progress information. A list of writings and sources of biographical and critical data are given when possible. The set is now in its 48th volume but many of the earlier volumes have been cumulated. Each volume is a separate alphabet but a cumulative name index is provided at the end of volume 48. (Gale Research Co., Detroit)

UNPUBLISHED STUDIES

American Dissertations on the Drama and the Theatre: a Bibliography
>Lists United States and Canadian doctoral dissertations to 1965. Author, KWIC, and subject indexes. Comp. by Frederick M. Litto. (Kent State Univ. Press, Kent, Ohio, 1969)

Dissertation Abstracts International
> The most complete source for abstracts of doctoral disserta-
> tions written in the United States. Most U. S. universities
> contribute to this system operated by a private corporation.
> Unfortunately, several important universities do not partici-
> pate. Microfilm or paper copies of the dissertations are
> available for purchase. Until recently, the indexing has been
> spotty and of poor quality. Fortunately, a much better (and
> very expensive) 37-volume cumulative index is now available.
> (University Microfilms, Ann Arbor, Mich.)

Dissertations in American Literature, 1891-1966
> Lists about 4,700 dissertations by subject. Author index.
> The newly revised and enlarged edition is comp. by James
> L. Woodress. (Duke Univ. Press, Durham, North Carolina,
> 1968)

Dissertations in English and American Literature
> Basic volume lists by subject dissertations accepted by Amer-
> ican, British, and German universities, 1865-1964. Indexed
> by authors of dissertations with a cross-index of authors as
> subjects. Supplement provides similar coverage for 1964-68.
> Comp. by Lawrence F. McNamee. (Bowker, New York,
> N. Y. , 1969)

Masters Abstracts
> This is a selective, classified and annotated list of master's
> theses produced by many, but by no means all, U. S. col-
> leges and universities. As with dissertations, microfilm or
> paper copies of the theses are available for purchase from
> the publisher of the Abstracts. Due to its selectivity, it is
> much easier to use than Dissertation Abstracts International.
> MA is presently being published quarterly. (University Mi-
> crofilms, Ann Arbor, Mich.)

PERIODICALS

American Literature (quarterly)
Canadian Literature (quarterly)
College English (8x yr.)
Columbia Journalism Review (bi-monthly)
Comparative Literature (quarterly)
Contemporary Literature (quarterly)
Critical Quarterly
Critique: Studies in Modern Fiction (3x yr.)
Drama (Br. Drama League) (quarterly)
Drama Review (quarterly)
English Language Notes (quarterly)
English Literary History (quarterly)
English Studies (bi-monthly)
Essays in Criticism (quarterly)

Explicator (10x yr.)
Extrapolation; a Journal of Science Fiction and Fantasy (semi-annual)
Hudson Review (quarterly)
Journal of American Folklore (quarterly)
Journal of Modern Literature (5x yr.)
Journalism Quarterly
Language Learning (bi-annual)
Modern Drama (quarterly)
Modern Fiction Studies (quarterly)
Modern Language Journal (10x yr.)
Modern Language Notes (6x yr.)
Modern Language Review (quarterly)
Modern Philology (quarterly)
New American Review (3x yr.)
Nineteenth Century Fiction (quarterly)
PMLA (6x yr.)
Paris Review (quarterly)
Philological Quarterly
Poetry (monthly)
Review of English Studies (quarterly)
Speculum (quarterly)
Studies in English Literature, 1500-1900
Studies in Short Fiction (quarterly)
Twentieth Century Literature (quarterly)
Victorian Studies (quarterly)

INDEXES AND ABSTRACTING SERVICES

Abstracts of English Studies (monthly)
> Articles on English language and literature from over 1,000
> periodicals covering American, English, and British Com-
> monwealth literature are abstracted, arranged geographically
> and chronologically, and indexed by names and subjects. (Na-
> tional Council of Teachers of English, Boulder, Colo.)

Abstracts of Folklore Studies (quarterly)
> Abstracts are arranged alphabetically by the journal in which
> the articles appeared and indexed annually by author, title,
> and subject. (American Folklore Society, Austin, Texas)

American Literature (quarterly)
> Each issue carries an unannotated, classified list of "Articles
> on American Literature Appearing in Current Periodicals."
> (Duke University Press, Durham, North Carolina)

Annual Bibliography of English Language and Literature (annual)
> Books and articles on English language and the literature of
> England, United States, and other English-speaking countries
> are classified by topic and/or period and indexed by author
> and subject. (Modern Humanities Research Association,
> Cambridge University Press, Cambridge, England)

Bibliographie Linguistique (annual)
> Lists books and articles on linguistics, arranged by various language groups. Also cites reviews for books included. Author index. (Permanent International Committee of Linguistics, Utrecht, The Netherlands)

British Humanities Index (quarterly)
> Subject index to over 350 British periodicals, including many on language and literature. Annual cumulation has author index. (The Library Association, London, England)

Essay and General Literature Index (semi-annual)
> Author, subject, and, where appropriate, title index to collections of essays and other composite works. (H. W. Wilson, Co., New York, N. Y.)

Index to Book Reviews in the Humanities (annual)
> Indexes all reviews in a specified list of about 160 humanities periodicals. Arranged alphabetically by author of the title reviewed. (Philip Thomson, Detroit, Mich.)

Index to Little Magazines (biennial)
> Author, and, occasionally, subject index to high quality literary reviews with limited circulations. Coverage varies. (Alan Swallow, Denver, Colo.)

LLBA: Language and Language Behavior Abstracts (quarterly)
> Abstracts of scholarly articles on language and language behavior, regardless of disciplinary focus. Classified with author, subject, book review, and source publication indexes. All indexes cumulate annually. (University of Michigan, Ann Arbor)

MLA Abstracts (annual)
> Supplements MLA International Bibliography with abstracts of selected journal articles from that bibliography. No indexes, but citations of articles abstracted are starred in the Bibliography. (Modern Language Association of America, New York, N. Y.)

MLA International Bibliography of Books and Articles on the Modern Languages and Literatures (annual)
> Covers literature in English, French, Spanish, German, Italian, Portuguese, Dutch, Modern Greek, and Scandinavian, Oriental, African and Eastern European languages; linguistics; and the teaching of foreign languages. Author index. (Modern Language Association of America, New York, N. Y.)

New York Theatre Critics Reviews (weekly)
> Brings together reviews of selected New York theatre productions. Annual index of plays, casts, authors, producers, etc. Cumulated index of play titles for 1940-60. (Critics' Theatre Reviews, New York, N. Y.)

Social Sciences and Humanities Index (quarterly)
>   Indexes over 200 scholarly journals, mostly American and
>   British. Published as International Index from 1907-1965.
>   (H. W. Wilson Co., Bronx, N.Y.)

BIBLIOGRAPHIC LISTS AND ESSAYS

Afro-American Writers
>   Selective guide to general and specialized works on Afro-
>   American literature. Emphasizes twentieth century and in-
>   cludes individual lists for 135 authors, as well as background
>   sections on historical and social setting of the literature.
>   Comp. by Darwin T. Turner. (Appleton-Century-Crofts, New
>   York, N.Y., 1970)

Articles on American Literature, 1900-1950
Articles on American Literature, 1950-1967
>   Most comprehensive classified list of periodical articles pub-
>   lished since 1900 on American literature. Includes foreign
>   periodicals, as well as English language works. Updated by
>   current listings in American Literature. Comp. by Lewis G.
>   Leary. (Duke Univ. Press, Durham, North Carolina, 1970)

Bibliographic Guide to the Study of the Literature of the U.S.A.,
3rd ed.
>   Classified arrangement of selected works on literature in the
>   United States, including book and periodical publishing. Some
>   annotations. Index. By Clarence L. Gohdes. (Duke Univer-
>   sity Press, Durham, North Carolina, 1970)

Bibliography of American Literature
>   When publication is completed, BAL will include detailed bib-
>   liographies for 300 American authors who died before 1930
>   and who enjoyed popularity among their contemporaries. Comp.
>   by Jacob Blanck for the Bibliographical Society of America.
>   (Yale University Press, New Haven, Conn., 1955+)

Bibliography of Comparative Literature
>   Classified list of books and articles on the literary influence
>   of one country on another. Up-dated through 1972 by annual
>   issues of Yearbook of Comparative and General Literature.
>   Ed. by Fernand Boldensperger and Werner Friedrich. (Uni-
>   versity of North Carolina Press, Chapel Hill, North Carolina,
>   1950)

Bibliography of General Linguistics: English and American
>   Annotated and classified list of basic publications in the field,
>   with special emphasis on recent works and reference materi-
>   als. Includes a section on periodicals and series. Author
>   and periodical title indexes. Comp. by Aleksandra K.
>   Wawrzyszko. (Archon Books, Hamden, Conn., 1971)

Bibliography of the American Theatre
>   Concerned with the history and development of theatre outside
>   New York City.   Arranged by state and city, with some anno-
>   tations and an index.   Comp. by Carl J. Stratman.   (Loyola
>   University Press, Chicago, 1965)

Cambridge Bibliography of English Literature
>   Most comprehensive bibliography for English literature, 600-
>   1900.   Arranged chronologically and by genre within five
>   main periods.   For important authors, bibliographies, col-
>   lected editions, separate works, biographical and critical
>   works are listed.   Includes brief sections on English litera-
>   ture of Commonwealth countries.   Indexed by subject, anony-
>   mous titles, and some authors.   Five volumes.   Ed. by
>   Frederick W. Bateson.   (Cambridge University Press, Cam-
>   bridge, England, 1940-57)

Concise Bibliography for Students of English.   5th ed.
>   Comprehensive, classified list of works useful for study of
>   literature in English.   Good for peripheral studies.   Index.
>   Ed. by Arthur G. Kennedy, et al.   (Stanford University Press,
>   Stanford, Calif., 1972)

Concise Cambridge Bibliography of English Literature.   2d ed.
>   Lists books and most important critical works for about 400
>   major authors of English literature, 600-1950.   Indexed by
>   names and anonymous titles.   Ed. by George Watson.   (Cam-
>   bridge University Press, Cambridge, England, 1965)

Fiction Catalog.   8th ed.
>   Annotated guide to adult fiction found most useful in American
>   libraries.   Indexed by author, title, and subject.   Annual sup-
>   plements.   (H. W. Wilson Co., New York, N.Y., 1971)

Guide to American Literature and Its Background Since 1890, 4th ed.
>   Works listed are selected to cover the "social and intellectual
>   setting of American literature."   Some annotations.   Index.
>   Ed. by Howard M. Jones and Richard M. Ludwig.   (Harvard
>   University Press, Cambridge, Mass., 1972)

Guide to English Literature, 2d ed.
>   Bibliographic essays covering, in period groupings, standard
>   editions, biographies, historical and critical works of English
>   literature to 1960.   Index.   Ed. by Frederick W. Bateson.
>   (Longmans, London, 1967)

Literary History of the United States, 3d ed.
>   Two supplements to this work contain selective bibliographic
>   essays on American literature since the colonial period and
>   on a number of individual authors.   Second supplement covers
>   through 1970.   Ed. by Robert E. Spiller, et al.   (Macmillan,
>   New York, 1963.   Bibliography Supplement II, 1972)

New Cambridge Bibliography of English Literature
        Revision and up-dating of CBEL, excluding Commonwealth
        countries, some "non-literary" topics, and some older mate-
        rial. When complete will cover 600-1950. Ed. by George Wat-
        son. (Cambridge University Press, Cambridge, Eng., 1969+)

Philological Quarterly
        One issue a year includes an interdisciplinary, annotated,
        current bibliography on the eighteenth century with strong
        coverage of English literature, 1660-1800, as well as French,
        German, Italian, Spanish, Scandinavian and Slavic literatures.
        (University of Iowa, Iowa City)

Play Index
        Annotated index of plays in collections and single plays, one-
        act and full-length, adult and juvenile. Indexed by author,
        title, subject, and cast. Present coverage from 1949 into
        the 1970's. (H. W. Wilson Co., New York, 1953+)

Reference Guide to English Studies, 2d ed.
        Survey of reference materials useful for study of English lit-
        erature. Some annotations. Index. Ed. by Donald F. Bond.
        (University of Chicago Press, Chicago, 1971)

Resources for American Literary Study (semi-annual)
        Includes annotated and evaluative checklists of critical and
        biographical scholarship on major and minor authors and
        evaluative bibliographic essays on major authors, works,
        genres, trends, and periods, etc. (Published jointly by
        Virginia Commonwealth University, Richmond, and University
        of Maryland, College Park)

Victorian Studies (quarterly)
        Since 1958, the June issue has carried an annotated bibliog-
        raphy of the past year's books, articles and dissertations on
        the Victorian period. From 1932 to 1957 the same bibliog-
        raphy was published in Modern Philology. (Indiana University,
        Bloomington)

ANNUAL REVIEWS AND STATE OF THE ART REPORTS

American Literary Scholarship (annual)
        Bibliographic essays provide a survey of research in Ameri-
        can literature published during the past year. Part I has
        chapters on eight major authors and Part II is arranged by
        genre and period.

Studies in English Literature, 1500-1900 (quarterly)
        Each issue contains a critical survey of recent studies on a
        specific period of English literature: winter issue, English
        Renaissance; spring issue, Elizabethan and Jacobean drama;

summer issue, Restoration and eighteenth century; autumn
issue, nineteenth century. (Rice University, Houston, Texas)

Year's Work in English Studies (annual)
Bibliographic essays cover recent work in English language
and literature, with two chapters devoted to American literature. Indexed by author and subject. (English Association,
London, England)

Year's Work in Modern Language Studies (annual)
Critical survey of recent studies on Romance, Germanic, and
Slavonic languages and literatures. Subject and name indexes.
(Modern Humanities Research Association, London, England)

BOOKS

Altick, Richard D. The English Common Reader: A Social History
of the Mass Reading Public, 1800-1900. Chicago: University of
Chicago Press, 1957.

Baugh, Albert C. A History of the English Language. 2d ed. New
York: Appleton-Century-Crofts, 1957.

Bloomfield, Leonard. Language. Rev. ed. New York: Rinehart
and Winston, 1933.

Brooks, Cleanth. Modern Poetry and the Tradition. Chapel Hill:
University of North Carolina Press, 1939.

_____. The Well-Wrought Urn; Studies in the Structure of Poetry.
New York: Reynal and Hitchcock, 1947.

Brooks, Van Wyck. America's Coming-of-Age. Rev. ed. New
York: Doubleday, 1934.

_____. The Flowering of New England, 1815-1865. New York:
Dutton, 1936.

Carroll, John B. The Study of Language: A Survey of Linguistics
and Related Disciplines in America. Cambridge, Mass.: Harvard
University Press, 1953.

Chomsky, Noam. Syntactic Structures. The Hague: Mouton, 1957.

Daiches, David. A Critical History of English Literature. New
York: Ronald, 1960. 2v.

_____. English Literature. Englewood Cliffs, N. J.: Prentice-
Hall, 1964.

Dowden, Edward. Shakespeare: A Critical Study of His Mind and

<u>Art.</u> London: Routledge, 1875.

Edel, Leon. <u>The Psychological Novel, 1900-1950.</u> Philadelphia:
Lippincott, 1955.

Fiedler, Leslie A. <u>Love and Death in the American Novel.</u> New
York: Criterion Books, 1960.

Forster, E. M. <u>Aspects of the Novel.</u> New York: Harcourt,
Brace and World, 1927.

Frye, Northrop. <u>Anatomy of Criticism.</u> Princeton, N. J.: Princeton University Press, 1957.

Halliday, Michael et al. <u>The Linguistic Sciences and Language
Teaching.</u> Bloomington: Indiana University Press, 1964.

Harris, Zellig. <u>Methods in Structural Linguistics.</u> Chicago: University of Chicago Press, 1951.

Hart, James D. <u>The Popular Book: A History of America's Literary Taste.</u> Berkeley: University of California Press, 1950.

Hayakawa, Samuel I. <u>Language in Thought and Action.</u> 2d ed.
New York: Harcourt, Brace and World, 1964.

Hyman, Stanley E. <u>The Armed Vision: A Study in the Methods of
Modern Literary Criticism.</u> New York: Knopf, 1948.

Hymes, Dell, ed. <u>Language in Culture and Society: A Reader in
Linguistics and Anthropology.</u> New York: Harper and Row, 1964.

Jarrell, Randall. · <u>Poetry and the Age.</u> New York: Random House,
1953.

Jesperson, Otto. <u>Language: Its Nature, Development and Origin.</u>
London: Allen and Unwin, 1922.

_____. <u>Philosophy of Grammar.</u> London: Allen and Unwin,
1924.

Jones, Howard M. <u>The Theory of American Literature.</u> Rev. ed.
Ithaca, N. Y.: Cornell University Press, 1967.

Leavis, F. R. <u>The Great Tradition.</u> New York: New York University Press, 1948.

Lewis, C. S. <u>The Allegory of Love: A Study in Medieval Tradition.</u> Oxford, England: Oxford University Press, 1936.

Lubbock, Percy. <u>The Craft of Fiction.</u> New York: Viking, 1921.

Martinet, Andre. <u>Elements of General Linguistics.</u> London:

Faber and Faber, 1964.

Pederson, Holger. The Discovery of Language; Linguistic Science
in the Nineteenth Century. Bloomington: Indiana University
Press, 1959.

Pike, Kenneth. Language in Relation to a Unified Theory of the
Structure of Human Behavior. 2d ed. The Hague: Mouton,
1967.

Ransom, John Crowe. The New Criticism. Norfolk, Conn.: New
Directions, 1941.

Richards, I. A. The Principles of Literary Criticism. New York:
Harcourt, Brace and World, 1924.

Robins, Robert H. Ancient and Medieval Grammatical Theory in
Europe with Particular Reference to Modern Linguistic Doctrine.
London: Bell, 1951.

_____. General Linguistics: An Introductory Survey. London:
Longmans, 1964.

Sapir, Edward A. Language: An Introduction to the Study of
Speech. New York: Harcourt,. Brace and World, 1949.

Spurgeon, Caroline F. E. Shakespeare's Imagery, and What It Tells
Us. Cambridge, England: Cambridge University Press, 1935.

Vygotsky, Lev S. Thought and Language. Cambridge, Mass.: MIT
Press, 1962.

ENCYCLOPEDIC SUMMARIES

American Authors and Books, 1640 to the Present Day, 3d ed.
        Entries for authors, titles, literary societies, book clubs,
        periodicals, movements, etc. Emphasizes American life and
        history as the setting for literature. Ed. by William J.
        Burke and Will D. Howe. (Crown, New York, 1972)

American Authors, 1600-1900
        About 1,300 biographical sketches, with portraits included
        for approximately one-third. Each sketch lists author's
        principal works and selected biographical and critical sources.
        Ed. by Stanley J. Kunitz and Howard Haycraft. (H. W. Wil-
        son, New York, 1938)

American Language, 4th ed.
        Historical account of the development of pronunciation, spel-
        ling, usage, etc. of English language in America. Index.

The Supplement is in two volumes.   By Henry L. Mencken.
(Knopf, New York, 1936-48)

American Novel, 1789-1959
Checklist of twentieth century criticism of American novels.
Alphabetical by author of works being criticized.   Comp. by
Donna Gerstenberger and George Hendrick.   (Alan Swallow,
Denver, 1961-70)

Bartlett's Familiar Quotations, 14th ed.
Subtitle: "collection of passages, phrases, and proverbs
traced to their sources in ancient and modern literature."
Standard work, arranged by authors chronologically and well-
indexed.   Ed. by Emily M. Beck.   (Little, Boston, 1968)

British Authors Before 1800
Over 600 biographical sketches, with portraits of about one-
third of the authors.   Each sketch includes a list of principal
works and of selected source material.   Ed. by Stanley J.
Kunitz and Howard Haycraft.   (H. W. Wilson, New York,
1952)

British Authors of the Nineteenth Century
Biographical sketches of over 1,000 authors, with lists of
authors' principal works and of source material.   Portraits
included for approximately one-third of the authors.   Ed. by
Stanley J. Kunitz and Howard Haycraft.   (H. W. Wilson,
New York, 1936)

Cambridge History of American Literature
Four-volume survey of literary history of the United States
to the early 1900's.   Valuable for coverage of early period
and peripheral areas, such as periodical publishing and children's literature.   Ed. by William Trent, et al.   (Putnam,
New York, 1917-21)

Cambridge History of English Literature
Surveys history from the beginnings to the end of the nine-
teenth century.   Includes English literature of the Empire.
Fifteen volumes.   Ed. by A. W. Ward and A. R. Waller.
(Cambridge University Press, Cambridge, England, 1907-33)

Contemporary Literary Criticism
Excerpts from criticism of novelists, poets, playwrights,
etc. who are now living or who died since 1960.   Claims to
give special attention to popular writers for whose work criticism is hard to find.   (Gale Research Co., Detroit, 1973+)

Contemporary Novel
Checklist of criticism of works of British and American
novelists who were most important after 1945.   Comp. by
Irving Adelman and Rita Dworkin.   (Scarecrow Press, Metuchen, N.J., 1972)

Contemporary Novelists
        Biographical sketches of about 600 living novelists who write
        in English.   Many entries are accompanied by signed essays
        by critics; some have a selected list of sources of further
        criticism.   (St. Martin's Press, New York, 1972)

Contemporary Poets of the English Language
        Biographical and bibliographical information on over 1, 000
        poets now writing in the English language.   Includes com-
        ments of critics where available.   (St. James Press, Chicago,
        1970)

Continental Novel
        Checklist of twentieth century criticism in English of novels
        in continental European languages.   Comp. by E. I. Kearney
        and L. S. Fitzgerald.   (Scarecrow Press, Metuchen, N. J.,
        1968)

Critical Temper
        Excerpts of criticism on English and American writers up to
        the twentieth century.   Broad chronological arrangement with
        author and critics indexes.   Three volumes.   Ed. by Martin
        Tucker.   (Ungar, New York, 1969)

Dictionary of American English on Historical Principles
        Attempts to show "those features by which the English of the
        American colonies and the United States is distinguished from
        that of England and the rest of the English-speaking world. "
        Coverage to the end of the nineteenth century.   Ed. by Wil-
        liam A. Craigie and James R. Hulbert.   Four volumes.
        (University of Chicago Press, Chicago, 1936-44)

Dictionary of Americanisms on Historical Principles
        Contains words and expressions that originated or derived
        new meanings in America.   Coverage to time of publication.
        Ed. by Mitford M. Matthews.   (University of Chicago Press,
        Chicago, 1951)

Dictionary of Modern English Usage, 2d ed.
        Defines terms and discusses usage of words, expressions,
        parts of speech, disputed spellings, etc.   By Henry W.
        Fowler.   (Oxford University Press, Oxford, England, 1965)

Dictionary of Phrase and Fable, 8th ed.
        Entries for phrases, names, titles, proverbs, quotations,
        fictitious characters, etc.   By Ebenezer C. Brewer.   (Harper,
        New York, 1964)

Dramatic Criticism Index
        Indexes English-language criticism of about 300 twentieth-
        century American and foreign playwrights.   (Gale Research
        Co., Detroit, 1972)

Encyclopedia of Poetry and Poetics
> Articles on poetic theory, form, history, etc. No entries
> for individual poets or poems. Ed. by Alexander Preminger,
> et al. (Princeton University Press, Princeton, N.J., 1965)

Encyclopedia of World Literature in the 20th Century
> Articles on twentieth-century authors whose works are avail-
> able to English-speaking audiences, also entries for literary
> movements and national literatures. A few portraits. Es-
> pecially useful for minor European writers. Three volumes.
> Ed. by Wolfgang B. Fleischmann. (Ungar, New York, 1967-
> 71)

English Novel, 1578-1956
> Checklist of twentieth-century criticism of English novels.
> Comp. by I. F. Bell and Donald Baird. (Alan Swallow, Den-
> ver, 1959)

European Authors: 1000-1900
> Nearly 1,000 biographical sketches are included, with por-
> traits for about one-third. Each includes a list of transla-
> tions into English of the author's principal works and a se-
> lected list of biographical and critical sources. Ed. by
> Stanley Kunitz and Vineta Colby. (H. W. Wilson Co., New
> York, 1967)

Explicator Cyclopedia
> Excerpts of comments from The Explicator, 1942-62, ar-
> ranged in separate volumes for modern poetry, traditional
> poetry, and prose. Three volumes. (Quadrangle Books,
> Chicago, 1966)

Granger's Index to Poetry, 6th ed.
> Indexes, by title, first line, author, and subject, poems from
> anthologies published through 1970. Ed. by William F. Bern-
> hardt. (Columbia University Press, New York, 1973)

Guide to Critical Reviews
> Indexes popular periodical reviews of twentieth-century Amer-
> ican drama, musicals, British and continental drama, and
> screen plays. Five volumes. Comp. by James M. Salem.
> (Scarecrow Press, Metuchen, N.J., 1966-71)

Handbook to Literature, 3d ed.
> Explanations of terms, concepts, literary schools, and move-
> ments. Based on original edition by Thrall and Hibbard. Ed.
> by Clarence H. Holman. (Odyssey Press, Indianapolis, 1972)

Library of Literary Criticism: Modern American Literature
> Excerpts of critical comments on about 300 twentieth century
> American authors, alphabetically by author with critic index.
> Three volumes. Ed. by Dorothy N. Curley. (Ungar, New
> York, 1969)

Library of Literary Criticism: Modern British Literature
　　　　Excerpts of critical comments on about 400 twentieth century
　　　　British authors, alphabetically by author with critic index.
　　　　Three volumes. Ed. by author with critic index. Three
　　　　volumes. Ed. by Ruth E. Temple and Martin Tucker. (Ungar,
　　　　New York, 1966)

Library of Literary Criticism: Modern German Literature
　　　　Excerpts of critical comments on works written since 1900.
　　　　Includes authors writing in German from East and West Ger-
　　　　many, Austria and Switzerland, arranged alphabetically by
　　　　author. Two volumes. Ed. by Agnes K. Domandi. (Ungar,
　　　　New York, 1972)

Library of Literary Criticism: Modern Romance Literatures
　　　　Excerpts of critical comments on twentieth century authors
　　　　writing in French, Italian, Spanish, or Portuguese, who have
　　　　become known in the United States. Ed. by Dorothy N.
　　　　Curley and Arthur Curley. (Ungar, New York, 1967)

Library of Literary Criticism of English and American Authors
Through the Beginning of the 20th Century
　　　　Excerpts of criticism published as late as 1964 on authors
　　　　who wrote through the Edwardian period. Broad chronologi-
　　　　cal arrangement. Index of critics. Four volumes. Ed. by
　　　　Charles W. Moulton. (Ungar, New York, 1966)

Literary History of the United States, 3d ed.
　　　　Survey from colonial times to the mid-twentieth century.
　　　　Bibliography supplements noted previously in this section.
　　　　Two volumes in one. Ed. by Robert E. Spiller, et al.
　　　　(Macmillan, New York, 1963. Bibliography supp., 1964.
　　　　Bibliography supp. II, 1973)

McGraw-Hill Encyclopedia of World Drama
　　　　Articles concentrate on major dramatists from Greco-Roman
　　　　times to the present. Tends to emphasize English-speaking
　　　　and European countries. Four volumes. (McGraw-Hill, New
　　　　York, 1972)

Modern Drama
　　　　Checklist of criticism of twentieth century plays. Comp. by
　　　　Irving Adelman and Rita Dworkin. (Scarecrow Press, Me-
　　　　tuchen, N. J. , 1967)

Oxford Companion to American Literature, 4th ed.
　　　　Entries for authors, novels, plays, literary schools, move-
　　　　ments, etc. Ed. by James D. Hert. (Oxford University
　　　　Press, Oxford, England, 1965)

Oxford Companion to Classical Literature, 2d ed.
　　　　Concentrates on principal Greek and Roman authors and their
　　　　works. Entries for authors, titles, characters, movements,

terms, etc.   Ed. by Paul Harvey.   (Oxford University Press, Oxford, England, 1937)

Oxford Companion to English Literature, 4th ed.
Entries for authors, titles, characters, movements, literary forms, literary societies, etc.   Ed. by Paul Harvey.   (Oxford University Press, Oxford, England, 1967)

Oxford Companion to French Literature
Articles on authors, individual works, allusions, places, institutions, movements, etc.   Covers French literary activity from medieval times to beginning of World War II.   Ed. by Paul Harvey and Janet Heseltine.   (Oxford University Press, Oxford, England, 1959)

Oxford Dictionary of Nursery Rhymes
Comprehensive collection of English nursery rhymes with notes and explanations concerning history, literary associations, social uses, etc.   Arranged alphabetically by first important word of rhyme.   Ed. by Iona Opie and Peter Opie. (Oxford University Press, Oxford, England, 1951)

Oxford History of English Literature
Updates Cambridge History of English Literature.   When completed it will cover English literature from Chaucer into the twentieth century.   The complete set will be 12 volumes. Ed. by Norman Davis and Bonamy Dobree.   (Oxford University Press, Oxford, England, 1945+)

Penguin Companion to American Literature
Covers most important writers in the United States with emphasis on twentieth century.   Separate section has entries for writers of Latin America, mostly those born after 1930. Ed. by Malcolm Bradbury, et al.   (McGraw-Hill, New York, 1971)

Penguin Companion to English Literature
Entries for writers in the British Isles and writers who used English in Commonwealth countries.   Ed. by David Daiches. (McGraw-Hill, New York, 1971)

Poetry Explication
Checklist of criticism written since 1925 on British and American poems of any time period.   Ed. by Joseph Kunitz. (Alan Swallow, Denver, 1962)

Reader's Encyclopedia, 2d ed.
Covers world literature with entries for authors, titles, characters, allusions, literary movements, etc.   Ed. by William R. Benet.   (Crowell, New York, 1965)

Reader's Encyclopedia of American Literature
Articles on authors, novels, plays, poems, stories, literary

groups, newspapers, and places and terms associated with American and Canadian writers from colonial times to the present. Ed. by Max J. Hertzberg, et al. (Crowell, New York, 1962)

Twentieth Century Authors
Combined coverage of two volumes includes autobiographical and biographical sketches of about 2,500 authors whose works are familiar to readers of English. Each sketch lists author's principal works and selected biographical and critical work. Most are accompanied by portraits. Ed. by Stanley J. Kunitz and Howard Haycraft. (H. W. Wilson, New York, 1942. First Supplement, 1955)

Twentieth-Century Short Story Explication
Indexes interpretations written since 1900 of short stories written since 1800. Basic volume covers 1900 to 1966; supplement covers 1967-1968. Arranged by authors of short stories with index. Comp. by Warren S. Walker. (Shoe String Press, Hamden, Conn., 1967. Supp. I, 1970. Supp. II, 1974)

World Authors, 1950-1970.
Almost 1,000 authors who achieved prominence, either for the quality of their work or its unusual popularity, during two decades, 1950-1970, are included here. Worldwide coverage has been attempted. As the latest addition (1975) to the Wilson Author Series this volume will supplement Twentieth Century Authors. Edited by John Wakeman. (H. W. Wilson, Bronx, N.Y.)

Search Procedure Form	LANGUAGE AND LITERATURE	
NAME OF USER		**DATE OF INQUIRY**

REDEFINED QUESTION STATEMENT

KEYWORDS

WORK IN PROGRESS

☐ American Literature
☐ American Quarterly
☐ Contemporary Authors

UNPUBLISHED STUDIES

☐ American Dissertations on the Drama and the Theatre: Bibliography
☐ Dissertation Abstracts International

☐ Dissertations in American Literature, 1891-1966
☐ Dissertations in English and American Literature
☐ Masters Abstracts

PERIODICALS

☐ American Literature
☐ Canadian Literature
☐ College English
☐ Columbia Journalism Review
☐ Comparative Literature
☐ Contemporary Literature
☐ Critical Quarterly
☐ Critique: Studies in Modern Fiction
☐ Drama
☐ Drama Review
☐ English Language Notes
☐ English Literary History
☐ English Studies
☐ Essays in Criticism
☐ Explicator
☐ Extrapolation; A Journal of Science Fiction and Fantasy
☐ Hudson Review
☐ Journal of American Folklore
☐ Journal of Modern Literature
☐ Journalism Quarterly
☐ Language Learning
☐ Modern Drama

☐ Modern Fiction Studies
☐ Modern Language Journal
☐ Modern Language Notes
☐ Modern Language Review
☐ Modern Philology
☐ New American Review
☐ Nineteenth Century Fiction
☐ PMLA
☐ Paris Review
☐ Philological Quarterly
☐ Poetry
☐ Review of English Studies
☐ Speculum
☐ Studies in English Literature, 1500-1900
☐ Studies in Short Fiction
☐ Twentieth Century Literature
☐ Victorian Studies

INDEXES AND ABSTRACTING SERVICES

☐ Abstracts of English Studies
☐ Abstracts of Folklore Studies
☐ American Literature
☐ Annual Bibliography of English Language and Literature
☐ Bibliographie Linguistique
☐ British Humanities Index
☐ Essay and General Literature Index
☐ Index to Book Reviews in the Humanities
☐ Index to Little Magazines
☐ LLBA: Language and Language Behavior Abstracts
☐ MLA Abstracts
☐ MLA International Bibliography of Books and Articles on the Modern Languages and Literatures
☐ New York Theatre Critics Reviews
☐ Social Sciences and Humanities Index

BIBLIOGRAPHIC LISTS AND ESSAYS

- ☐ Afro-American Writers
- ☐ Articles on American Literature, 1900-1950
- ☐ Articles on American Literature, 1950-1967
- ☐ Bibliographic Guide to the Study of the Literature of the U.S.A., 3rd ed.
- ☐ Bibliography of American Literature
- ☐ Bibliography of Comparative Literature
- ☐ Bibliography of General Linguistics: English and American
- ☐ Bibliography of the American Theatre
- ☐ Cambridge Bibliography of English Literature
- ☐ Concise Bibliography for Students of English
- ☐ Concise Cambridge Bibliography of English Literature
- ☐ Fiction Catalog, 8th ed.
- ☐ Guide to American Literature and Its Background Since 1890
- ☐ Guide to English Literature
- ☐ Literary History of the United States
- ☐ New Cambridge Bibliography of English Literature
- ☐ Philological Quarterly
- ☐ Play Index
- ☐ Reference Guide to English Studies
- ☐ Resources for American Literary Study
- ☐ Victorian Studies

ANNUAL REVIEWS AND STATE-OF-THE-ART REPORTS

- ☐ American Literary Scholarship
- ☐ Studies in English Literature, 1500-1900
- ☐ Year's Work in English Studies
- ☐ Year's Work in Modern Language Studies

ENCYCLOPEDIC SUMMARIES

- ☐ American Authors and Books, 1640 to the Present Day
- ☐ American Authors, 1600-1900
- ☐ American Language
- ☐ American Novel, 1789-1959
- ☐ Bartlett's Familiar Quotations
- ☐ British Authors Before 1800
- ☐ British Authors of the Nineteenth Century
- ☐ Cambridge History of American Literature
- ☐ Cambridge History of English Literature
- ☐ Contemporary Literary Criticism
- ☐ Contemporary Novel
- ☐ Contemporary Novelists
- ☐ Contemporary Poets of the English Language
- ☐ Continental Novel
- ☐ Critical Temper
- ☐ Dictionary of American English on Historical Principles
- ☐ Dictionary of Americanisms on Historical Principles
- ☐ Dictionary of Modern English Usage
- ☐ Dictionary of Phrase and Fable
- ☐ Dramatic Criticism Index
- ☐ Encyclopedia of Poetry and Poetics
- ☐ Encyclopedia of World Literature in the 20th Century
- ☐ English Novel, 1578-1956
- ☐ European Authors: 1000-1900
- ☐ Explicator Cyclopedia
- ☐ Granger's Index to Poetry
- ☐ Guide to Critical Reviews
- ☐ Handbook to Literature
- ☐ Library of Literary Criticism: Modern American Literature
- ☐ Library of Literary Criticism: Modern British Literature
- ☐ Library of Literary Criticism: Modern German Literature
- ☐ Library of Literary Criticism: Modern Romance Literature
- ☐ Library of Literary Criticism of English and American Authors Through the Beginning of the 20th Century
- ☐ Literary History of the United States
- ☐ McGraw-Hill Encyclopedia of World Drama
- ☐ Modern Drama
- ☐ Oxford Companion to American Literature
- ☐ Oxford Companion to Classical Literature
- ☐ Oxford Companion to English Literature
- ☐ Oxford Companion to French Literature
- ☐ Oxford Dictionary of Nursery Rhymes
- ☐ Oxford History of English Literature
- ☐ Penguin Companion to American Literature
- ☐ Penguin Companion to English Literature
- ☐ Poetry Explication
- ☐ Reader's Encyclopedia
- ☐ Reader's Encyclopedia of American Literature
- ☐ Twentieth Century Authors
- ☐ Twentieth Century Short Story Explication

COMMENTS:

SEARCHER'S SIGNATURE   **DATE COMPLETED**

Discipline Resource Package

FINE ARTS

Francis W. Peters
Detroit Institute of Arts

The Fine Arts are those arts where the primary purpose for
creating is to express beauty, and the primary criterion for judging
it is aesthetics. The Fine Arts include painting, sculpture, draw-
ing, graphics, architecture, music, etc.

WORK IN PROGRESS

Contemporary Authors

A comprehensive source for biographical data on contemporary
authors, many of which may not yet appear in traditional biographical sources. Entries are short, with personal, career,
and work-in-progress information. A list of writings and
sources of biographical and critical data are given when possible. The set is now in its 48th volume but many of the
earlier volumes have been cumulated. Each volume is a separate alphabet but a cumulative name index is provided at the
end of volume 48. (Gale Research Co., Detroit)

UNPUBLISHED STUDIES

Dissertation Abstracts International

The most complete source for abstracts of doctoral dissertations written in the United States. Most U.S. universities
contribute to this system operated by a private corporation.
Unfortunately, several important universities do not partici-
pate. Microfilm or paper copies of the dissertations are
available for purchase. Until recently, the indexing has been
spotty and of poor quality. Fortunately, a much better (and
very expensive) 37-volume cumulative index is now available.
(University Microfilms, Ann Arbor, Mich.)

Masters Abstracts

This is a selective, classified and annotated list of master's
theses produced by many, but by no means all, U.S. colleges
and universities. As with dissertations, microfilm or paper
copies of the theses are available for purchase from the publisher of the Abstracts. Due to its selectivity, it is much

easier to use than <u>Dissertation Abstracts International.</u>   MA
is presently being published quarterly.   (University Microfilms, Ann Arbor, Mich.)

PERIODICALS

A. I. A.   (American Institute of Architects) <u>Journal</u> (monthly)
African Arts (quarterly)
American Artist (monthly)
American Choral Review (quarterly)
American Journal of Art Therapy (quarterly)
American Music Teacher (bi-monthly)
Antike Kunst (semi-annual)
Antique Dealer and Collectors Guide (monthly)
Antiques Journal (monthly)
Aperture (quarterly)
Apollo, the Magazine of the Arts (monthly)
Architects Journal (weekly)
Architectural Forum (10x yr.)
Architectural Record (monthly)
Architectural Review (monthly)
Art Bulletin (quarterly)
Art Gallery (monthly, Oct.-July)
Art in America (bi-monthly)
Art Journal (quarterly)
Art Quarterly
Arts Magazine (monthly)
Arts of Asia (bi-monthly)
Artscanada (bi-monthly)
Classical America (2x yr.)
Clavier, a Magazine for Pianists and Organists (9x yr.)
Design (monthly)
Design and Environment (quarterly)
Ethnomusicology (3x yr.)
Graphic Arts Progress (monthly)
Graphics: International Journal of Graphic Art and Applied Art (bi-
          monthly)
Greek, Roman and Byzantine Studies (quarterly)
Industrial and Commercial Photographer (monthly)
Italix, the Calligrapher Quarterly
Jazz Journal (monthly)
Journal of Aesthetics and Art Criticism (quarterly)
Journal of Music Theory (semi-annual)
Journal of the Society of Architectural Historians (quarterly)
Landscape Architecture (quarterly)
Magazine Antiques (monthly)
Metropolitan Museum of Arts Bulletin (6x yr.)
Modern Photography (monthly)
Museum (quarterly)
Museum News (monthly)
Museums Journal (quarterly)

National Sculpture Review (quarterly)
Opera News (monthly)
Oriental Art (quarterly)
Popular Photography (monthly)
Print (bi-monthly)
Schwann Record and Tape Guide (monthly)
Spinning Wheel, the National Magazine About Antiques (10x yr.)
Studies in Art Education (3x yr.)
Studies in Conservation (quarterly)
Studio International (monthly)

INDEXES AND ABSTRACTING SERVICES

Architectural Index
A highly selective annual index to journal literature in the field of architecture. It indexes the eight principal journals in its area of specialty. It is arranged by subject and, within that, by title. A list of subject headings used is appended for easy reference. (Architectural Index, P.O. Box 1168, Boulder, Colo.)

Art Index
This Wilson index covers art and art related subjects, such as archaeology, architecture, art history, crafts, city planning, graphics, design, etc. It is published quarterly with annual cumulations. It indexes over a hundred journals by subject and author. (H. W. Wilson, Bronx, N.Y.)

Avery Index to Architectural Periodicals
This set is a comprehensive, recently revised (1973) index to the Avery Library of Architecture at Columbia University. It consists of photoreproductions of the catalog cards of this famous library. It is a dictionary catalog, mixing author, title, and subject entries. The 18-volume set is supplemented by an obituary index, and regular supplementary volumes are anticipated. (G. K. Hall, Boston, Mass.)

"Graphic Arts Index" section of Graphic Arts Progress Magazine
The index section of this journal is one of the major methods of controlling literature in the graphic arts. It indexes well over 100 magazines in ten different subject categories. The journal is issued monthly. (Graphic Arts Research Center, Rochester Institute of Technology, Rochester, N.Y.)

Guide to the Performing Arts
An annual subject index to about 50 journals related to all aspects of the performing arts, including television. Citations, within the subject headings, are arranged by author. Lists of abbreviations and periodicals indexed are provided. (Scarecrow, Metuchen, N.J.)

Index to Book Reviews in the Humanities
        An annual index to citations to book reviews in the humanities.
        Since 1971 all reviews, except juvenile books, that appear in
        the journals covered are indexed.   Within the author and name
        of the book, the citations are listed.   The list of periodicals
        in the front is numbered and these numbers are used, in lieu
        of abbreviated titles, in the citations.   (Phillip Thompson,
        Williamston, Mich.)

Music Article Guide
        A useful quarterly subject index to over 100 current music
        periodicals.   It supplies a full citation, but with somewhat
        different abbreviations than other indexes.   Excellent for the
        small library that cannot use (or afford) the Music Index.
        (Music Article Guide, P. O. Box 12216, Philadelphia, Pa.)

Music Index
        The most comprehensive index to music and music related
        magazine literature available.   It indexes nearly 200 journals
        by subject and author.   Reviews are extensively indexed,
        and first performances and obituaries are indexed.   Most
        music periodicals are completely indexed and music articles
        in many general periodicals are included.   (Information Co-
        ordinators, Detroit, Mich.)

                BIBLIOGRAPHICAL LISTS AND ESSAYS

Bibliography of Costume
        This bibliography is a dictionary catalog-arranged list of
        over 8, 000 items in the area of costume and adornment.   The
        citations are complete and emphasize the type and size of il-
        lustrations, with notes, where appropriate.   Bibliography notes
        and LC card numbers are also provided.   (H. W. Wilson,
        Bronx, N. Y.)

Bibliography of Early Secular American Music
        The 18th century is the focus of this comprehensive bibliog-
        raphy of music published in the United States before 1900.
        Edited by Oscar Sonneck in 1917, it was revised and reissued
        in 1964.   It is arranged by main entry.   The music is de-
        scribed in a brief abstract that often includes such information
        as first line, where it was advertised, etc.   Bibliographic
        data of the copy examined is included.   Appendixes cover first
        lines and publishers.   A good general index is included.   (Da
        Capo Press, N. Y. , N. Y.)

Guide to Art Reference Books
        The best basic guide to reference works on art and art his-
        tory.   Its 2, 500 entries include bibliographies, indexes, di-
        rectories, sales records, reproductions, dictionaries, en-
        cyclopedias, biography, histories, architecture, as well as

the traditional division of art, such as sculpture, painting, etc. Sections on periodicals and special collections (by country) are provided, as well as an index. (American Library Association, Chicago, Ill.)

Harvard List of Books on Art
This list, which comprises a basic collection for an art research library, is now somewhat dated (1950). However, it is nearly comprehensive to the time of publication (only a few titles, included in the previous edition, were dropped). Foreign titles were included, but not periodical articles. An author/artist index is appended. Ed. by Edna Lucas. (Harvard Univ. Press., Cambridge, Mass.)

ANNUAL REVIEWS AND STATE OF THE ART REPORTS

American Art Directory
An all purpose almanac/annual, it is sponsored by the American Federation of Artists. It is a compendium of data on museums, schools, exhibits, booking agencies, etc. Included are lists of magazines, scholarships, etc. The title has varied, but it has been continuously published since 1913. (Bowker, N.Y., N.Y.)

Art News Annual
This annual does have an "art news of the year" section and several long essays on current art topics, but it all seems to be an excuse to publish the magnificent color plates that illustrate it. It is a supplement to Art News Magazine. (Art Foundation Press, N.Y., N.Y.)

The Structurist
The Structurist is an annual publication dedicated to artists concerned with "the building-growing processes of creation in Art and Nature." It consists of lengthy essays loosely related to that broad approach to art. Some good black and white illustrations are included. There was a list of current exhibits in the issue I examined. It is produced by the University of Saskatchewan. (Wittenborn & Co., N.Y., N.Y.)

BOOKS

Adams, Ansel. Making a Photograph. N.Y.: Studio Publications, 1935.

Anderson, Donald M. Elements of Design. N.Y.: Holt, 1961.

Baines, Harry. The Science of Photography. N.Y.: Wiley, 1958.

Baldinger, Wallace S.   The Visual Arts.   N. Y.:   Holt, 1960.

Burland, Cottie A.   Man and Art.   N. Y.:   Studio Publications, 1959.

Clark, Kenneth.   The Nude: a Study in Ideal Form.   N. Y.:   Pantheon, 1956.

Cook, R. M.   Greek Painted Pottery.   Chicago: Quadrangle Books, 1960.

Copland, Aaron.   Copland on Music.   N. Y.:   Doubleday, 1960.

Easton, Malcolm.   Artists and Writers in Paris: the Bohemian Idea, 1803-1867.   London: Arnold, 1964.

Elson, Albert E.   Purposes of Art.   N. Y.:   Holt, 1962.

Feibleman, James.   Aesthetics, a Study of the Fine Arts in Theory and Practice.   N. Y.:   Humanities, 1949.

Francastle, Pierre.   La Réalité Figurative: Eléments Structurels de Sociologie de l'Art.   Paris: Gonthier, 1965.

Gimple, Jean.   The Cathedral Builders.   N. Y.:   Grove, 1958.

Gombrich, E. H.   Meditations on a Hobby Horse, and Other Essays on the Theory of Art.   London: Phaidon, 1963.

Griff, Mason.   "The Commercial Artist: a Study in Changing and Consistent Identities, " in Maurice Stein, A. Vidich, and D. White (editors), Identity and Anxiety.   Glencoe, Ill.:   Free Press, 1960, pp. 219-241.

Harrison, Jane E.   Ancient Art and Ritual.   London: Butterworth, 1913.

Haskell, Francis.   Patrons and Painters: a Study in the Relations Between Italian Art and Society in the Age of Baroque.   N. Y.:   Knopf, 1963.

Hauser, Arnold.   Social History of Art.   2 vols.   London: Routledge, 1951.

Martingale, Andrew.   "The Rise of the Artist, " in Joan Evans (editor), the Flowering of the Middle Ages.   N. Y.:   McGraw-Hill, 1966, pp. 281-314.

Moholy-Nagy, Laszlo. • The New Vision.   N. Y.:   Wittenborn, 1929.

Mumford, Lewis.   Art and Technics.   N. Y.:   Columbia Univ. Press, 1952.

Parker, Paul. "The Analysis of the Style of Advertising Art."
Master's thesis, Univ. of Chicago, Department of Art, 1937.

Pevsner, Nikolaus. Academies of Art: Past and Present. Cambridge Univ. Press; N. Y.: Macmillan, 1940.

Rank, Otto. Art and Artist: Creative Urge and Personality Development. N. Y.: Knopf, 1932.

Spaeth, Sigmund G. The Common Sense of Music. N. Y.: Boni, 1924.

Tomasini, Wallace J. "The Social and Economic Position of the
Florentine Artist in the 15th Century." Ph. D. dissertation, Univ.
of Michigan, 1953.

Willetts, William. Chinese Art. 2 vols. N. Y.: Braziller, 1958.

ENCYCLOPEDIC SUMMARIES

American Architects Directory
         A good, one-volume source for brief biographies of Americans
         in the art specified in the title.   The entries give specializa-
         tion, birth-death dates, etc., in addition to the short narrative
         biography.   This edition (1965) has an addendum and a short
         bibliography of other sources.   (James F. Carr, N. Y., N. Y.)

Dictionary of American Painters, Sculptors, and Engravers
         Although produced by the American Institute of Architects,
         this directory is not limited to its membership.   The editors
         included every qualified person who returned the question-
         naire, making it somewhat more comprehensive than the av-
         erage association directory.   Entries are of the Who's Who
         style, with vital statistics, educational data, etc., in list
         form.   A geographical index (state and city) and a necrology
         are among the appendixes.   Ed. by Mantle Fielding.   (R. R.
         Bowker, N. Y., N. Y.)

Encyclopaedia of Modern Architecture
         This edition is a translation of a 1963 German encyclopedia
         which provides brief articles on topics related to architecture
         since the mid-nineteenth century.   Although brief, the articles
         are signed and bibliographies are provided.   Ed. by G. Hatje.
         (Thames & Hudson, London, England)

Encyclopedia of Painting
         A good one-volume survey of painting now in its 3rd edition
         (1970), it has a good supply of color illustrations of varying
         quality.   The entries are short and the majority seem to be
         biography.   There are somewhat longer articles on various
         types of painting, etc.   Ed. by Bernard S. Meyers.   (Crown
         Pub., N. Y., N. Y.)

Encyclopedia of World Art
        A monumental, 15-volume work provided by the International
        Council of Scholars in 1958. Its intention is to "encompass
        our present knowledge of the arts within a single work that
        is factually complete within the limits of possibility..."
        They succeed admirably with long scholarly, signed articles
        on all fields of the fine arts. Long bibliographies are ap-
        pended to most articles. Each volume is almost half text
        and half color and black and white plates--good reproductions
        for the most part. Vol. 15 is an index. It was produced in
        Italy. (McGraw-Hill, N. Y., N. Y.)

Harvard Dictionary of Music
        Editor Willi Apel has produced a good, general reference dic-
        tionary on music, but a restrictive one. Limited strictly to
        "musical topics," it excludes biographies and articles on in-
        dividual organizations, orchestras, etc. Entries are short
        and readable. Word origins are provided for foreign language
        and like terminology. Now somewhat dated (1944), but the
        exclusions mentioned above make this less important. (Har-
        vard Univ. Press, Cambridge, Mass.)

History of Art
        A definitive text (revised in 1969) on the "visual arts from
        the dawn of history to the present day." Written by H. W.
        Janson, it is arranged chronologically with lengthy chapters
        on each important era in art history. Profusely illustrated
        with excellent black and white drawings and photos. It has a
        few so-so color reproductions. Synoptic tables, an extensive
        bibliography, and what seems to be an excellent index are ap-
        pended. (Prentice-Hall, Englewood Cliffs, N. J.)

Oxford Companion to Art
        Another excellent contribution to the Oxford Companion series.
        it was edited by Harold Osborne and published in 1970. It
        was devised to be a non-specialist's compendium for the fine
        arts; thus the "handicraft" arts were arbitrarily excluded.
        Most entries are brief and the cross-references are adequate.
        The illustrations are good and it has a lengthy, classified bib-
        liography at the end. (Oxford Univ. Press, London, England)

Oxford Companion to Music
        Like its many "companions," the music volume is an excel-
        lent one-volume source for both brief general articles and
        short biographies. A good source for song titles. Its illus-
        trations are black and white and, for the most part, excel-
        lent. (Oxford Univ. Press, London, England)

Praeger Encyclopedia of Art
        Starting with an impressive, international list of editors, the
        publisher attempted to compose an "authoritative reference
        guide for both student and general reader..." for world art.
        The result is an impressive, 5-volume set with short articles

and concise bibliographies. Profusely illustrated, about one-
third of them are in color. Volume 5 contains an adequate
(if not impressive) index. (Praeger, N. Y., N. Y.)

Who's Who in American Art

Produced for the American Federation of Arts, this volume
takes the traditional format familiar to users of "who's
who's." The entries stress educational and professional
data. The address is there unless the artist requested its
exclusion. This edition was dated 1970--its frequency was
not indicated. A geographic index and list of obituaries are
appended. (R. R. Bowker, N. Y., N. Y.)

Search Procedure Form	FINE ARTS

NAME OF USER | **DATE OF INQUIRY**

REDEFINED QUESTION STATEMENT

KEYWORDS

WORK IN PROGRESS

☐ Contemporary Authors

UNPUBLISHED STUDIES

☐ Dissertation Abstracts International
☐ Masters Abstracts

PERIODICALS

☐ AIA
☐ African Arts
☐ American Artist
☐ American Choral Review
☐ American Journal of Art Therapy
☐ American Music Teacher
☐ Antike Kunst
☐ Antique Dealer and Collectors Guide
☐ Antiques Journal
☐ Aperture
☐ Apollo
☐ Architects Journal
☐ Architectural Forum
☐ Architectural Record
☐ Architectural Review
☐ Art Bulletin
☐ Art Gallery
☐ Art in America
☐ Art Journal
☐ Art Quarterly
☐ Arts Magazine
☐ Arts of Asia
☐ Artscanada
☐ Classical America
☐ Clavier
☐ Design
☐ Design and Environment

☐ Ethnomusicology
☐ Graphic Arts Progress
☐ Graphics: International Journal of Graphic Art and Applied Art
☐ Greek, Roman and Byzantine Studies
☐ Industrial and Commercial Photographer
☐ Italix, the Calligrapher Quarterly
☐ Jazz Journal
☐ Journal of Aesthetics and Art Criticism
☐ Journal of Music Theory
☐ Journal of the Society of Archtectural Historians
☐ Landscape Architecture
☐ Magazine Antiques
☐ Metropolitan Museum of Arts Bulletin
☐ Modern Photography
☐ Museum
☐ Museum News
☐ Museums Journal
☐ National Sculpture Review
☐ Opera News
☐ Oriental Art
☐ Popular Photography
☐ Print
☐ Schwann Record and Tape Guide
☐ Spinning Wheel
☐ Studies in Art Education
☐ Studies in Conservation
☐ Studio International

INDEXES AND ABSTRACTING SERVICES

☐ Architectural Index
☐ Art Index
☐ Avery Index to Architectural Periodicals
☐ Guide to the Performing Arts
☐ Index to Book Reviews in the Humanities
☐ Music Article Guide
☐ Music Index

BIBLIOGRAPHIC LISTS AND ESSAYS

- ☐ Bibliography of Costume
- ☐ Bibliography of Early Secular American Music
- ☐ Guide to Art Reference Books
- ☐ Harvard List of Books on Art

ANNUAL REVIEWS AND STATE-OF-THE-ART REPORTS

- ☐ American Art Directory
- ☐ Art News Annual
- ☐ The Structurist

ENCYCLOPEDIC SUMMARIES

- ☐ American Architects Directory
- ☐ Dictionary of American Painters, Sculptors, and Engravers
- ☐ Encyclopedia of Modern Architecture
- ☐ Encyclopedia of Painting
- ☐ Encyclopedia of World Art
- ☐ Harvard Dictionary of Music
- ☐ History of Art
- ☐ Oxford Companion to Art
- ☐ Oxford Companion to Music
- ☐ Praeger Encyclopedia of Art
- ☐ Who's Who in American Art

COMMENTS:

SEARCHER'S SIGNATURE	DATE COMPLETED

Discipline Resource Package

PHYSICAL SCIENCES

Elma M. Stewart
Eastern Michigan University

It is unrealistic to regard the natural sciences as easily categorized. There are significant overlaps between the physical and life sciences (e.g., biochemistry, the relationship between geology and palentology, etc.) as well as within the physical sciences (e.g., astrophysics, geophysics, etc.). However, the division between the physical and life sciences is adequate for the purposes of the Discipline Resource Packages.

Physical Sciences represent that division of the sciences that deal primarily with nonliving matter. They are concerned with the properties of matter and its interaction. Included here under the heading of physical sciences are:

> Astronomy
> Chemistry
> Earth Sciences
> Engineering
> Mathematics
> Physics

WORK IN PROGRESS

Contemporary Authors
> A comprehensive source for biographical data on contemporary authors, many of which may not yet appear in traditional biographical sources. Entries are short, with personal, career, and work-in-progress information. A list of writings and sources of biographical and critical data are given when possible. The set is now in its 48th volume but many of the earlier volumes have been cumulated. Each volume is a separate alphabet but a cumulative name index is provided at the end of volume 48. (Gale Research Co., Detroit)

UNPUBLISHED STUDIES

Dissertation Abstracts international
> The most complete source for abstracts of doctoral dissertations written in the United States. Most U.S. universities

contribute to this system operated by a private corporation. Unfortunately, several important universities do not participate. Microfilm or paper copies of the dissertations are available for purchase. Until recently, the indexing has been spotty and of poor quality. Fortunately, a much better (and very expensive) 37-volume cumulative index is now available. (University Microfilms, Ann Arbor, Mich.)

Masters Abstracts
This is a selective, classified and annotated list of master's theses produced by many, but by no means all, U.S. colleges and Universities. As with dissertations, microfilm or paper copies of the theses are available for purchase from the publisher of the Abstracts. Due to its selectivity, it is much easier to use than Dissertation Abstracts International. MA is presently being published quarterly. (University Microfilms, Ann Arbor, Mich.)

PERIODICALS

Acoustical Society of America Journal (monthly)
Advances in Physics (bi-monthly)
American Chemical Society Journal (semi-monthly)
American Journal of Mathematics (quarterly)
American Journal of Physics (monthly)
American Mathematical Society Bulletin (bi-monthly)
American Mineralogist (bi-monthly)
American Statistical Association Journal (quarterly)
Analytical Chemistry (monthly)
Annals of Mathematics (bi-monthly)
Astronomical Journal (monthly)
Astronomy and Astrophysics (monthly)
Chemical and Engineering News (weekly)
Chemical Engineering (fortnightly)
Chemical Reviews (bi-monthly)
Chemical Technology (monthly)
Chemistry (monthly)
Chemistry and Industry (semi-monthly)
Civil Engineering (monthly)
Contemporary Physics (monthly)
Earth and Extraterrestrial Sciences (irregular)
Earth Science (bi-monthly)
Electronics (fortnightly)
Engineering (monthly)
Engineering Geology (4x yr.)
Geological Society of America Bulletin (monthly)
Geophysics (bi-monthly)
Inorganic Chemistry (monthly)
International Chemical Engineering (quarterly)
International Geology Review (monthly)
Journal for Research in Mathematics Education (quarterly)

Journal for the History of Astronomy (quarterly)
Journal of Applied Mechanics (quarterly)
Journal of Applied Physics (monthly)
Journal of Basic Engineering (quarterly)
Journal of Chemical Documentation (quarterly)
Journal of Geophysical Research (36x yr.)
Journal of Heat Transfer (quarterly)
Journal of Mathematical Physics (monthly)
Journal of Organic Chemistry (monthly)
Journal of Physical Chemistry (semi-monthly)
Journal of Physics (in 6 parts; various frequencies)
Mathematics Teacher (monthly - October/May)
Mineralological Magazine (quarterly)
Nuclear Physics (weekly)
Physics Teacher (9x yr.)
Physics Today (monthly)
Quarterly Journal of Mathematics
Review of Physics in Technology (3x yr.)
Reviews of Geophysics and Space Physics (quarterly)
Russian Chemical Reviews (monthly)
Science (weekly)
Science News (weekly)
Sedimentology (8x yr.)
Sky and Telescope (monthly)
Soviet Astronomy (bi-monthly)
Technology and Culture (quarterly)

REPORTS AND MONOGRAPHS

Government Reports Announcements
Announcements of Government-sponsored research and development reports, and other Government analyses prepared by Federal agencies, their contractors or grantees. Also included are federally-sponsored translations and some reports written in foreign languages. The announcements are arranged in 22 subject fields and each field is divided into groups. The arrangement is alphanumeric by accession number. (Government Printing Office, Washington, D.C.)

Government Reports Index
Designed as a companion volume to Government Reports Announcements (GRA) this publication indexes the corresponding issue of GRA by Corporate Author, Subject, Personal Author, Contract Number, and Accession/Report Number. Each index is arranged alphanumerically. Research titles are included in all indexes except the Contract Number Index and prices are given in the Accession/Report Number Index only. (Government Printing Office, Washington, D.C.)

Nuclear Science Abstracts
A comprehensive abstracting and indexing service covering

the international nuclear science literature.   Included are
scientific and technical reports of the U. S. Atomic Energy
Commission and its contractors, other U. S. Government
agencies, other governments, universities, and industrial and
research organizations.   Books, conference proceedings, individual conference papers, patents, and journal literature on
a worldwide basis are also abstracted and indexed.   Each issue includes four indexes: subject, personal author, corporate author, and report number.   (Government Printing Office, Washington, D. C.)

Scientific and Technical Aerospace Reports (STAR)
    A comprehensive abstracting and indexing service covering
    current worldwide report literature on the science and tech-
    nology of space and aeronautics.   Abstracts of scientific and
    technical reports issued by NASA and its contractors, other
    U. S. Government agencies, corporations, universities, and
    research organizations throughout the world are included.
    The citations and abstracts are grouped in 34 subject cate-
    gories.   The five indexes included in each issue are: sub-
    ject, personal author, corporate source, contract number,
    and report/accession number.   (Government Printing Office,
    Washington, D. C.)

INDEXES AND ABSTRACTING SERVICES

Applied Mechanics Reviews
    AMR is a critical review of the world literature in applied
    mechanics and related engineering science.   It is arranged
    by major subject categories and then subdivided within each
    category.   Annual subject and author index.   Photocopies of
    articles indexed generally provided whenever possible.   (Amer-
    ican Society of Mechanical Engineers, New York, N. Y.)

Applied Science and Technology Index
    A cumulative subject index to English language periodicals in
    the fields of aeronautics and space science, automation, chem-
    istry, construction, earth sciences, electricity and electronics,
    engineering, industrial and mechanical arts, materials math-
    ematics, metallurgy, physics, telecommunications, transporta-
    tion and related subjects.   Published monthly with an annual
    cumulation.   (H. W. Wilson Co. , New York, N. Y.)

Chemical Abstracts
    Detailed and accurate abstracts of nearly all scientific and
    technical papers containing new information of chemical and
    chemical engineering interest.   New information revealed in
    the patent literature is also included.   Semi-annual author,
    subject, formula and chemical substance indexes.   Also in-
    cludes numerical patent index and the patent concordance.
    There are cumulative 10-year indexes.   (Chemical Abstracts,
    Columbus, Ohio)

Computing Reviews
        Monthly abstracts of critical information about all current
        publications in any area of computer sciences.   Especially
        useful to computer-oriented persons in mathematics, engi-
        neering, the natural and social sciences, the humanities and
        other fields.   Many book reviews are included.   (Association
        for Computing Machinery, New York, N. Y.)

Engineering Index
        A transdisciplinary guide to world engineering developments.
        This index is an organized compilation of abstracts and items
        covering all significant technological literature and conferences
        encompassing all engineering disciplines.   The annual cumula-
        tion is alphabetically arranged by main subject headings and
        subheadings.   (Engineering Index, Inc., New York, N. Y.)

Mathematical Reviews
        Reviews of books, periodical articles and other printed mate-
        rials in the field of mathematics.   Published monthly with two
        issues (one of them an index issue) in June and in December.
        (American Mathematical Society, Providence, R. I.)

Metals Abstracts
        Provides, each month, abstracts of the metals developments
        that appear in engineering and industrial journals published
        in the United States and abroad.   The abstracts are arranged
        in subject categories to facilitate scanning of the material.
        For more precise searching, a companion volume, Metals
        Abstracts Index, published simultaneously with the Metals
        Abstracts should be used.   (The Institute of Metals, London,
        England, and the American Society for Metals, Metals Park,
        Ohio)

Science Abstracts, Series A: Physics Abstracts
        This publication covers all aspects of physics, from the gen-
        eral to interdisciplinary subjects.   The information is derived
        from a wide range of sources including journals, reports,
        books, dissertations, patents and conference papers published
        in all countries and languages of the world.   Semi-annual
        cumulations of the author and subject indexes.   (Institution of
        Electrical Engineers, New York, N. Y.)

Science Abstracts, Series B: Electrical & Electronics Abstracts
        The major purpose of this publication is to cover all aspects
        of electrical and electronics engineering.   The abstracts are
        derived from many sources including journals, reports, books,
        dissertations, patents and conference papers published in all
        countries and languages of the world.   (Institution of Electri-
        cal Engineers, New York, N. Y.)

Science Citation Index
        An index to references cited in the bibliography of a published
        article, book, letter, etc.   Coverage includes over 90% of

the world's important scientific and technical journals published each year.   There is a multidisciplinary coverage that
includes practically every possible scientific and technical
subject area.   Extremely useful in helping one to locate other
articles related to ones subject interest.   (Institute for Scientific Information, Philadelphia, PA.)

Technical Book Review Index
An alphabetically arranged monthly index of over 100 scientific, technical and commercial books, giving brief quotations
from reviews from leading scientific, technical and trade
journals.   Devoted almost exclusively to English-language material, this index is published monthly except July and August.
The listing of much material not given in Book Review Digest
will be found in this index.   (Special Libraries Assoc., New
York, N.Y.)

BIBLIOGRAPHICAL LISTS AND ESSAYS

Guide to Science Reading (AAAS)
A selected annotated list of paperbound science books.   This
title is an especially useful aid in the development of personal
or home library collections.   The entries were selected with
the collaboration of professional representatives of the biological, physical, behavioral, medical, engineering, agricultural and mathematical sciences.   (American Association for
the Advancement of Science; New American Library, New
York, N.Y., 1964)

McGraw-Hill Basic Bibliography of Science and Technology
Brief annotations of titles covering more than 7,000 subjects.
Numerous cross-references facilitate access to very specialized topics.   It is especially useful to the individual who
wishes to read beyond the articles in the McGraw-Hill Encyclopedia of Science and Technology and into the materials
of science, on those specialized topics treated in the Encyclopedia itself.   (McGraw-Hill, New York, N.Y., 1966)

Quarterly Bibliography of Computers and Data Processing
A selective subject author index to current computer literature, with some abstracts.   Issues replaced by an annual
cumulation.   (Applied Computer Research, Phoenix, Arizona)

Science Books, A Quarterly Review
Published to improve science education and public understanding of science.   Included are reviews of trade books, textbooks, and reference works in pure and applied science for
students in the elementary school, in the secondary school
and in the first two years of college.   Also included are selected advanced and professional books useful for reference
by students and faculty members.   (American Association
for the Advancement of Science, Washington, D.C.)

ANNUAL REVIEWS AND STATE OF THE ART REPORTS

Annual Review of Information Science and Technology
      The basic reviews of current research for the fields of com-
puter information searching, library automation, user studies,
document retrieval, information systems and networks, etc.
Most chapters (e. g. , Information needs and uses) are repeated
each year with different editors.   Overall editor for the
ARIST is Carlos Cuadra.   Started in 1966.   (Encyclopaedia
Britannica, Inc. , Chicago)

The National Council of Teachers of Mathematics Yearbooks
      The NCTM's yearbook focuses on various topics of particular
interest to teachers of mathematics.   Each year is entirely
devoted to one particular aspect of mathematics teaching.
Past topics have included the teaching of secondary mathematics, geometry in the curriculum, the slow learner in
mathematics, etc.   (The Council, National Education Assn. ,
Washington, D. C.)

BOOKS

Abro, A. d'.   The Evolution of Scientific Thought: From Newton to
Einstein, 2nd ed.   Gloucester, Mass. :   Peter Smith, 1950.

Amrine, Michale.   The Great Decision: the Secret History of the
Atomic Bomb.   N. Y. :   Putnam, 1959.

Bawden, Arthur T.   Man's Physical Universe: a Survey of Sciences
for Colleges, 4th ed.   N. Y. :   Macmillan, 1950.

Bohr, Niels.   Atomic Physics and Human Knowledge.   N. Y. :   Wiley,
1958.

Boyle, Robert.   The Sceptical Chymist.   N. Y. :   Dutton, 1911.

Buchheim, Robert W. , et. al.   Space Handbook: Astronautics and
Its Applications.   N. Y. :   Random, 1959.

Burtt, Edwin A.   The Metaphysical Foundations of Modern Science...
N. Y. :   Doubleday, 1932.

Campbell, Norman.   Foundations of Experimental Science.   N. Y. :
Dover, 1957.

Carrington, Richard.   The Story of Our Earth.   N. Y. :   Harper, 1956.

Coleman, James A.   Relativity for the Layman: a Simplified Account of the History, Theory and Proofs of Relativity.   N. Y. :
Macmillan, 1959.

Copernicus, Nicolaus. Three Copernican Treatises, 2nd ed. Trans.
by Edward Rosen. Gloucester, Mass.: Peter Smith, 1953.
(circa 1530)

Derry, T. K. and Williams, Trevor I. A Short History of Technology: From the Earliest Times to A.D. 1900. Oxford, England: Oxford Univ. Press, 1961.

Dunlap, Orin E., Jr. Communications in Space: From Wireless
to Satellite Relay. N.Y.: Harper, 1962.

Einstein, Albert. Relativity: the Special and General Theory.
Gloucester, Mass.: Peter Smith, 1920.

Euclid. The Elements of Euclid, 2nd ed. (3 vols.) Ed. by T. L.
Heath. N.Y.: Everyman's, 1933. (circa 300 B.C.)

Farb, Peter. The Face of North America: the Natural History of
a Continent. N.Y.: Harper, 1963.

Freeman, T. W. A Hundred Years of Geography. Chicago: Aldine
Pub., 1962.

Galileo. The Achievement of Galileo. Ed. by James Brophy and
Henry Paolucci. N.Y.: Twayne, 1962. (circa 1600)

Hoyle, Fred. The Nature of the Universe, rev. ed. N.Y.: Harper,
1960.

Hughes, Donald J. On Nuclear Energy: Its Potential for Peacetime
Uses. Cambridge, Mass.: Harvard Univ. Press, 1957.

Jones, Harold S. Life on Other Worlds. N.Y.: New American
Library, n.d.

Kaiser, Hans K. Rockets and Spaceflight. N.Y.: Pitman, 1962.

Moore, Patrick. The Planets. N.Y.: Norton, 1962.

Newman, James R., ed. The World of Mathematics. 4 vols.
N.Y.: Simon and Schuster, 1956.

Newton, Isaac. Sir Isaac Newton's Mathematical Principles of Natural Philosophy and His System of the World. Ed. by Floren
Cajori. Berkeley: Univ. of California Press, 1947. (circa 1700)

Oparin, A. and Fesenkov, V. Life in the Universe. N.Y.: Twayne,
1962.

Pannekoek, A. A History of Astronomy. N.Y.: Wiley, 1962.

Ptolemy. Works. Cambridge, Mass.: Harvard Univ. Press,
1940. (circa 150 A.D.)

Read, John. Through Alchemy to Chemistry: a Procession of
Ideas and Personalities. N. Y.: Harper, 1957.

Shapley, Harlow. Galaxies. Cambridge, Mass.: Harvard Univ.
Press, 1943.

Struve, Otto and Zebergs, Velta. Astronomy of the 20th Century.
N. Y.: Macmillan, 1962.

Toulmin, Stephen and Goodfield, Jane. The Fabric of the Heavens:
the Development of Astronomy... N. Y.: Harper, 1961.

Udall, Stewart L. The Quiet Crisis. N. Y.: Holt, 1963.

Whitehead, Alfred N. Science and the Modern World. N. Y.: Macmillan, 1926.

Wiener, Norbert. The Human Use of Human Beings: Cybernetics
and Society, 2nd ed. N. Y.: Houghton, 1954.

ENCYCLOPEDIC SUMMARIES

AMA Drug Evaluations
        Practically all therapeutic agents in the official compendia,
        United States Pharmacopeia (U. S. P.) and National Formulary
        (N. F.), are selected for individual evaluations. This includes
        drugs, including mixtures, most commonly prescribed or ad-
        ministered by physicians in the United States. The chapters
        contain introductory statements that discuss the overall thera-
        peutic category, followed by brief evaluative monographs for
        individual drugs in the class. (American Medical Assn. ,
        Chicago)

Chambers' Dictionary of Science and Technology
        A successor to Chambers' Technical Dictionary, this volume
        presents the level of vocabulary required by those interested
        in understanding current scientific and technological develop-
        ments and problems. The arrangement is basically alpha-
        betical and a number of tables are included in the appendices.
        These tables endeavor to treat certain topics with more de-
        tailed information. For example, there are traditional and
        modern tables of the plant kingdom, tables of chemical ele-
        ments, etc. (W & R Chambers, London, England)

Computer Dictionary and Handbook
        This volume is replete with the information needed by stu-
        dents, workers, users and others involved in the applications
        of computers to their specific job or livelihood. There is an
        uncomplicated explanation of rules, procedures, and applica-
        tions of the specific fundamental languages and the many spe-
        cialized computer programming and language techniques.

Aside from the dictionary section (490 pages), there are 288 pages of appendices with more detailed information about computer languages, statistical definitions, a section on acronyms and abbreviations etc. Ed. by Charles Sippl. (Bobbs-Merrill, Indianapolis, Indiana)

A Directory of Information Resources in the United States: Physical Sciences and Engineering

An alphabetical listing of organizations having knowledge or expertise that they wish to share with others. This includes professional societies, university research bureaus and institutes, Federal or State agencies, industrial laboratories, museum specimen collections, testing stations, and individual experts as well as the more traditional sources, such as technical libraries, information and documents centers, and abstracting and indexing services. Names, addresses, telephone numbers, and brief descriptions of the organizations are given. There is a subject index. Material on the biological sciences, included in previous editions, will be published in a separate volume. (Government Printing Office, Washington, D.C.)

Encyclopedia of Astronomy

Alphabetically arranged by subject, this volume offers definitions and other detailed information to individuals, professional or amateur, who wish to study space and the planets. Included also are numerous biographical notes on distinguished astronomers of the past, both amateur and professional. Although limited information is offered on actual space flight achievements, details of the fundamental astronomical background to them is provided. Ed. by Gilbert.Satterthwaite. (St. Martin's Press, New York, N.Y., 1971)

Handbook of Chemistry and Physics

A biennial ready-reference book of chemical and physical information. This title is published in collaboration with a large number of professional chemists and physicists. The handbook is divided into six sections and includes: mathematics tables, the elements and inorganic compounds, organic compounds, general chemistry, general physical constants, and miscellaneous information. The basic format is tabular and the information included is continually updated. (Chemical Rubber Co., Cleveland, Ohio)

Handbook of Tables for Mathematics

This volume is especially useful to the astronomer, the mathematician, the physicist, the biologist, the scientist, the engineer, the student, and any other individual needing detailed information on mathematical nomenclature and symbolism. Although the basic format is tabular, there are many complete sections on mathematical concepts. (Chemical Rubber Co., Cleveland, Ohio)

McGraw-Hill Encyclopedia of Science and Technology
        A multivolume encyclopedia aimed at authoritative compre-
hensive coverage of the physical, natural and applied sciences.
Each new edition is completely revised and updated. The latest edition contains over 7,600 articles written by more than
2,500 scientists and engineers. Although there is some variance in the depth and detail of treatment, each article is designed and written to be understandable to the nonspecialist.
(McGraw-Hill, New York, N.Y.)

Mathematics Dictionary
        The guiding objective in the publication of this dictionary was
to make it useful for students, scientists, engineers, and others concerned with the meaning of mathematical terms.
There is near complete coverage of topics frequently included
in precollege or undergraduate college mathematics courses.
In addition, however, there are other interesting and important mathematical concepts included. Thus, this dictionary
is a valuable reference book for both amateur and professional
mathematicians. There is a multilingual index including
French, German, Russian, and Spanish. Ed. by Glenn James
and Robert James. (Van Nostrand, Princeton, N.J., 1959)

Merck Index
        Although the Merck Index has strong medicinal overtones, it
is essentially an organic chemical work with the inclusion of
useful substances and a separate section on organic name re-
actions. The latest edition contains nearly 10,000 descriptions of individual substances, more than 4,500 structural
formulas, and about 45,000 names of chemicals and drugs.
(Merck & Co., Rahway, N.J.)

The New Larousse Encyclopedia of the Earth
        The story of the earth itself unfolds in this volume. Detailed
explanations of the interplay of the oceans and atmosphere,
the forces of mountain building and those which ultimately de-
stroy them. Information detailing natural physical phenomena
to the evolution of life on earth is covered in this book. The
contents are divided into three subdivisions: the present,
earth in the service of man, and the past. There are numerous color plates and there is an index. (Larousse and Co.,
New York, N.Y.)

Van Nostrand's Scientific Encyclopedia
        This encyclopedia is a basic reference work on science, en-
gineering mathematics and medicine. It is extremely useful
for the scientist, engineer, mathematician, medical doctor,
student, teacher and general reader. All articles in this
volume begin with broad fundamental concepts and progress
to specific, more detailed information. In addition to the
detailed articles, the Encyclopedia defines and explains over
16,500 alphabetically arranged terms of fundamental interest.
(Van Nostrand, New York, N.Y., 1968)

Search Procedure Form	PHYSICAL SCIENCES
NAME OF USER	DATE OF INQUIRY

REDEFINED QUESTION STATEMENT

KEYWORDS

WORK IN PROGRESS

☐ Contemporary Authors

UNPUBLISHED STUDIES

☐ Dissertation Abstracts International
☐ Masters Abstracts

PERIODICALS

☐ Acoustical Society of America Journal
☐ Advances in Physics
☐ American Chemical Society Journal
☐ American Mineralogist
☐ American Journal of Mathematics
☐ American Journal of Physics
☐ American Mathematical Society Bulletin
☐ American Statistical Association Journal
☐ Analytical Chemistry
☐ Annals of Mathematics
☐ Astronomical Journal
☐ Astronomy and Astrophsics
☐ Chemical and Engineering News
☐ Chemical Engineering
☐ Chemical Reviews
☐ Chemical Technology
☐ Chemistry
☐ Chemistry and Industry
☐ Civil Engineering
☐ Contemporary Physics
☐ Earth and Extraterrestrial Sciences
☐ Earth Science
☐ Electronics
  Engineering
☐ Engineering Geology
☐ Geological Society of America Bulletin
☐ Geophysics
☐ International Geology Review
☐ Journal of Applied Mechanics

☐ Journal for Research in Mathematics Education
☐ Journal for the History of Astronomy
☐ Journal of Applied Physics
☐ Journal of Basic Engineering
☐ Journal of Chemical Documentation
☐ Journal of Geophysical Research
☐ Journal of Heat Transfer
☐ Journal of Mathematical Physics
☐ Journal of Organic Chemistry
☐ Journal of Physical Chemistry
☐ Journal of Physics
☐ Inorganic Chemistry
☐ International Chemical Engineering
☐ Mathematics Teacher
☐ Mineralological Magazine
☐ Nuclear Physics
☐ Physics Teacher
☐ Physics Today
☐ Quarterly Journal of Mathematics
☐ Review of Physics in Technology
☐ Reviews of Geophysics and Space Physics
☐ Russian Chemical Reviews
☐ Science
☐ Science News
☐ Sedimentology
☐ Sky and Telescope
☐ Soviet Astronomy
☐ Technology and Culture

REPORTS AND MONOGRAPHS

☐ Government Reports Announcements
☐ Government Reports Index
☐ Nuclear Science Abstracts
☐ Scientific and Technical Aerospace Reports

INDEXES AND ABSTRACTING SERVICES

- [ ] Applied Mechnics Reviews
- [ ] Applied Science and Technology Index
- [ ] Chemical Abstracts
- [ ] Computing Reviews
- [ ] Engineering Index
- [ ] Mathematical Reviews
- [ ] Metals Abstracts
- [ ] Science Abstracts, Series A: Physics Abstracts
- [ ] Science Abstracts, Series B: Electrial & Electronics Abstracts
- [ ] Science Citation Index
- [ ] Technical Book Review Index

BIBLIOGRAPHIC LISTS AND ESSAYS

- [ ] Guide to Science Reading
- [ ] McGraw-Hill Basic Bibliography of Science and Technology
- [ ] Quarterly Bibliography of Computers and Data Processing
- [ ] Science Books, A Quarterly Review

ANNUAL REVIEWS AND STATE-OF-THE-ART REPORTS

- [ ] Annual Review of Information Science and Technology
- [ ] The National Council of Teachers of Mathematics Yearbooks

ENCYCLOPEDIC SUMMARIES

- [ ] AMA Drug Evaluations
- [ ] Chambers Dictionary of Science and Technology
- [ ] Computer Dictionary and Handbook
- [ ] A Directory of Information Resources in the United States: Physical Sciences and Engineering
- [ ] Encyclopedia of Astronomy
- [ ] Handbook of Chemistry and Physics
- [ ] Handbook of Tables for Mathematics
- [ ] The New Larousse Encyclopedia of the Earth
- [ ] McGraw-Hill Encyclopedia of Science and Technology
- [ ] Mathematics Dictionary
- [ ] Merck Index
- [ ] Van Nostrand's Scientific Encyclopedia

COMMENTS:

SEARCHER'S SIGNATURE   **DATE COMPLETED**

Discipline Resource Package

LIFE SCIENCES

Elma M. Stewart
Eastern Michigan University

It is unrealistic to regard the natural sciences as easily categorized. There are significant overlaps between the physical and life sciences (e.g., biochemistry, the relationship between geology and paleontology, etc.) As well as within the physical sciences (e.g., astrophysics, geophysics, etc.) However, the division between the physical and life sciences is adequate for the purposes of the Discipline Resource Packages.

The life sciences deal with living organisms and their interaction in nature, as well as in controlled experiments. Included here under the heading of life sciences are:

> Agriculture
> Anthropology
> Biological Sciences
> Health Sciences
> Paleontology

WORK IN PROGRESS

Contemporary Authors
> A comprehensive source for biographical data on contemporary authors, many of which may not yet appear in traditional biographical sources. Entries are short, with personal, career, and work-in-progress information. A list of writings and sources of biographical and critical data are given when possible. The set is now in its 48th volume but many of the earlier volumes have been cumulated. Each volume is a separate alphabet but a cumulative name index is provided at the end of volume 48. (Gale Research Co., Detroit)

UNPUBLISHED STUDIES

Dissertation Abstracts International
> The most complete source for abstracts of doctoral dissertations written in the United States. Most U.S. universities contribute to this system operated by a private corporation.

Unfortunately, several important universities do not partici-
pate. Microfilm or paper copies of the dissertations are
available for purchase. Until recently, the indexing has been
spotty and of poor quality. Fortunately, a much better (and
very expensive) 37-volume cumulative index is now available.
(University Microfilms, Ann Arbor, Mich.)

Masters Abstracts
This is a selective, classified and annotated list of master's
theses produced by many, but by no means all, U.S. colleges
and universities. As with dissertations, microfilm or paper
copies of the theses are available for purchase from the publisher of the Abstracts. Due to its selectivity, it is much
easier to use than Dissertation Abstracts International. MA
is presently being published quarterly. (University Microfilms, Ann Arbor, Mich.)

PERIODICALS

Agricultural Economics Research (quarterly)
Agricultural Engineering (monthly)
Agricultural History (quarterly)
Agricultural Science Review (quarterly)
American Anthropologist (bi-monthly)
American Antiquity (quarterly)
American Biology Teacher (monthly)
American Journal of Anatomy (monthly)
American Journal of Archaeology (quarterly)
American Journal of Botany (10x yr.)
American Journal of Medicine (monthly)
American Journal of Nursing (monthly)
American Journal of Physical Anthropology (bi-monthly)
American Journal of Physiology (monthly)
American Medical Association Journal (weekly)
American Naturalist (bi-monthly)
American Zoologist (bi-monthly)
Anthropological Linguistics (9x yr.)
Anthropological Quarterly
Applied Microbiology (monthly)
Behavior Genetics (quarterly)
Biochemistry (semi-monthly)
Biological Bulletin (bi-monthly)
BioScience (monthly)
Botanical Review (quarterly)
British Medical Journal (weekly)
Bulletin of the History of Medicine (bi-monthly)
Crops and Soils (9x yr.)
Developmental Biology (monthly)
Ecology (bi-monthly)
Evolution (quarterly)
Farm Journal (monthly)

Foreign Agriculture (weekly)
Genetical Research (bi-monthly)
Human Biology (quarterly)
Human Organization (quarterly)
Journal of Heredity (bi-monthly)
Journal of Molecular Biology (semi-monthly)
Journal of Natural History (bi-monthly)
Journal of Paleontology (bi-monthly)
Life Sciences (semi-monthly)
Mankind (semi-annual)
Medical Economics (bi-weekly)
National Wildlife (bi-monthly)
Natural History (monthly)
Organic Gardening & Farming
Quarterly Review of Biology
Smithsonian (monthly)
Successful Farming (monthly)
Today's Health
World Archaeology (3x yr.)

REPORTS AND MONOGRAPHS

Government Reports Announcements
        Announcements of Government-sponsored research and develop-
        ment reports, and other Government analyses prepared by
        federal agencies, their contractors or grantees.   Also in-
        cluded are federally-sponsored translations and some reports
        written in foreign languages.   The announcements are ar-
        ranged in 22 subject fields and each field is divided into
        groups.   The arrangement is alphanumeric by accession num-
        ber.   (Government Printing Office, Washington, D.C.)

Government Reports Index
        Designed as a companion volume to Government Reports An-
        nouncements (GRA) this publication indexes the corresponding
        issue of GRA by Corporate Author, Subject, Personal Author,
        Contract Number, and Accession/Report Number.   Each in-
        dex is arranged alphanumerically.   Research titles are in-
        cluded in all indexes except the Contract Number Index and
        prices are given in the Accession/Report Number Index only.
        (Government Printing Office, Washington, D.C.)

Scientific and Technical Aerospace Reports (STAR)
        A comprehensive abstracting and indexing service covering
        current worldwide report literature on the science and tech-
        nology of space and aeronautics.   Abstracts of scientific and
        technical reports issued by NASA and its contractors, other
        U.S. Government agencies, corporations, universities, and
        research organizations throughout the world are included.
        The citations and abstracts are grouped in 34 subject cate-
        gories.   The five indexes included in each issue are: sub-

ject, personal author, corporate source, contract number,
and report/accession number. (Government Printing Office,
Washington, D. C.)

INDEXES AND ABSTRACTING SERVICES

Abridged Index Medicus
   Especially designed for the individual practitioner and libraries of small hospitals and clinics, the Abridged Index Medicus
   is based on articles from 100 English-language journals. Very
   useful for that student needing only limited detail on any particular medical topic. Published monthly with an annual cumulation. (Government Printing Office, Washington, D. C.)

Abstracts in Anthropology
   This publication abstracts information in four subfields of
   anthropology. These subfields are: cultural anthropology,
   archaeology, linguistics, and physical anthropology. The primary sources of material for these abstracts are journal articles, papers presented at meetings of interest to anthropologists, and monographs. Each issue includes author and subject indexes. (Greenwood Press, Westport, Conn.)

Air Pollution Abstracts
   An annotated guide to selected technical literature, covering
   most phases of air pollution, recently accessioned by the Air
   Pollution Technical Information Center (APTIC). Each issue
   contains six major sections: APTIC Publications; a list of
   Recent Contract Awards including amount of award; Subject
   Fields and Space Notes; Abstract Bulletin; a Subject Index;
   and Author Index. Published monthly, this title has a semi-
   annual author and title index. (Government Printing Office,
   Washington, D. C.)

Bibliography and Index of Geology
   This title follows very closely the format of its predecessor,
   the Bibliography and Index of Geology Exclusive of North
   America. The monthly issues are divided into 21 interdisciplinary categories. The citations under each category are
   listed alphabetically by author. There are also separate sections, within each issue, which include an in-depth, alphabetically arranged subject index and an alphabetically arranged
   author listing. (Geological Society of America, Boulder, Colorado)

Biological Abstracts
   Abstracts of articles concerning theoretical and applied biology
   from the world's biological research literature. Beginning in
   1927 with 14,506 abstracts the Biological Abstracts now runs
   as high as a quarter million abstracts originating in over 100
   countries. Over 600 subject sections covering the wide

diversity of the life sciences comprise each issue. In each
issue, the abstracts are arranged by section and subsection
with subject, author, systematic, and cross indexes.   The
coverage runs from general biology and health sciences to
soil science and horticulture.   Published monthly, there are
semi-annual cumulations of each section.   (Biological Abstracts, Philadelphia, Pa.)

Biological and Agricultural Index
A cumulative subject index to English-language periodicals
in the fields of agriculture (all phases), biology (many areas),
conservation, dairying, food sciences, soil science, veterinary
medicine and related fields.   It is published monthly with an
annual cumulation.   (H. W. Wilson Co., New York, N.Y.)

Cumulative Index to Nursing Literature
CINL is an authoritative subject-author index to a wide selection of subjects important to nurses and other health-related
scientists.   The articles found in current journals and serials
are indexed in depth.   Each issue includes a list of journals
and serials indexed, an alphabetical subject section, and an
alphabetical author section.   (Glendale Adventist Hospital Publications Service, Glendale, California)

Index Medicus
An alphabetical subject listing of references to current articles from about 2,250 of the world's bio-medical journals.
Aside from the subject section, there is also an author section and a separate Bibliography of Medical Reviews.   The
coverage is limited to periodical literature and an effort is
made to maintain a reasonable balance of subject matter.   A
publication of the National Medical Library, this index is published monthly and cumulated annually.   (Government Printing
Office, Washington, D.C.)

Pollution Abstracts
A summation, organization and indexing of the world's technical literature on the environment.   This title includes abstracts of information covering air pollution, general environmental quality, noise, pesticides, radiation, solid waste, and
water pollutions.   This publication is especially useful to researchers in universities, libraries, research centers, businesses, engineering firms, and government agencies.   Each
issue includes a keytalpha (rotating keywords) subject index
and an author index.   (Paul Janensch, La Jolla, California)

Technical Book Review Index
An alphabetically arranged monthly index of over 100 scientific, technical and commercial books, giving brief quotations
from reviews from leading scientific, technical and trade
journals.   Devoted almost exclusively to English language material, this index is published monthly except July and August.
Much material not listed in Book Review Digest will be found

in this index.   (Special Libraries Assn. , New York, N. Y.)

Water Pollution Abstracts
        Information is subdivided into five major categories: Water
        supplies, Analysis and examination of water, Sewage, Trade
        waste, and Pollution of natural waters.   Thousands of items
        are abstracted annually and a special feature is the noting of
        additional references at the end of the sections.   Cumulative
        author and subject indexes are issued annually.   (Her Maj-
        esty's Stationery Office, London, England)

                BIBLIOGRAPHIC LISTS AND ESSAYS

Bibliography of Agriculture
        An index to the literature of agriculture and allied sciences
        received in the National Agricultural Library.   The topics
        covered range from general agricultural information to human
        nutrition and food programs.   There is an author/subject
        cumulation annually.   (Government Printing Office, Washing-
        ton, D. C.)

Guide to Science Reading (AAAS)
        A selected annotated list of paperbound science books.   This
        title is an especially useful aid in the development of per-
        sonal or home library collections.   The entries were selected
        with the collaboration of professional representatives of the
        biological, physical, behavioral, medical, engineering, agri-
        cultural and mathematical sciences.   (American Association
        for the Advancement of Science; New American Library, New
        York, N. Y. , 1964)

Guide to Reference Material, Volume 1:   Science and Technology
        Although somewhat British in coverage, this publication has
        an international scope.   Its objective is to provide a guide to
        reference books and bibliographies published in recent years.
        Critical annotations have been provided for each title, thus
        making this a good source for librarians in the building up or
        revision of reference collections as well as for the student of
        library science.   Edited by A. J. Walford.   (The Library
        Association, London, England)

McGraw-Hill Basic Bibliography of Science and Technology
        Brief annotations of titles covering more than 7, 000 subjects.
        Numerous cross-references facilitate access to very special-
        ized topics.   It is especially useful to the individual who
        wishes to read beyond the articles in the McGraw-Hill Ency-
        clopedia of Science and Technology and into the materials of
        science, on those specialized topics treated in the Encyclo-
        pedia itself.   (McGraw-Hill, New York, N. Y. , 1966)

Science Books, A Quarterly Review

Published to improve science education and public understanding of science. Included are reviews of trade books, textbooks, and reference works in pure and applied sciences for students in the elementary school, in secondary school and in the first two years of college. Also included are selected advanced and professional books useful for reference by students and faculty members. (American Association for the Advancement of Science, Washington, D. C.)

ANNUAL REVIEWS AND STATE OF THE ART REPORTS

Biennial Review of Anthropology
A review that describes and summarizes important papers and monographs in several fields of major current interest. In the past, these fields have included: social and cultural change, physical anthropology, linguistics, social organization, and the psychological dimensions of culture. (Stanford Univ. Press, Stanford, California)

U. S. Department of Agriculture. Yearbooks.
Originally designed (1894) to "be specially suited to the interest and instruct the farmers of the country, " this publication has broadened its scope to include material of interest to practically every segment of the population. Each Yearbook is devoted to a specific topic. Recent topics have included: "Landscape for Living"-1972; "A Good Life for More People"-1971; and "Food for All"-1969. (Government Printing Office, Washington, D. C.)

BOOKS

Ardrey, Robert. African Genesis: a Personal Investigation into the Animal Origins and Nature of Man. N. Y.: Atheneum, 1961.

Bacon, Edward. Digging for History: Archaeological Discoveries Throughout the World, 1945-1959. N. Y.: John Day, 1961.

Bates, Marston. Man in Nature. N. Y.: Prentice, 1961.

Beerbower, James R. Search for the Past, an Introduction to Paleontology. N. Y.: Prentice, 1960.

Benedict, Ruth. Patterns of Culture. N. Y.: Houghton, 1934.

Berman, Lamar T. Farm Relief. N. Y.: H. W. Wilson, 1927.

Birket-Smith, Kaj. Primitive Man and His Ways: Patterns of Life in Some Nature Societies. N. Y.: World, 1961.

Black, John. Agricultural Reform in the U.S. N.Y.: McGraw-
Hill, 1929.

Calder, Peter Richie. Medicine and Man, a Comprehensive History.... N.Y.: New American Library, 1958.

Carson, Hampton L. Heredity and Human Life. N.Y.: Columbia,
1963.

Carson, Rachel. The Edge of the Sea. N.Y.: Houghton, 1955.

Ceram, C. W. Gods, Graves, and Scholars, the Story of Archaeology. N.Y.: Knopf, 1951.

Cloudsley-Thompson, J. L. Animal Behavior. N.Y.: Macmillan,
1961.

Cousteau, Jacques Y. and Dumas, Frederic. The Silent World.
N.Y.: Harper, 1963.

Darwin, Charles. On the Origin of the Species by Means of Natural
Selection. N.Y.: Doubleday, 1960 (c1859).

_____. The Voyage of the Beagle. N.Y.: Doubleday, 1962
(c1860).

Desroches-Noblecourt, Christiane. Tutankhamen: Life and Death
of a Pharaoh. N.Y.: New York Graphic Society, 1963.

Doblhofer, Ernst. Voices in Stone: The Decipherment of Ancient
Scripts and Writings. Clifton, N.J.: Kelley, 1961.

Eisley, Loren. The Mind as Nature. N.Y.: Harper, 1962.

Frisch, Karl von. The Dancing Bees: an Account of the Life and
Senses of the Honey Bee. N.Y.: Harcourt, 1955.

Harvey, William. Lectures on the Whole of Anatomy: an Annotated
Translation of... 'Prelectiones Anatomiae Universalis.' Berkeley:
Univ. of California Press, 1961. (circa 1630)

Heyerdahl, Thor. Kon-Tiki. Chicago: Rand McNally, 1950.

Hippocrates. The Medical Works. Trans. by W. H. S. Jones.
4 vols. Cambridge, Mass.: Harvard Univ. Press, 1927.
(circa 400 B.C.)

Howells, William W., ed. Ideas on Human Evolution: Selected
Essays, 1949-1961. Cambridge, Mass.: Harvard Univ. Press,
1962.

Huxley, Julian. Man in the Modern World. N.Y.: New American
Library, 1948.

Leakey, L. S. B., et al. Olduvai Gorge, 1951-1961. 3 vols.
    London: Butterworth, 1964.

Lilly, John W. Man and Dolphin. N. Y.: Doubleday, 1961.

Mead, Margaret. Coming of Age in Samoa. N. Y.: Morrow, 1930.

Muir, John. The Wilderness World of John Muir. N. Y.: Hough-
    ton, 1954. (circa 1900)

Rapport, Samuel and Wright, Helen, eds. Great Adventures in
    Medicine. N. Y.: Dial, 1961.

Russell, Franklin. Watchers at the Pond. N. Y.: Knopf, 1961.

Schmeck, Harold. The Semi-Artificial Man: A Dawning Revolution
    in Medicine. N. Y.: Walker & Co., 1964.

Singer, Charles. A History of Biology to About the Year 1900.
    3rd ed. N. Y.: Abelard, 1950.

_____. and Underwood, E. A. A Short History of Medicine,
    2nd ed. Oxford, England: Oxford, 1962.

Stirton, Ruben A. Time, Life, and Man: the Fossil Record, an
    Introduction to Paleontology. N. Y.: Wiley, 1959.

Tax, Sol, ed. Evolution after Darwin. 3 vols. Chicago: Univ.
    of Chicago Press, 1960.

Teale, Edwin W. North with the Spring. N. Y.: Dodd, 1951.

Teilhard de Chardin, Pierre. The Phenomenon of Man. N. Y.:
    Harper, 1959.

Thorndike, Lynn. Science and Thought in the Fifteenth Century.
    N. Y.: Harper, 1963.

Turnbull, Colin. The Forest People. N. Y.: Simon and Schuster,
    1961.

Walker, Kenneth. The Story of Medicine. Oxford, England: Ox-
    ford, 1955.

Williams, Greer. Virus Hunters. N. Y.: Knopf, 1959.

ENCYCLOPEDIC SUMMARIES

American Men and Women of Science
        An alphabetically arranged guide to current biographies of
    American men and women in the physical and biological

sciences.   The criteria for inclusion in <u>American Men and
Women of Science</u> are:
  a.   Achievement (by experience and training) equivalent to
       that associated with the doctoral degree
  b.   Research activity of high quality as evidenced by pub-
       lication in reputable scientific journals
or c. A position of substantial responsibility requiring sci-
       entific training and experience to the extent described
       for (a) and (b).
Biographees who are retired, in private practice, or who have
not submitted new information during the past ten years have
been deleted.   (R. R. Bowker, New York, N. Y.)

Anatomy of the Human Body

An extensively illustrated atlas covering almost every structure in the human body.   The latest American edition of this
title includes new drawings on the peripheral nerves and the
number of x-ray pictures has been increased.   The nomenclature used in this edition follows the Nomina Anatomica adopted
by the International Anatomical Nomenclature Committee and
the International Congress of Anatomists.   This volume is an
excellent reference source for any serious student in the
health sciences.   Originated by the late Henry Gray, it is
now edited by Charles M. Goss.   (Lea and Febiger, Philadelphia, Pa.)

Chambers' Dictionary of Science and Technology

A successor to <u>Chambers' Technical Dictionary,</u> this volume
presents the level of vocabulary required by those interested
in understanding current scientific and technological developments and problems.   The arrangement is basically alphabetical and a number of tables are included in the appendices.
These tables endeavor to treat certain topics with more detailed information.   For example, there are traditional and
modern tables of the plant kingdom, tables of chemical elements, etc.   (W & R Chambers, London, England)

Dictionary of Agricultural and Allied Terminology

This dictionary includes definitions of terms from every
phase of agriculture (from the general to engineering), animal
husbandry, beekeeping, plant diseases, meat products and
processing, veterinary medicine and many other related subdivisions of the agricultural sciences.   The words from the
various sciences were collected by culling the terms used in
250 carefully selected books, magazines, pamphlets, and
catalogs.   The entries and definitions follow a common pattern: the head word; the scientific name; a general description; the agricultural implications; synonyms; and cross-references.   Edited by John Winburne.   (Michigan State Univ.
Press, East Lansing, Mich.)

Dictionary of Biological Terms

This title includes very brief definitions of terms in biology,

botany, and zoology. Also included are the terms of anatomy,
cytology, embryology, genetics, physiology, and some other
cognate subjects. Although the method of spelling is, for the
most part, that used in Britain, some attention has been
given to American orthography. ˙ This is done by the use of
cross-references or by reproducing in the original lettering
terms taken from scientific literature published in the United
States. (Van Nostrand Reinhold, New York, N. Y.)

A Directory of Information Resources in the United States: Physical Sciences and Engineering

An alphabetical listing of organizations having knowledge or
expertise that they wish to share with others. This includes
professional societies, university research bureaus and institutes, federal or state agencies, industrial laboratories,
museum specimen collections, testing stations, and individual
experts as well as the more traditional sources, such as
technical libraries, information and documents centers, and
abstracting and indexing services. Names, addresses, telephone numbers, and brief descriptions of the organizations
are given. There is a subject index. Material on the biological sciences, included in previous editions, will be published in a separate volume. (Government Printing Office,
Washington, D. C.)

Dorland's Illustrated Medical Dictionary

A carefully arranged repository of precise and specific medical term meanings. Much additional related information in
tables and illustrations is also included. Throughout the dictionary, the main entries appear in bold print. Subentries
consisting of two words, which are ordinarily defined under
the second (or principal) word, run on in the same paragraph
and also appear in bold face print. For example, more than
120 types of anemia appear as subentries under the main entry
anemia. (W. B. Saunders Co., Philadelphia, Pa.)

The Encyclopedia of the Biological Sciences, 2nd ed.

This is a comprehensive reference source for those needing
information about biology even though biology is not the field
of their specialization. Especially useful for teachers and
students who seek more than a short definition and more than
a general encyclopedia can offer. Except for a few biographies, all of the articles are over 500 words. The 800
articles cover the broad field of the biological sciences in
their developmental, ecological, functional, genetic, structural
and taxonomic aspects. An interesting entry, "Names, Group,
Gender and Juvenile, " gives the collective nouns for many
animals (a rafter of turkeys) as well as gender names and
the terminology for immature animals. Ed. by Peter Gray.
(Van Nostrand Reinhold, New York, N. Y., 1970.)

McGraw-Hill Encyclopedia of Science and Technology

A multivolume encyclopedia aimed at authoritative comprehensive coverage of the physical, natural and applied sciences. Each new edition is completely revised and updated. The latest edition contains over 7,600 articles written by more than 2,500 scientists and engineers. Although there is some variance in the depth and detail of treatment, each article is designed and written to be understandable to the nonspecialist. (McGraw-Hill, New York, N.Y.)

Physician's Desk Reference

Published annually, this reference source includes the latest available information on approximately 2,500 drug products. The four major sections of information are: Product Information, Diagnostic Products Information, Drug Classification Index, and Generic and Chemical Name Index. Especially useful also is the alphabetical index by manufacturer and the alphabetical index by brand name. (Medical Economics Co., Oradell, N.J.)

Van Nostrand's Scientific Encyclopedia

This encyclopedia is a basic reference work on science, engineering mathematics and medicine. It is extremely useful for the scientist, engineer, mathematician, medical doctor, student teacher and general reader. All articles in this volume begin with broad fundamental concepts and progress to specific, more detailed information. In addition to the detailed articles, the Encyclopedia defines and explains over 16,500 alphabetically arranged terms of fundamental interest. (Van Nostrand, New York, N.Y., 1968)

Search Procedure Form	LIFE SCIENCES
NAME OF USER	**DATE OF INQUIRY**

REDEFINED QUESTION STATEMENT

KEYWORDS

WORK IN PROGRESS

☐ Contemporary Authors

UNPUBLISHED STUDIES

☐ Dissertation Abstracts International
☐ Masters Abstracts

PERIODICALS

☐ Agricultural Economics Research
☐ Agricultural Engineering
☐ Agricultural History
☐ Agricultural Science Review
☐ American Anthropologist
☐ American Antiquity
☐ American Biology Teacher
☐ American Journal of Anatomy
☐ American Journal of Archaeology
☐ American Journal of Botany
☐ American Journal of Medicine
☐ American Journal of Nursing
☐ American Journal of Physical Anthropology
☐ American Journal of Physiology
☐ American Medical Association Journal
☐ American Naturalist
☐ American Zoologist
☐ Anthropological Linquistics
☐ Anthropological Quarterly
☐ Applied Microbiology
☐ Behaivor Genetics
☐ Biochemistry
☐ Biological Bulletin
☐ BioScience
☐ Botanical   ew
☐ British Medical Journal

☐ Bulletin of the History of Medicine
☐ Crops and Soils
☐ Developmental Biology
☐ Ecology
☐ Evolution
☐ Farm Journal
☐ Foreign Agriculture
☐ Genetical Research
☐ Human Biology
☐ Human Organization
☐ Journal of Heredity
☐ Journal of Molecular Biology
☐ Journal of Natural History
☐ Journal of Paleontology
☐ Life Sciences
☐ Mankind
☐ Medical Economics
☐ National Wildlife
☐ Natural History
☐ Organic Gardening & Farming
☐ Quarterly Review of Biology
☐ Smithsonian
☐ Successful Farming
☐ Today's Health
☐ World Archaeology

REPORTS AND MONOGRAPHS:

☐ Government Reports Announcements
☐ Government Reports Index
☐ Scientific and Technical Aerospace Reports

INDEXES AND ABSTRACTING SERVICES

☐ Abridged Index Medicus
☐ Abstracts in Anthropology
☐ Air Pollution Abstracts
☐ Bibliography and Index of Geology
☐ Biological Abstracts
☐ Biological and Agricultural Index

☐ Cumulative Index to Nursing Literature
☐ Index Medicus
☐ Pollution Abstracts
☐ Technical Book Review Index
☐ Water Pollution Abstracts

BIBLIOGRAPHIC LISTS AND ESSAYS

☐ Bibliography of Agriculture
☐ Guide to Science Reading
☐ Guide to Reference Material. Volume 1 Science and Technology
☐ McGraw-Hill Basic Bibliography of Science and Technology
☐ Science Books, A Quarterly Review

ANNUAL REVIEWS AND STATE-OF-THE-ART REPORTS

☐ Biennial Review of Anthropology
☐ U.S. Department of Agriculture. Yearbooks

ENCYCLOPEDIC SUMMARIES

☐ American Men and Women of Science
☐ Anatomy of the Human Body
☐ Chambers Dictionary of Science and Technology
☐ Dictionary of Agricultural and Allied Terminology
☐ Dictionary of Biological Terms
☐ A Directory of Information Resources in the United States: Physical
  Sciences & Engineering
☐ Dorland's Illustrated Medical Dictionary
☐ The Encyclopedia Of the Biological Sciences
☐ McGraw-Hill Encyclopedia of Science and Technology
☐ Physicians Desk Reference
☐ Van Nostrand's Scientific Encyclopedia

COMMENTS:

SEARCHER'S SIGNATURE | **DATE COMPLETED**

Discipline Resource Package

GENERAL WORKS

Thomas W. Mulford
Detroit Public Library

This last of the Discipline Resource Packages has been created to serve as a catchall for miscellaneous reference resources, and for items that are clearly interdisciplinary in character.

Therefore, its arrangement will be somewhat different than the arrangement used for the subject-oriented Discipline Resource Packages. The subject-oriented Packages are arranged by the printed formats of the Bibliographic Chain. Due to the interdisciplinary nature of its inclusions, this Package will be arranged by the following eight general types of resources:

-Almanacs
-Biography location tools
-Book location tools
-Book review location tools
-Dictionaries
-Encyclopedias
-Periodical location tools
-Statistical sources

ALMANACS

Guinness Book of World Records
An annual published in 12 different languages. The American edition contains 12 sections which categorize the extremes and all kinds of records in the world. There is a subject index in the back and pictures accompany some entries. The name "Guinness" appears because of the sponsorship of the Guinness Brewery of Dublin, Ireland. (Sterling Pub. Co., N.Y., N.Y.)

Information Please Almanac
It contains popular facts, statistics, names, and dates in one volume. Many chronological lists cover events in the United States and abroad. Capsulized treatments of world history and events are included as well as sports data. An alphabetical index is provided. (Simon & Schuster, N.Y., N.Y.)

Official Associated Press Almanac

A one-volume, convenient popular reference source formerly entitled the New York Times Almanac, it contains many facts, lists, and statistics grouped under about 30 subject headings. News reviews for the year preceding end with a "news flash" section in November. An atlas section in color, and one on the world's nations, cover the international scene. An extensive section on the United States provides descriptions of states, cities, and presidential administrations. An index is provided. (Almanac Pub. Co., N.Y., N.Y.)

Statesman's Yearbook

A one-volume annual that summarizes political, geographic, and economic information for over 150 countries. It is arranged in four parts, the first of which describes the background and operation of world organizations like the UN. The next part describes in rough alphabetical order British Commonwealth countries, the third covers the United States and its states, and the last covers other countries of the world. Countries like the United Kingdom, Canada, and the USSR are covered in some depth, and smaller countries in less detail. In addition to encyclopedia-type descriptions, there are tables comparing product shipments of countries, a few fold-out maps, an extensive table of contents, and a detailed index. (St. Martin's Press, N.Y., N.Y.)

World Almanac

Containing an alphabetical index, it is published annually and intended for general use. Sizable sections cover summarized facts on U.S. states, government, sports, last year's chronology, population, and economy. Useful lists cover names, dates, and events. (Newspaper Enterprise Assn., N.Y., N.Y.)

BIOGRAPHY LOCATION TOOLS

Biography Index

This index, published since 1946, is intended to be a comprehensive source of individual and collective biographies published in English and of biographies in journals, diaries, memoirs, etc. The main section of each bound volume (or current issue) is arranged by the name of the biographee. The second section indexes the first by profession or occupation. Quarterly issues are cumulated into annual volumes. (H. W. Wilson, Bronx, N.Y.)

Contemporary Authors

A comprehensive source for biographical data on contemporary authors, many of which may not yet appear in traditional biographical sources. Entries are short, with personal, career, and work-in-progress information. A list

of writings and sources of biographical and critical data are
given when possible. The set is now in its 48th volume but
many of the earlier volumes have been cumulated. Each volume is a separate alphabet but a cumulative name index is
provided at the end of volume 48. (Gale Research Co., Detroit)

Current Biography
A source of fairly lengthy biographical articles on people
prominent in the news. All fields and interest areas are included. It is international in scope. The biographical information comes from various sources but, as the editors point
out, they are "objective rather than authorized biographies."
Citations to journal and newspaper articles on the biographee
are listed at the end of each article. Each issue also contains a list of current obituaries of people who previously
appeared in Current Biography, along with a citation to the
newspaper obituary. Each monthly issue contains an index
that cumulates biographies and obituaries for that year. The
issues and indexes are cumulated into annual bound volumes.
Decennial indexes and one for the entire set to 1970 have
been published. (H. W. Wilson, Bronx, N.Y.)

Dictionary of American Biography
A large compendium of fairly short biographies of Americans,
no longer alive, who "have made some contribution to American life in its manifold aspects." The 20-volume set presently has three supplements. (Scribners, N.Y., N.Y.)

Dictionary of National Biography
The major reference work for short biographies of British and
colonial figures, both important and minor. Colonial Americans are included. It is limited to people no longer alive.
The original set is in 21 volumes and several supplements
bring it up to 1960. (Oxford University Press, N.Y., N.Y.)

Directory of American Scholars
Although now somewhat dated (1969) this four-volume set is
still the best single source for brief biographical data on
prominent American scholars. Some personal data is sup-
plied in addition to the usual positions held, subject field,
education, professional memberships, etc. The four volumes
cover: history; English; speech; drama; foreign languages,
linguistics, and philology; and philosophy, religion, and law.
There's a cumulative index in volume four. A new edition
is now in press. (Bowker, N.Y., N.Y.)

Twentieth Century Authors
A standard source for brief biographies of authors "who, in
the literary sense, have flourished since 1900." Although
dated (1942), it is an excellent source for authors of this
period. The text of the biography is followed by bibliographies of principal works and works about the subject.

Nearly all have pictures--a unique and useful feature.   A
supplementary volume was produced in 1955.   Both were
edited by Stanley Kunitz.   (H. W. Wilson, N. Y., N. Y.)

Webster's Biographical Dictionary
An excellent one-volume source for very brief biographies
of the world's prominent of the present and past.   Dated
1970, it seems to be reasonably up to date.   Its real value
as a quick reference tool, however, is the fact that last
names are divided and marked for pronunciation.   A pro-
nouncing list of prenames is appended, as are other helpful
tables and charts.   (G. & C. Merriam, Springfield, Mass.)

Who's Who
A good, basic source for very brief biographical entries for
prominent people in all fields who are still alive.   Worldwide
in scope, but it heavily emphasizes the United Kingdom and
the rest of Europe.   The entries are factual: personal information, education, publications, etc.   The selection policy
must be cumbersome, since the 1974 edition notes Agnew's
resignation but doesn't include Ford.   A list of the previous
year's prominent obituaries is included, as is a good list of
the British royal family.   (A. & C. Black, London, England)

Who's Who in America
This standard reference work, now in two volumes, is the
best single source for brief, descriptive biographies of prominent Americans in all fields.   Prominence, or "reference
value," is the principal criterion for inclusion.   Data in the
entries is personal, statistical, education, positions held, etc.
It is presently in its 37th edition.   (Marquis Who's Who, Chicago, Ill.)

BOOK LOCATION TOOLS

Books in Print/Subject Guide to Books in Print
This is an annual author-title index (in 4 volumes) to books
published in the United States with one supplement section to
update halfway through the year.   The subject guide (2 volumes) contains 62,000 subject categories adapted from the
Library of Congress headings.   Data sufficient for ordering
books is included with each entry.   Excluded are fictional
books, microforms, periodicals, free materials, and books
without a U.S. distributor.   (R. R. Bowker, N. Y., N. Y.)

British Museum Catalogue of Printed Books
This set, now over 325 volumes, serves as the catalog of
books owned by the British Museum. which serves as England's national library.   The Catalogue is alphabetical by the
name of the author.   Works are listed alphabetically after
the authors' names, except for periodicals which are

interfiled with the author entries. It is a valuable bibliographic tool for locating listings written in the authors' own
languages.   The first general catalogue appeared in 1787.
The current one appeared at the rate of one volume per
month during the 1960's as copied from the British Museum
staff's work copy. A 10- and 5-year supplement have been
issued to up-date the main 263 volume set. (The British
Museum, London, England)

Cumulative Book Index

"A world list of books in the English language" published
every one or two years since the early 1900's (formerly the
United States Catalog) and cumulated quarterly.   Entries are
listed by author, title, and subject.   Author entries contain
author's names (or pseudonyms), titles, dates, prices, publishers, code numbers, and editions. Pamphlets, cheaper
paperback books, and government documents are excluded.
A list of publishers and their addresses appears at the back.
(H. W. Wilson, Bronx, N. Y.)

Forthcoming Books/Subject Guide to Forthcoming Books

Bi-monthly paperbound index to books scheduled for publication within five months from the date of its issue.   The first
half is a list of new books by author and the last half is a
list by titles.   In addition to including forecasted authors and
titles of their books to be published and the postponed titles,
it cumulates titles which have been published since the annual
summer issues of another Bowker publication, Books in Print.
A smaller companion publication is the bi-monthly Subject
Guide to Forthcoming Books. Entries for each of the author,
title, and subject listings contain sufficient information and
data for ordering--price, reading level, etc.   A list of publishers, publisher code keys, and addresses is provided.
(R. R. Bowker, N. Y. , N. Y.)

National Union Catalog (Library of Congress)

Published periodically since 1956, it combines, in one alphabetical cumulative author list, monographs reported by 950
North American libraries and acquisitions added to the U. S.
Library of Congress collection and printed on its catalog
cards.   Major supplements represent 20- or 5-year cumulations of these cards.   A complete supplement may reach 90
volumes.   Entries are photoreductions of the printed catalog
cards.   Entries appear alphabetically by main entry.   Bi-
weekly, quarterly, and annual supplements are published.
MARC II tapes (Machine-readable computer cards) provide
coded Library of Congress catalog cards on magnetic tape
for libraries with automated printing systems.   In addition to
the cumulative author list (the National Union Catalog), the
Library of Congress publishes a companion set Books: Subjects, which is a multi-volumed cumulative listing of printed
catalog card entries arranged by subject.   Other supplements
issued annually in the National Union Catalog series are the

Register of Additional Features, Motion Pictures and Film-
strips, Music and Phonorecords, National Register of Micro-
form Masters, and National Union Catalog of Manuscript Collections. (U.S. Library of Congress, Washington, D.C.)

Paperbound Books in Print
     Published quarterly, it indexes over 100,000 titles of paper-
bound books currently in print. Each issue is divided by
title, author, and subject. Each entry contains the book's
author, title, price, International Standard Book Number, and
the publisher order number. A subject classification table
provides an index to the alphabetical subject section; each entry in other sections contains a classification number from
this table. A section in the back provides a key to publishers' abbreviations and their addresses. (R. R. Bowker,
N.Y., N.Y.)

Popular Names of U.S. Government Reports
     Like laws, U.S. government reports seem to attract popular
nicknames, usually the person in charge of the group that
produced the report (e.g., "Kerner Commission Report," or
the "Moynihan Report"). This makes locating them in a card
catalog nearly impossible without this excellent little publication which indexes these reports by their popular name. The
result is a photoreduction of the LC card giving main entry,
tracings, full title, etc. (U.S. Government Printing Office,
Washington, D.C.)

Subject Collections (Ash)
     Now in its 4th edition, this excellent one-volume publication
indexes, by subject, specialized library collections all over
the U.S. and Canada. Certain purely local sources, such as
local history societies, are excluded, but everything else of
importance is there. Within the subject, entries are arranged
by state. Entries include name, address, data like volume
count, description of the scope of the collection, and contact
person. (R. R. Bowker, N.Y., N.Y.)

Titles in Series (Baer)
     A revised, two-volume second edition of this was published
in 1964. Volume 1 lists about 40,000 book titles in series
as they have been published prior to January 1963 under their
series names as used by the U.S. Library of Congress. Included after each series entry (which are listed alphabetically)
are the publishers, titles, series, numbers, dates, and con-
secutive index numbers. Volume 2 is an alphabetical listing
by the titles of each title in the series; code numbers referring back to the same title number are listed after the
appropriate series name. Three supplements combine alphabetical entries and alphabetical series names and their sub-
classed titles in single volumes for 1967, 1971, and 1974.
Useful for filling in missing books that belong to publishers'
series. (Scarecrow Press, Metuchen, N.J.)

<u>World Bibliography of Bibliographies</u> (Besterman)

> The fourth and reportedly final edition, covering over 100,000 bibliographies through 1963, arranges bibliographies, written in over 40 languages (lists of books on subjects), under near-ly 40 general subject headings. The entries of the bibliographies are in chronological order by the date of publication, the earliest first. Each entry includes the author's name, the title, publisher, date, page, and number of entries. The last volume (5) is an index arranging alphabetically the authors, titles, and library locations of the bibliographies. Each entry has a column number which refers back to the appropriate page and column in the first four volumes. (Societas Bibliographica, Lausanne, Switzerland)

BOOK REVIEW LOCATION TOOLS

<u>Book Review Index</u>

> An annual cumulative edition and supplements published three times a year provide an index to book reviews of about 35,000 different books appearing in over 200 periodicals. The index is arranged alphabetically by the authors' names. Each entry lists the source, date, and page for each review. (Gale Research Co., Detroit, Mich.)

<u>Book Review Digest</u>

> Books published or distributed in the United States and re-ceiving two or more reviews (for non-fiction) and four or more reviews (for fiction) in selected periodicals are included in this digest. Annual cumulations and periodic cumulative supplements list condensed reviews alphabetically by the au-thor of the books reviewed. Both the sources of the reviews and ordering information about each book are included. A combined subject-title index is found in the back of each vol-ume. The latter cumulates every five years. (H. W. Wilson, Bronx, N. Y.)

<u>Media Review Digest</u>

> Originally titled <u>Multi Media Reviews Index,</u> this publication has been expanded to include very brief reviews covering all types of non-book materials. In addition to the review state-ment, it includes all bibliographic and cataloging data, includ-ing Dewey number and tracings. Thus it becomes both a cataloging and an ordering tool as well as a location aid. Other reviews are cited, as well as technical data on length, etc., and grade level. It has separately published subject indexes and supplements to the annual bound volumes. (Pierian Press, Ann Arbor, Mich.)

DICTIONARIES

Acronyms and Initialisms Dictionary, 4th ed.
> Although the original concentrated on government acronyms, succeeding editions expanded into other fields. The fourth edition is presently the best single source of acronyms and initialisms. Annual paperbacks entitled New Acronyms and Initialisms are produced between editions. There is also a less useful companion volume: Reverse Acronyms and Initialisms Dictionary which arranges acronyms by meaning instead of strict alphabet. (Gale Research Co., Detroit, Mich.)

Dictionary of Slang and Unconventional English
> A unique and valuable source of, as the subtitle says, "colloquialisms and catch phrases, solecisms and catachreses, nicknames, vulgarisms, and such Americanisms as have been naturalized." Slang and cant account for 50% of the entries and colloquialisms another 35%. Vulgarisms, its most controversial aspect, represent only 1/2 of 1% of the entries. (Macmillan Co., N.Y., N.Y.)

New English Dictionary on Historic Principals
> The first, great, comprehensive English language dictionary. It was compiled by readers who scanned the world's English literature to place a word in historical perspective, as well as define it. Thus, in addition to spelling, part of speech, pronunciation, and definition, actual quotes from authors who used the word, with dates, are supplied in chronological order. The dictionary thus serves as a major etymological source as well. Begun at the University of Oxford in 1857, it is composed of 10 volumes and one supplement. (Oxford Univ. Press, Oxford, England)

Origins, a Short Etymological Dictionary
> A handy, one-volume, etymological dictionary edited by one of the field's acknowledged experts, Eric Partridge. It has few definitions, saving its space for the data on word origins and evolution. The editor states that "I have concentrated upon civilization rather than upon science and technology; dialect and cant have been ignored; slang is represented only by a very few outstanding examples...." He also deleted most colonialisms. (Routledge and Kegan Paul, London, England)

Oxford English Dictionary
> The OED, now more famous than its predecessor, is actually a reissue of the New English Dictionary on Historic Principals (see above) with some corrections and additions. A supplement to the OED is now in progress. (Oxford University Press, Oxford, England)

Random House Dictionary
>An entirely new dictionary designed, according to the editor, "to keep pace with the dynamic growth of ... language." Its most useful aspect is the strong collection of newer words and it is a valuable supplement to Webster's Third in that respect. It also claims to have avoided excessively concise wordings "We have tried to express ourselves clearly and simply, using normal English and normal punctuation...." © 1970. (Random House, N.Y., N.Y.)

Webster's New International Dictionary of the English Language, 2nd ed.
>A major, completely revised unabridged dictionary published in 1934, containing about 600,000 words. Its strong points include its comprehensiveness, including many obsolete Middle English words, its notations of the status of usage (e.g., slang) and its useful appendices, notably two pronouncing dictionaries (geographical and biographical). Due to limitations of the 3rd edition, it is still the authority for good usage, preferred pronunciation, and words obsolete before 1755. (G. & C. Merriam Co., Springfield, Mass.)

Webster's Third New International Dictionary of the English Language
>A complete revision of the 2nd edition, it contains 450,000 words--a significant drop from the 600,000 of the 2nd edition. Most deleted words were those obsolete before 1755. Useful appendices were also deleted from the 3rd edition, notably the pronouncing dictionaries. Its two major advantages are availability (the 2nd edition is out of print), and the inclusion of 100,000 new terms (since 1934). Published in 1961, it is considered inferior to the 2nd edition. (G. & C. Merriam Co., Springfield, Mass.)

ENCYCLOPEDIAS

Chambers's Encyclopaedia
>The present encyclopedia is a complete revision of the classic encyclopedia. It was published in 1950 with only minor revisions since then. Its major usefulness is that it is, unlike Encyclopaedia Britannica, still a British publication. Thus it stresses British topics and viewpoints and supplements the great American encyclopedias in that respect. Although mainly composed of brief entries, it gives longer treatment to some broad topics. An index/atlas volume is appended. (International Learning Systems Ltd., London, England)

Enciclopedia Universal Illustrada (Espasa)
>Espasa is the major Spanish-language encyclopedia. The main set was completed in 1933, and regular supplements have kept it up to date. Fortunately, it is strong in Latin American as well as Spanish coverage and excellent for biographies. (Espasa, Barcelona, Spain)

Encyclopaedia Britannica
Still considered the major English-language encyclopedia, it
is no longer British and is published in Chicago. Up to the
1971 edition, it was conventionally arranged and known for
its long, scholarly articles. EB (especially the 11th ed.) is
famous for its highly qualified contributors and excellent
writing. The 1974 (15th) edition, however, was completely
revised and radically rearranged into three sections: a "mi-
cropaedia" with short articles, a "macropaedia" with long
articles, and a "propaedia, " a sort of study guide. Obvious-
ly done to attract school and home sales, it is difficult to
use and significantly diminishes its value as a serious research tool. (Encyclopaedia Britannica, Chicago, Ill.)

Encyclopedia Americana
Originally a "popular" encyclopedia, EA has grown into a
scholarly reference work. It contains long, scholarly articles
and is especially good for American place names and excellent brief descriptions of U. S. government agencies. Since
the recent downfall of Encyclopaedia Britannica, it has become the major American scholarly encyclopedia. It has
an index volume and color maps scattered through the set.
(Americana Corp., N. Y., N. Y.)

Encyclopedia of Associations
The major source, now in its 8th edition, for brief information on business, government, scientific, cultural, social,
hobby, and like associations, societies, and organizations.
It has all the famous ones but its most useful aspect is the
plethora of obscure, oddball associations it controls. It's
hard to locate the Aaron Burr Society or the Shetland Pony
Identification Bureau anywhere else. A good index, and a
separate volume with geographic and executive indexes are
provided. The serial New Associations updates it between
editions. (Gale Research Co., Detroit, Mich.)

PERIODICAL LOCATION TOOLS

Ayer Directory of Publications
This annual, now in its 106th edition, is the best single
source for advertising price and setup information and subscription price, for newspapers and periodicals in most of
North America and the Philippines. The entries include
price, mechanical specifications, and rate data. Added features are a section of maps; short descriptions of states,
towns, etc. In addition to the alphabetical index, there are
separate lists of specialty publications: agricultural, college,
foreign language, Jewish, fraternal, black, etc. Tabular
data and mailing list information are also provided. (Ayer
Press, Philadelphia, Pa.)

Irregular Serials and Annuals

It is similar to Ulrich's International Periodicals Directory (also by Bowker), but covers about 25,000 irregularly published serials from throughout the world. Titles, dates, frequencies, purchasing information, and Dewey library call numbers are included under each title entry. Each title entry is grouped alphabetically with other titles according to their subject classification. There are two indexes: one for titles and another for publications of international organizations. A separate section lists serials that have ceased publication. (R. R. Bowker, Bronx, N.Y.)

Magazines for Libraries

Put together by Bill Katz with the help of many contributors who are also librarians and educators, it is a guide which classifies about 4,500 magazine titles in significant subject areas (both scientific and general). Under each subject category (roughly those corresponding to subjects established by the the same publisher in Ulrich's International Periodicals Directory) are arranged alphabetical listings of magazines and long paragraph annotations describing them. Data of use to potential subscribers is included (like kinds of reading audiences appealed to, prices, and types of book reviews). Separate sections at the back list subject bibliographies for the periodical titles and an alphabetical index to the periodical titles annotated. Subject headings used to classify the magazine titles are found in the front under a "Contents" section. A useful section, also in the front, annotates abstracts and indexes of magazines. It is now in its 2nd edition. (R. R. Bowker, N.Y., N.Y.)

New Serial Titles

The four-volume cumulation of this work collects titles and data on over 280,000 serials which were published between 1950 and 1970. It supplements an earlier publication (by the H. W. Wilson Co.), the Union List of Serials. Entries are listed alphabetically by title (or issuing organization). Codes representing major libraries in the United States that have that serial title in their collections are listed after each entry. City of publication, date of first issue, identifying code number, and a library Dewey call number are also included after each entry. Updating issues are published in eight monthly and four quarterly issues. These are cumulated annually and every five and ten years. (U.S. Library of Congress, Washington, D.C.; and R. R. Bowker, N.Y., N.Y.)

Ulrich's International Periodicals Directory

International in scope, it provides a directory of about 55,000 in-print periodicals published more often than once a year and at regular intervals. It is a subject listing subarranged alphabetically by the title of the periodical. Data like date of first publication, frequency, price (often in U.S. money), editor, and publisher's address are included. A section

explaining the international standard serial numbers is included. Dewey library call numbers are added to each periodical entry. An alphabetical title and subject index is appended. Lists of new periodicals added and cessations are
also included. During alternate years, Bowker Serials Bibliography Supplement updates the regular directory and has
the same basic format. (R. R. Bowker, N.Y., N.Y.)

Union List of Serials
    The third edition of this publication (in five volumes) is a
    master compilation of serial (periodical) holdings in nearly
    1,000 major libraries throughout the U.S. and Canada. The
    original edition was published in 1927 under the sponsorship
    of library associations. Each entry is listed alphabetically
    by title or issuing organization. Included after the entries
    are the geographical code letters of libraries subscribing to
    them as well as city and first date of publication. News-
    papers and government documents are excluded. (H. W. Wil-
    son, Bronx, N.Y.)

STATISTICAL SOURCES

County and City Data Book (U.S.)
    Published every year by the U.S. Bureau of the Census, its
    tables provide census data for counties, for Standard Metro-
    politan Statistical Areas, for urbanized areas, and for cities
    in the United States. Appendices rank census units by popu-
    lation, cover housing units for SMSA's, compute percentages,
    list SMSA's, and list maps for states. (U.S. Bureau of the
    Census, Washington, D.C.)

Directory of Federal Statistics for States (U.S.)
    A companion document to the Directory of Federal Statistics
    for Local Areas, it is published irregularly by the U.S. Bu-
    reau of the Census "to serve as a comprehensive finding
    guide to available published sources of federal statistics on
    social, political, and economic subjects." A classified sub-
    ject index at the back of the book and an appendix listing
    statistics available from each federal department's divisions
    facilitate locating appropriate sources. Entries are listed
    under nearly 25 general topics. Each entry gives the source,
    tabular detail, frequency, most recent reference period, other
    areas included, and the source citation itself. (U.S. Bureau
    of the Census, Washington, D.C.)

Historical Statistics of the United States (Colonial-1962)
    This is updated approximately every ten years, with a five-
    year supplement between editions. It is a one-volume com-
    pendium of statistics which appear in back issues of the an-
    nual Statistical Abstracts of the U.S. Specific statistics ap-
    pearing over the years may be conveniently accessed through

the table of contents in the front or the index in the back.
Tables resemble those of Statistical Abstracts of the U.S.,
except that they may extend back a number of years. The
consumer price index, for example, goes back as far as
1851. (U.S. Bureau of the Census, Washington, D.C.)

Statistical Abstract of the United States
        An annual publication of the U.S. Bureau of the Census since
        1878, it serves as a one-volume guide to many more exten-
        sive government statistical publications. It contains more
        than 1,300 tables and charts and covers mainly national and
        state data. Its tables are grouped together in over 30 sec-
        tions and it is indexed extensively in the back. Appendices
        provide weights and measures, guides to historical statistical
        series, guides to other sources of government statistics, and
        lists of other abstracts and censuses. (U.S. Bureau of the
        Census, Washington, D.C.)

Statistics Sources
        Published irregularly by Gale Research Co. and edited by
        Paul Wasserman, it lists published print sources for statis-
        tics both for the United States and internationally in an alpha-
        betical list of subject headings that indicate both item and
        topic or country. The entry also identifies the publisher, ad-
        dress, title, and source of the statistics. Special care has
        been given to include statistical sources listed in the United
        Nations Statistical Yearbook, Statistical Abstract of the United
        States, and the Encyclopedia of Associations (to locate organ-
        izations having unpublished statistics). (Gale Research Co.,
        Detroit, Mich.)

U.N. Demographic Yearbook
        Demographic statistics from almost 250 countries and areas
        cover different aspects of data gathered by the Statistical Of-
        fice of the UN from various population censuses repeated at
        regular intervals over the years. For example, population
        of 100,000 or more were repeated for the yearbooks of 1960
        and again in 1970. Population statistics for countries of the
        world by sex and age were repeated in 1962, 1963, 1964,
        and 1971 yearbooks. Life and mortality tables for countries
        of the world may be found in both the 1971 Yearbook and
        the World Health Statistics Annual. Census-taking techniques
        as well as captions to various tables are written in both
        English and French. A subject index at the back of each
        yearbook provides references to the periods covered in which
        yearbook issues for each type of demographic statistical se-
        ries. (United Nations, N.Y., N.Y.)

U.N. Statistical Yearbook
        A compilation, in English and French, of marketing statistics
        from over 150 countries and territories. The first section
        contains a "world summary" of "global aggregates divided in-

to geographic and economic areas, " which are followed by a
group of chapters with statistics on population, manpower,
production, transportation, communication, and consumption.
Another group of chapters deal with financial statistics like
wages, prices, and the balance of payments. The last group
of chapters relate to social aspects like health, housing, education, science, and culture. Statistics cover the entire year
in question and often are standardized to make them comparable between different countries and different years. The
table of contents serves as an index to subject, and a special
index at the back provides page numbers for statistics on
various countries. It is updated by <u>Monthly Bulletins of Sta-</u>
<u>tistics</u> and an annual <u>Supplement</u>. (United Nations, N. Y.,
N. Y.)

U. S. <u>Census of Housing</u>
    Companion to the population census, it is also taken every
    ten years. Interim data is available in paperback form but
    the final, bound volumes are usually published one or two
    years after the census. Data includes number of units, oc-
    cupancy characteristics, vacancy data, size, plumbing, struc-
    tural information, type of fuel, value, etc. Breakdowns are
    by state, SMSA, etc. with U. S. summary volume. Really
    sophisticated use, however, almost requires access to the
    census computer tapes, available at many universities. (U. S.
    Bureau of the Census, Washington, D. C.)

U. S. <u>Census of Manufacturers</u>
    It covers types of firms engaged in manufacturing as defined
    by the latest <u>Standard Industrial Classification</u> Manual and is
    published every five years. Volume 1 contains statistics
    summarizing data about U. S. firms; volume 2 has statistics
    arranged by type of industry; volume 3 covers manufacturing
    by state; volume 4 contains data about the location of manu-
    facturing plants; and volume 5 has production indexes. Data
    for manufacturing groups and specific SIC numbers are in-
    dexed alphabetically in volume 2. Appendices to the bound
    volumes explain terms, standard metropolitan statistical
    areas, and descriptions. (U. S. Bureau of the Census, Wash-
    ington, D. C.)

U. S. <u>Census of Population</u>
    The decennial census, mandated by the Constitution to appor-
    tion Congressional districts, also provides a fascinating tabu-
    lar history of the growth of the U. S. Originally merely a
    count, it has grown to include data on age, race, nationality,
    school enrollment, family and marital status, income, and a
    wealth of other data. Each census is first published in a
    plethora of preliminary editions, finally cumulating into per-
    manent volumes by state, SMSA, and the like. Really so-
    phisticated use of such massive data now requires access to
    the census computer tapes. These are available at many
    large universities. (U. S. Bureau of the Census, Washington, D. C.)

Search Procedure Form	GENERAL
NAME OF USER	**DATE OF INQUIRY**

REDEFINED QUESTION STATEMENT

KEYWORDS

ALMANACS:

- ☐ Guinness Book of World Records
- ☐ Information Please Almanac
- ☐ Official Associated Press Almanac
- ☐ Statesman's Yearbook
- ☐ World Almanac

BIOGRAPHY LOCATION AIDS:

- ☐ Biography Index
- ☐ Contemporary Authors
- ☐ Current Biography
- ☐ Dictionary of American Biography
- ☐ Dictionary of National Biography
- ☐ Directory of American Scholars
- ☐ Twentieth Century Authors
- ☐ Webster's Biographical Dictionary
- ☐ Who's Who
- ☐ Who's Who in America

BOOK LOCATION AIDS:

- ☐ Books in Print/Subject Guide to Books in Print
- ☐ British Museum Catalogue of Printed Books
- ☐ Cumulative Book Index
- ☐ Forthcoming Books/Subject Guide to Forthcoming Books
- ☐ National Union Catalog (Library of Congress)
- ☐ Paperbound Books in Print
- ☐ Popular Names of the U.S. Government Reports
- ☐ Subject Collections
- ☐ Titles in Series
- ☐ World Bibliography of Bibliographies

BOOK REVIEW LOCATION AIDS:

- ☐ Book Review Index
- ☐ Book Review Digest
- ☐ Media Review Digest

DICTIONARIES:

- ☐ Acronyms and Initialisms Dictionary
- ☐ Dictionary of Slang and Unconventional English
- ☐ New English Dictionary on Historic Principals
- ☐ Origins, a Short Etymological Dictionary
- ☐ Oxford English Dictionary
- ☐ Random House Dictionary
- ☐ Webster's New International Dictionary of the English Language, 2nd ed.
- ☐ Webster's Third New International Dictionary of the English Language

ENCYCLOPEDIAS:

- ☐ Chambers Encylopaedia
- ☐ Enciclopedia Universal Illustrada
- ☐ Encyclopaedia Britannica
- ☐ Encyclopedia Americana
- ☐ Encyclopedia of Associations

PERIODICAL LOCATION AIDS:

- ☐ Ayer Directory of Publications
- ☐ Irregular Serials and Annuals
- ☐ Magazines for Libraries
- ☐ New Serial Titles
- ☐ Ulrich's International Periodicals Directory
- ☐ Union List of Serials

STATISTICAL SOURCES:

- ☐ County and City Data Book
- ☐ Directory of Federal Statistics for States
- ☐ Historical Statistics of the United States
- ☐ Statistical Abstract of the United States
- ☐ Statistics Sources
- ☐ U.N. Demographic Yearbook
- ☐ U.N. Statistical Yearbook
- ☐ U.S. Census of Housing
- ☐ U.S. Census of Manufacturers
- ☐ U.S. Census of Population

COMMENTS:

SEARCHER'S SIGNATURE   **DATE COMPLETED**

APPENDIX A

"HOW TO..." BOOKS

Although the Discipline Resource Packages identify the basic reference resources of academic scholarship, the user should be aware that most fields also depend upon more esoteric sources of information.

To aid the user who may wish to pursue his researches beyond the range of the basic resources, the following selected unannotated list of "guides to the literature" is provided. Often called "how-to" books, they usually give comprehensive coverage of the library and other research tools available within their fields of interest.

GENERAL

Barton, M. N. Reference Books, a Brief Guide..., 7th ed. Baltimore, Md.: Enoch Pratt Free Library, 1970.

Chandler, G. How to Find Out: a Guide to Sources of Information For All..., 3rd ed. N. Y.: Pergamon, 1967.

Cheney, F. N. Fundamental Reference Sources. Chicago: American Library Association, 1971.

Galin, S. and Spielberg, P. Reference Books: How to Select and Use Them. N. Y.: Random, 1969.

Gates, J. K. Guide to the Use of Books and Libraries, 3rd ed. N. Y.: McGraw, 1974.

Gray, R. A. Guide to Book Review Citations, a Bibliography of Sources.... Columbus, Ohio: Ohio State University Press, 1968.

Hillard, James M. Where to Find What: A Handbook to Reference Questions. Metuchen, N. J.: Scarecrow, 1975.

How-to-Do-It Books; a Selected Guide, 3rd ed. N. Y.: Bowker, 1963.

Katz, W. A. Introduction to Reference Work, Vol. 1: Reference Sources, Vol. 2: Reference Services, 2nd ed. N. Y.: McGraw, 1973, 1974.

Kline, J. Biographical Sources for the United States. Washington,
  D. C.: Reference Department, Library of Congress, 1961.

Krathwohl, D. R. How to Prepare a Research Proposal; Suggestions for Those Seeking Funds for Behavioral Science Research.
  Syracuse, N. Y.: Syracuse University Bookstore, 1966.

Limbacher, J. L. Reference Guide to Audiovisual Information.
  N. Y.: Bowker, 1972.

Lodge, A. A Guide to Research Materials for Graduate Students.
  Los Angeles: University of California Library, 1964.

Morse, G. W. Concise Library Guide to Research. N. Y.: Washington Square Press, 1966.

Murphey, R. W. How and Where to Look It Up, a Guide to Standard Sources of Information. N. Y.: McGraw, 1958.

Schmeckebier, L. F. and Eastin, R. B. Government Publications
  and Their Use, revised ed. Washington, D. C.: Brookings Institution, 1961.

Shores, L. Basic Reference Sources. Chicago: American Library
  Association, 1954.

U. S. Library of Congress. General Reference and Bibliography
  Division. Biographical Sources for the United States. Washington, D. C.: Library of Congress, 1961.

U. S. Library of Congress. National Referral Center. A Directory
  of Information Resources in the U. S.: Federal Government, revised ed. Washington, D. C.: Library of Congress, 1974.

Walford, A. J. Guide to Reference Material, 3rd ed. London:
  The Library Association, 1973.

Wasserman, P., et. al. Statistics Sources, 4th ed. Detroit,
  Mich.: Gale Research Co., 1974.

Wheeler, H. Womanhood Media: Current Resources About Women.
  Metuchen, N. J.: Scarecrow, 1972. Supplement, 1975.

Winchell, C. M. Guide to Reference Books, 8th ed. Chicago:
  American Library Association, 1967.

Wynkoop, S. Subject Guide to Government Reference Books. Littleton, Colo.: Libraries Unlimited, 1972.

BUSINESS AND ECONOMICS

Alexander, R. Business Pamphlets and Information Sources. N. Y.:

Exceptional Books, 1967.

Babb, J. B. and Dordick, B. F. Real Estate Information Sources.
Detroit: Gale Research Co., 1963.

Bakewell, K. G. B. How to Find Out: Management and Productivity: a Guide to Sources of Information.... N.Y.: Pergamon,
1966.

Ball, J. Foreign Statistical Documents, a Bibliography of General,
International Trade, and Agricultural Statistics.... Stanford,
Calif.: Stanford, University, 1967.

Blaisdell, R. F. Sources of Information in Transportation. Evans-
ton, Ill.: Transportation Center, Northwestern University, 1964.

Burgess, N. How to Find Out About Banking and Investment. N.Y.:
Pergamon, 1969.

_____. How to Find Out About Secretarial and Office Practice.
N.Y.: Pergamon, 1967.

Carpenter, R. N. Guidelist for Marketing Research and Economic
Forecasting. N.Y.: American Management Association, 1966.

Christian, P. Ethics in Business Conduct, a Guide to Information
Sources. Detroit: Gale Research Co., 1970.

Coman, E. T. Sources of Business Information, revised ed.
Berkeley, Calif.: University of California Press, 1964.

Demarest, R. R. Accounting: Information Sources. Detroit, Mich.:
Gale Research Co., 1970.

Flood, K. U. Research in Transportation: Legal/Legislative and
Economic Sources and Procedure. Detroit: Gale Research Co.,
1970.

George, C. The Literature of Executive Management, Selected
Books and Reference Sources.... N.Y.: Special Libraries Association, 1963.

Harvard University. Graduate School of Business Administration.
Baker Library. Business Literature: An Annotated List for
Students and Businessmen. Cambridge, Mass.: Harvard Uni-
versity, 1968.

Harvard University. Graduate School of Business Administration.
Baker Library. Selected Business Reference Sources. Cambridge, Mass.: Harvard University, 1965.

Hunt, F. E. Public Utilities Information Sources. Detroit: Gale
Research Co., 1965.

Johnson, H. W. How to Use the Business Library..., 4th ed.
Cincinnati, Ohio: South-Western Pub. Co., 1972.

Klingman, H. F., et al. Management Planning and Control, an
Annotated Bibliography. N. Y.: Controllership Foundation, 1955.

Knox, V. H. Public Finance Information Sources. Detroit: Gale
Research Co., 1964.

Kopycinski, J. V. Textile Industry Information Sources. Detroit:
Gale Research Co., 1964.

Lightwood, M. B. Public and Business Planning in the U.S., a
Bibliography. Detroit: Gale Research Co., 1972.

Lovett, R. W. American Economic and Business History Information Sources.... Detroit, Mich.: Gale Research Co., 1971.

McDermott, B. S. Government Regulation of Business, Including
Antitrust Information Sources.... Detroit, Mich.: Gale Research
Co., 1967.

Melnyk, P. Economics, Bibliographic Guide to Reference Books
and Information Resources. Littleton, Colo.: Libraries Unlimited, 1971.

Metcalf, K. N. Transportation Information Sources. Detroit: Gale
Research Co., 1965.

Morrill, C. Systems and Procedures Including Office Management,
a Guide to Information Sources. Detroit: Gale Research Co.,
1967.

Pendleton, O. W. How to Find Out About Insurance, a Guide to
Sources of Information. N. Y.: Pergamon, 1967.

Randle, G. R. Electronic Industries, Information Sources. Detroit:
Gale Research Co., 1968.

Robert Morris Associates. Sources of Composite Financial Data,
a Bibliography, 2nd ed. Philadelphia: Robert Morris Associates,
1967.

Sherman, M. Industrial Data Guide. N. Y.: Scarecrow, 1962.

Wales, H. G. A Basic Bibliography on Marketing Research.
Chicago: American Marketing Association, 1956.

Wheeler, L. J. International Business and Foreign Trade, a Guide
to Information Sources. Detroit: Gale Research Co., 1968.

Woy, J. B. Business Trends and Forecasting: Information
Sources.... Detroit, Mich.: Gale Research Co., 1965.

_____. Investment Information, a Guide to Information Sources. Detroit: Gale Research Co., 1970.

Zerden, S. Best Books on the Stock Market, an Annotated Bibliography. N. Y.: Bowker, 1972.

EDUCATION

Burke, A. J. and Burke, M. A. Documentation in Education. N. Y.: Teachers College Press, 1967.

Foskett, D. J. How to Find Out: Educational Research. N. Y.: Pergamon, 1965.

Gates, J. L. and Altman, J. W. Handbook of Information Sources in Education and the Behavioral Sciences. Washington, D. C.: U. S. Dept. of Health Education and Welfare, 1968.

Manheim, T., et al. Sources in Educational Research, a Selected Annotated Bibliography. Detroit: Wayne State Univ. Pr., 1969.

Rufsvold, M. I. and Guss, C. Guides to Educational Media, 3rd ed. Chicago: American Library Association, 1971.

Willingham, W. W., et al. Source Book for Higher Education, a Critical Guide to Literature and Information on Access to Higher Education. N. Y.: College Entrance Examination Board, 1973.

FINE ARTS

Baker, B. Theatre and Allied Arts: a Guide to Books Dealing with the History, Criticism and Technique of the Drama and Theatre.... N. Y.: Wilson, 1952.

Carrick, N. How to Find Out About the Arts, a Guide to Sources of Information. N. Y.: Pergamon, 1965.

Chamberlain, M. W. Guide to Art Reference Books. Chicago: American Library Association, 1959.

Cheshire, D. F. Theatre; History, Criticism and Reference. London: Bingley, 1967.

Duckles, V. H. Music Reference and Research Materials, an Annotated Bibliography. London: Free Press of Glencoe, 1964.

McCoy, G. Archives of American Art, a Directory of Resources. N. Y.: Bowker, 1972.

Smith, D. L. How to Find Out in Architecture and Building, a Guide to Sources of Information. N. Y.: Pergamon, 1967.

LANGUAGE AND LITERATURE

Altick, R. D. and Wright, A.   A Selective Bibliography for the
   Study of English and American Literature, 3rd ed.   N. Y.:   Macmillan, 1967.

Bateson, F. W.   A Guide to English Literature.   Chicago: Aldine,
   1965.

Bond, D. F.   A Reference Guide to English Studies.   Chicago: University of Chicago Press, 1962.

Chandler, G.   How to Find Out About Literature.   N. Y.:   Pergamon,
   1968.

Columbia University.   Columbia College.   A Guide to Oriental Clas-
   sics.   N. Y.:   Columbia University Press, 1964.

Cotton, G. B. and McGill, H. M.   Fiction Guides, General: British
   and American.   Hampden, Conn.:   Shoestring, 1967.

Cross, T. P.   Bibliographical Guide to English Studies, 10th ed.
   Chicago: University of Chicago Press, 1951.

Gohdes, C. L. F.   Bibliographical Guide to the Study of the Literature of the U. S. A., 3rd ed.   Durham, N. C.:   Duke University
   Press, 1970.

Jones, H. M.   Guide to American Literature and Its Backgrounds
   Since 1890, 3rd ed.   Cambridge, Mass.:   Harvard University
   Press, 1964.

Neiswender, R.   Guide to Russian Reference and Language Aids.
   N. Y.:   Special Libraries Association, 1962.

Osburn, C. B.   Research and Reference Guide to French Studies.
   Metuchen, N. J.:   Scarecrow, 1968.   Supplement, 1972.

Rice, F. A. and Guss, A.   Information Sources in Linguistics; a
   Bibliographical Handbook.   Washington, D. C.:   Center for Applied
   Linguistics, 1965.

Vitale, P. H.   Basic Tools of Research: an Annotated Guide for
   Students of English.   Great Neck, N. Y.:   Barrons, 1963.

LAW

Cohen, M. L.   Legal Research in a Nutshell.   St. Paul, Minn.:
   West Pub. Co., 1968.

Price, M. O. and Bitner, H.   Effective Legal Research, 3rd ed.
   Boston: Little, 1969.

Roalf, W. R.   How to Find the Law, with Special Chapters on Legal Writing, 6th ed.   St. Paul, Minn.: West Pub. Co., 1965.

Robinson, J.   International Law and Organization, General Sources of Information.   Leyden: A. W. Sijthoff, 1967.

PHILOSOPHY, RELIGION AND PSYCHOLOGY

Borchardt, D. H.   How to Find Out in Philosophy and Psychology. N. Y.: Pergamon, 1968.

De George, R. T.   A Guide to Philosophical Bibliography and Research.   N. Y.: Appleton, 1971.

Glanzman, G. S. and Fitzmyer, J. A.   An Introductory Bibliography for the Study of Scripture, an Annotated Guide to Basic Works.... Westminster, Md: Newman Press, 1962.

Higgins, C. L.   Bibliography of Philosophy, a Descriptive Account. Ann Arbor, Mich.: Campus Publishers, 1965.

Louttit, C. M.   Handbook of Psychological Literature.   N. Y.: Gordon Press, n. d.

McCabe, J. P.   Critical Guide to Catholic Reference Books.   Littleton, Colo.: Libraries Unlimited, 1971.

Rothenberg, J.   Judaica Reference Materials, a Selective Annotated Bibliography, preliminary ed.   Waltham, Mass.: Brandeis Univ. Library, 1971.

SCIENCES

Alexander, R.   Sources of Medical Information....   N. Y.: Exceptional Books, 1969.

American Chemical Society.   Searching the Chemical Literature. Washington, D. C.: the Society, 1961.

Bottle, R. T.   Use of Chemical Literature.   London: Butterworths, 1962.

Brown, R. and Campbell, G. A.   How to Find Out About the Chemical Industry.   N. Y.: Pergamon, 1969.

Burkett, J.   How to Find Out in Electrical Engineering, a Guide to Sources of Information....   N. Y.: Pergamon, 1967.

Burman, C. R.   How to Find Out in Chemistry, a Guide to Sources of Information.   N. Y.: Pergamon, 1965.

Crane, E. J. A Guide to the Literature of Chemistry, 2nd ed.
   N. Y.: Wiley, 1957.

Dick, E. M. Current Information Sources in Mathematics, an Annotated Guide.... Littleton, Colo.: Libraries Unlimited, 1973.

Dyson, G. M. A Short Guide to Chemical Literature, 2nd ed.
   N. Y.: Longmans, 1958.

Gibson, E. B. and Tapia, E. W. Guide to Metallurgical Information, 2nd ed. N. Y.: Special Libraries Association, 1965.

Harvey, A. P. and Bancroft, R. F. L. A Directory of Scientific
   Directories, a World Guide to Scientific Directories Including
   Medicine, Agriculture, Engineering, Manufacturing, and Industrial
   Directories. London: Francis Hodgson Ltd., 1969

Herner, S. A Brief Guide to Sources of Scientific and Technical
   Information. Washington, D. C.: Information Resources Press,
   1970.

Jackson, B. D. Guide to the Literature of Botany.... N. Y.:
   Hafner, 1964.

Jenkins, F. B. Science Reference Sources, 5th ed. Cambridge,
   Mass.: MIT Press, 1969.

Kaplan, S. R. A Guide to Information Sources in Mining, Minerals,
   and Geosciences. N. Y.: Wiley, 1965.

Lasworth, E. J. Reference Sources in Science and Technology.
   Metuchen, N. J.: Scarecrow, 1972.

Luik, J. Van. Searching the Chemical and Chemical Engineering
   Literature..., revised ed. Lafayette, Ind.: Purdue University,
   1957.

Malinowsky, H. R. Science and Engineering Reference Sources....
   Rochester, N. Y.: Libraries Unlimited, 1967.

Mellon, M. G. Chemical Publications, Their Nature and Use, 4th
   ed. N. Y.: McGraw, 1965.

Morrill, C. Computers and Data Processing: Information Sources;
   an Annotated Guide.... Detroit, Mich.: Gale Research Co.,
   1969.

Organization for Economic Cooperation and Development. Guide to
   European Sources of Technical Information. Paris: OECD, 1964.

Parke, N. G. Guide to the Literature of Mathematics and Physics.... N. Y.: Dover, 1958.

Smith, R. C. Guide to the Literature of the Zoological Sciences,
    6th ed. Minneapolis, Minn.: Burgess, 1962.

Sternberg, V. A. How to Locate Technical Information. Water-
    ford, Conn.: National Sales Development Institute, 1964.

Struglia, E. J. Standards and Specifications Information Resources.
    Detroit: Gale Research Co., 1965.

Turnbull, W. R. Scientific and Technical Dictionaries, an Annotated
    Bibliography; vol. 1: Physical Sciences and Engineering. San
    Bernadino, Calif.: Bibliothek Press, 1966+.

U. S. Library of Congress. National Referral Center. A Directory
    of Information Resources in the U.S.: Biological Sciences. Wash-
    ington, D. C.: Library of Congress, 1972.

U. S. Library of Congress. National Referral Center. A Directory
    of Information Resources in the U.S.: Physical Sciences, En-
    gineering. Washington, D. C.: Government Printing Office, 1971.

U. S. Library of Congress. Reference Department. Science and
    Technology Division. Directories in Science and Technology, a
    Provisional List. Washington, D. C.: Library of Congress, 1963.

Waiser, S. Guide to the Literature of Engineering, Mathematics,
    and the Physical Sciences, 3rd ed. Silver Spring, Md: Applied
    Physics Laboratory, Johns Hopkins University, 1972.

Whitford, R. H. Physics Literature, a Reference Manual, 2nd ed.
    Metuchen, N. J.: Scarecrow, 1968.

Yates, B. How to Find Out About Physics, a Guide to Sources of
    Information.... N. Y.: Pergamon, 1965.

SOCIAL SCIENCES

American Historical Association. Guide to Historical Literature.
    N. Y.: Macmillan, 1961.

Baer, M. F. and Roeher, E. C. Occupational Information: the
    Dynamics of Its Nature and Use. Chicago: Science Research
    Associates, 1964.

Bengston, H. Introduction to Ancient History. Berkeley, Calif.:
    University of California Press, 1970.

Blum, E. Basic Books in the Mass Media, an Annotated, Selected
    Booklist.... Urbana, Ill.: University of Illinois Press, 1972.

Brimmer, B., et al. Guide to the Use of United Nations Docu-
    ments. Dobbs Ferry, N. Y.: Oceana, 1962.

Brock, C. The Literature of Political Science.... N.Y.: Bowker, 1969.

Bureau of Social Science Research. International Communication and Political Opinion, a Guide to the Literature. Princeton, N.J.: Princeton University Press, 1956.

Campbell, H. C. How to Find Out About Canada. N.Y.: Pergamon, 1967.

Carter, R. M. Communication in Organizations, a Guide to Information Sources. Detroit: Gale Research Co., 1972.

Clarke, J. A. Research Materials on the Social Sciences. Madison, Wis.: University of Wisconsin Press, 1959.

Cosgrove, C. A. Reader's Guide to Britain and the European Communities. London: Chatham House, 1970.

Cox, E. G. A Reference Guide to the Literature of Travel, Including Voyages, Geographical Descriptions, Adventures, Shipwrecks and Expeditions. Seattle, Wash.: University of Washington, 1950. 3 vols.

Cumming, J. Guide to the Writing of Local History. Lansing, Mich.: Michigan American Revolution Bicentennial Commission, 1974.

Griffin, C. C. Latin America, a Guide to the Historical Literature. Austin, Texas: University of Texas Press, 1971.

Handlin, O., et al. Harvard Guide to American History. Cambridge, Mass.: Harvard University Press, 1954.

Harmon, R. B. Political Science: a Bibliographical Guide to the Literature. N.Y.: Scarecrow, 1965. Supplements, 1968, 1972, 1974.

Hepworth, P. How to Find Out in History. N.Y.: Pergamon, 1966.

Kalvelage, C., et al. Research Guide for Undergraduates in Political Science. Morristown, N.J.: General Learning Press, 1972.

Larson, A. D. National Security Affairs, a Guide to Information Sources. Detroit, Mich.: Gale Research Co., 1973.

Lewis, P. R. The Literature of the Social Sciences, an Introductory Survey and Guide. London: The Library Association, 1960.

Lock, C. B. M. Geography, a Reference Handbook. London: C. Bingley, 1968.

Maichel, K. Guide to Russian Reference Books. Stanford, Calif.: Stanford University Press, 1964. 2 vols.

Mandelbaum, D. G., et al. Resources for the Teaching of Anthropology. Berkeley, Calif.: University of California Press, 1963.

Mason, J. B. Research Resources, Annotated Guide to the Social Sciences. Santa Barbara, Calif.: ABC-Clio, 1968+. (multivolume; in progress)

Merritt, R. L. and Pyszka, G. J. The Student Political Scientist's Handbook. N.Y.: Harper, 1969.

Minto, C. S. How to Find Out in Geography, a Guide.... N.Y.: Pergamon, 1966.

Moor, C. C. and Chamberlin, W. How to Use United Nations Documents. N.Y.: New York University Press, 1952. •

Morley, C. Guide to Research Literature in Russian History. Syracuse, N.Y.: Syracuse University Press, 1951.

Neal, J. A. Reference Guide for Travellers. N.Y.: Bowker, 1969.

Norton, A. Public Relations, a Guide to Information Resources. Detroit: Gale Research Co., 1970.

Paetow, L. J. Guide to the Study of Medieval History. N.Y.: F. S. Crofts, 1931.

Pemberton, J. E. How to Find Out About France, a Guide to Sources of Information. N.Y.: Pergamon, 1966.

Pinson, W. M. Resource Guide to Current Social Issues. Waco, Texas: Word Books, 1968.

Plischke, E. American Foreign Relations, a Bibliography of Official Sources. College Park, Md.: University of Maryland, 1955.

Poulton, H. J. Historian's Handbook, a Descriptive Guide to Reference Works. Norman: University of Oklahoma Press, 1972.

ReQua, E. G. and Statham, J. The Developing Nations, a Guide to Information Sources. Detroit: Gale Research Co., 1965.

Roach, H. Spoken Records, 3rd ed. Metuchen, N.J.: Scarecrow Press, 1970.

Special Libraries Association. A Source List of Selected Labor Statistics, revised ed. N.Y.: S.L.A., 1953.

Teng, S. and Biggerstaff, K. An Annotated Bibliography of Selected

Chinese Reference Works, 3rd ed.   Cambridge, Mass.:   Harvard University Press, 1971.

Thiele, W.   Official Map Publications, a Historical Sketch and a Bibliographical Handbook for Current Maps and Mapping Services....   Chicago: American Library Association, 1938.

U. S. Bureau of Labor Statistics.   Counselor's Guide to Occupational and Other Manpower Information, an Annotated Bibliography of Selected Government Publications.   Washington, D. C.:   Government Printing Office, 1964.

U. S. Library of Congress.   General Reference and Bibliography Division.   A Guide to Bibliographic Tools for Research in Foreign Affairs.   Washington, D. C.:   Library of Congress, 1956.

U. S. Library of Congress.   National Referral Center.   A Directory of Information Resources in the U. S.:   Social Sciences, rev. ed. Washington, D. C.:   Library of Congress, 1973.

Welsch, E. K.   The Negro in the United States; a Research Guide. Bloomington, Ind.:   Indiana University Press, 1965.

White, C. M.   Sources of Information in the Social Sciences, 2nd ed.   Chicago: American Library Association, 1973.

Wright, J. K.   Aids to Geographical Research..., 2nd ed.   N. Y.: Columbia University Press, 1947.

Wynar, L. R.   Guide to Reference Materials in Political Science. Denver, Colo.:   Bibliographic Institute, 1966.

QUESTION NEGOTIATION SIMULATION EXERCISE

Purpose

The purpose of the oral presentation, and the simulation game to follow, is to make the learner familiar with the basic concepts inherent in negotiation of a reference question, the process which constitutes the heart of the librarian/information specialist's professional responsibilities.

The presentation will define the concept of reference searching, outline the types of people who qualify as searchers, and provide a basic model of the searching process. The detailed steps in the negotiation of the reference question will be discussed.

The simulation game will then test the learner's understanding of these concepts by placing him in a hypothetical situation where he will either be a user asking a question, an information specialist negotiating a user's question, or an impartial observer critiquing this process.

Learner Characteristics

This exercise is intended for use in training adults in understanding the basic concepts of question negotiation. It is applicable to library science students, to librarians in an in-service training situation, and to laymen interested in acquiring skills in framing questions for personal library searching.

Terminal Objectives of the Presentation:

1) The learner will be able to demonstrate his understanding of the concept "search" with an appropriate response to a question from the lecturer.

2) The learner will be able to list and define the three major types of searches when asked to do so by the lecturer.

3) The learner will be able to demonstrate his knowledge of the logical sequence of the ten steps in the suggested model of the searching process by using them to renegotiate a typical question during the simulation exercise to follow.

4) The learner will be able to list and define the three major steps in question definition when asked to do so by the lecturer.

5) The learner will be able to demonstrate his knowledge of the logical sequence of the nine basic, or key, questions asked in limit- ing and redefining a reference question by redefining such a question in the simulation exercise to follow.

Terminal Objectives of the Simulation

During the simulation exercise, the learner will demonstrate his ability to:

1) apply the knowledge acquired in the lecture to an actual situation requiring creative thinking; specifically, an ability to:
    --analyze the initial statement;
    --devise key words related to the initial statement;
    --adequately narrow and polish the initial statement into an ac- ceptable redefined question.

2) demonstrate the interpersonal communication skills necessary to renegotiate a reference question.   Specifically:
    --an ability to deal effectively with another person verbally, on a one-to-one basis;
    --an ability to participate in an interrogation that identifies spe- cific needs.

3) satisfactorily fill the role of observer, when assigned that role. Specifically:
    --to be able to understand the point of view of both user and in- formation specialist.
    --to demonstrate an ability to observe a question negotiation and to critique it constructively.

Activities and Materials for the Presentation

        The presentation, encompassing the concepts summarized by the objectives (above), will be presented orally (live or tape) with ap- propriate visual aids.   A handout, essentially an outline of the oral presentation and visuals, will be supplied to the learners to reduce notetaking and increase attention.

Activities and Materials for the Simulation

        The purpose and procedures for the simulation will be ex- plained orally before the game begins.   A one-page handout sum- marizing this explanation will be provided simultaneously with the explanation.   The learners will be divided into groups of three.   The members of each group will play the roles of "user, " "information specialist, " and "observer. "   Each group will be provided with several "typical" initial questions asked by users of libraries and other information facilities.   (A specific list of handouts appears below.)

The simulation will progress as follows:

1)   The person playing the role of the user will present one of the initial questions for discussion.

2)   The person playing the role of the information specialist will then begin the negotiation process by asking questions designed to focus in on the actual need of the user.   The role-playing user must depend upon his imagination and his knowledge of the types of users and their needs (presented in the lecture) to respond intelligently to the information specialist's questions.   The information specialist must depend upon similar knowledge to ask the right questions in the first place.   The result should be a polished, redefined, and narrowed reference question statement.   The steps of the simulated negotiation process can be summarized as follows:

   a)   discussion of what the initial question means;

   b)   compilation of a list of key words, to standardize the concepts discussed by both parties in a;

   c)   a consensus is achieved between the two parties as to what the user "really needs," in light of:
        i) the user's expressed wants
        ii)   the information specialist's understanding of the user's actual need
        iii)   the type and amount of information it is feasible to obtain.

   d)   writing a redefined, concise question statement based on the above consensus.

3)   The person playing the role of the observer serves as a moderator for the exercise (time-keeping, distributing handouts, etc.). His major task is to observe the negotiation process and compare it to a checklist of key questions.   These questions are central to the negotiation process and the quality of the simulation game can be judged by how many of these questions the user and the information specialist use during their simulated negotiation.

Materials for Each Simulation

1)   a one-page "Explanation Sheet. "

2)   a "Negotiation Record Sheet, " with an initial question typed in.

3)   an "Observer Record Sheet, " which consists of a checklist of key questions to be covered, and a place for the observer's comments.

4) scrap paper and pencils for each person.

INSTRUCTIONAL MATERIALS

The oral presentation:
 -a script
 -a slide-tape presentation

PARTICIPANTS HANDOUTS

A written summary of the presentation for participants:
 -with wide right margins for note taking

A one-page "Explanation Sheet" for participants:
 -introduction to the simulation exercise
 -definitions of the three roles
 -steps in the simulation process summarized

A stapled handout for participants:
 -terminal objectives
 -3 types of searcher
 -10 steps - model searching process
 -3 steps - question definition
 -9 key questions - redefinition of the question

EXERCISE MATERIALS

Negotiation Record Sheet (with the initial question typed in)
 -space for rewriting the question, recording key words, etc.

Observer Record Sheet
 -a rating form for the observer. A checklist to assure that
 the 9 key questions are covered, and space for observer
 comments.

APPENDIX C

CONTRIBUTORS

James M. DOYLE
(Co-Author)
Public Service Librarian
Macomb County Community College
Warren, Michigan

As co-author Mr. Doyle's primary responsibility was for the sections on the searching process and question negotiation, and for overseeing the development of Part III materials relating to Discipline Resource Packages.

Mr. Doyle was Head of Reference for the University of Detroit Library for six years, before being employed by Macomb Community College. He has also been an Information Services Specialist with the Michigan-Ohio Regional Educational Laboratory (MOREL). The development of the concept of the Bibliographic Chain was developed at MOREL in conjunction with co-author George Grimes, based on original work done by Thelma Friedes, formerly of the Wayne State University Libraries.

Mr. Doyle took his undergraduate and library science degrees at Wayne State University. He is currently completing a Ph. D. in Instructional Technology at the same institution.

Joan W. GARTLAND
(Editor-General Social Sciences)
Head of Reference
University of Detroit Library
Detroit, Michigan

Ms. Gartland is an Egyptologist as well as a librarian. Before joining the staff of the University of Detroit Library she was Research Assistant and Registrar at the Oriental Institute's museum in Chicago. She also spent two summers on an archaeological dig at Mendes in the Egyptian delta. Ms. Gartland is a Counselor at Crossroads, a community guidance center in Detroit and reviews books for Library Journal.

Ms. Gartland's undergraduate work in history was taken at Barnard College, she completed her M. A. in Egyptology at the University of Chicago, and received her M. A. L. S. from the University of Michigan.

George H. GRIMES
(Co-Author)
Consultant, Learning Resources
Wayne County Intermediate School District
Detroit, Michigan

Dr. Grimes' primary responsibility as co-author related to creation of the draft for Parts I and II of the book with particular attention to sections on knowledge utilization and user characteristics.

Dr. Grimes has acted as a school, public, and community college librarian as well as elementary/secondary and college instructor. He had system-wide coordinative responsibility for curriculum laboratories in the Detroit Public Schools and worked as Coordinator, Information Services for the Michigan-Ohio Regional Educational Laboratory (MOREL). His present responsibility is general consultation in learning resources and media for the Wayne County Intermediate School District.

After completion of undergraduate work and an M. Ed. in Social Studies at Wayne State University, Dr. Grimes obtained his M. L. S. from the School of Library and Information Science, State University of New York College at Geneseo. Returning to Wayne State University Dr. Grimes received his Ed. D. in Curriculum Development, writing his dissertation in the area of educational information systems.

Jovian P. LANG
(Editor - Philosophy and Religion; Psychology)
Assistant Professor
Department of Library and Information Science
St. John's University
Jamaica, New York

In addition to teaching speech and hearing therapy Fr. Lang has had wide experience in librarianship, working both in public service and administration, as well as being deeply involved in the Library-College movement.

Fr. Lang was Librarian at Quincy College (Illinois) and archivist for the Sacred Heart Province (St. Louis, Missouri). He taught audiovisual and library science at Rosary College (Illinois) and at the University of South Florida (Tampa, Florida), prior to his present similar teaching position. Currently a member of the ALA Council, Fr. Lang has held numerous other library association positions including President of the Catholic Library Association.

After completing undergraduate work and further study at St. Joseph Seminary, Fr. Lang was ordained a priest. He earned his M. S. in L. S. and M. A. in Speech and Hearing Therapy from Case Western Reserve University.

Rose Mary MAGRILL
(Editor - Language and Literature)

Associate Professor
School of Library Science
University of Michigan
Ann Arbor, Michigan

Dr. Magrill has had a varied work experience in academic
libraries in addition to teaching responsibility at Ball State University and the University of Michigan. She is a co-author of the 4th
edition of Building Library Collections.
Dr. Magrill received a B. S. and M. A. from East Texas
State University and her M. S. L. S. and Ph. D. from the University
of Illinois.

Thomas W. MULFORD
(Editor - Business and Economics; General Works)
Reference Librarian
Business and Finance Department
Detroit Public Library, Main Branch
Detroit, Michigan

Mr. Mulford worked in various aspects of public library work
in New York City before coming to the Detroit Public Library. He
has also had professional experience in advertising and marketing
libraries. He has a particular interest in computer applications to
libraries.
Mr. Mulford holds degrees from Duke University and the
School of Library Science, Syracuse University.

Francis W. PETERS
(Editor - Fine Arts)
Librarian
Detroit Institute of Arts
Detroit, Michigan

Mr. Peters was a reference librarian at the Ryerson and
Burnham Libraries of the Art Institute of Chicago for two years before coming to the Research Library of the Detroit Institute of Arts
as Assistant Librarian in 1951. He has been the head Librarian
there since 1968.
Mr. Peters did his undergraduate work in the history of art
at the University of Michigan (BA, 1949). He received his M. A. L. S.
from the University of Michigan in 1950.

Elma M. STEWART
(Editor - Physical Sciences; Life Sciences)
Assistant Science and Technology Librarian
and Assistant Professor
Eastern Michigan University Library
Ypsilanti, Michigan

Miss Stewart has worked in public and academic libraries and has compiled an index of <u>Douglass' Monthly</u> and has several other indexes in process.

Miss Stewart's undergraduate and library science degrees were obtained from Wayne State University and a Specialist's degree was received from Eastern Michigan University. She has also taken postgraduate training in library administration and the science of personal achievement. Miss Stewart is currently working toward a Ph. D. in Higher Education at the University of Michigan.

Kent D. TALBOT
(Editor-Director, Policy Reference Services - Law)
Lyndon B. Johnson School of Public Affairs
University of Texas at Austin
Austin, Texas

Mr. Talbot is both a librarian and a lawyer. Prior to accepting his present position he was head of the University of Detroit Law Library, a reference librarian at the University of Chicago Law School, an Assistant Attorney General for the State of Illinois, and a librarian for the U. S. Bureau of Labor Statistics. His teaching specialties are legal research and writing as well as equitable remedies.

After completion of undergraduate work at Knox College, Mr. Talbot completed his J. D. at Loyola of Chicago. He received his library science degree from the University of Chicago Library School.

REFERENCE LIST

Allen, T. J.   The Utilization of Information Sources during R & D
Proposal Preparation; working paper no. 97-64.   Cambridge, Mass.:
Massachusetts Institute of Technology, Alfred P. Sloan School of
Management, 1964.

Allen, T. J.   "Communications in the research and development
laboratory."   Technology Review, 70 (1), 1967 (Oct.-Nov.), 31-
37.

_____.   and Cohen, S. I.   "Information flow in two R & D labo-
ratories."   Administrative Science Quarterly, 14 (1), 1969 (March),
12-19.

_____.   and Gerstberger, P. G.   Criteria for selection of an in-
formation source; working paper no. 284-67.   Cambridge, Mass.:
Massachusetts Institute of Technology, Alfred P. Sloan School of
Management, 1967.

_____., Piepmeier, J., and Cooney, S.   The international tech-
nological gatekeeper.   Technology Review, 73(5), 1971 (March),
36-43.

American Psychological Association, Project on Scientific Information Exchange in Psychology.   Reports, volume I; Overview Report and Reports 1-9.   Washington, D.C.: The Association,
1963.

_____.   _____.   Reports, volume II, Reports 10-15.   Wash-
ington, D.C.:   The Association, 1965.

_____.   _____.   Report 16: Innovations in Scientific Commu-
nication in Psychology.   Washington, D.C.:   The Association,
1966.

Atherton, P. (ed.).   Large Scale Information Processing Systems,
Section IV-B: the User Component of System B.   Syracuse,
N.Y.:   Syracuse University, School of Library Science, 1971.

Boswell, L.   Life of Dr. Johnson.   Everyman ed.   2 vols.   N.Y.:
Dutton, 1949 (c. 1791).

Clemens, T.   "Information transfer and research utilization in education"; an address before the staff of the Michigan Department

of Education, July 14, 1969; appendix D of G. Grimes, A Proposed Educational Information System for the State of Michigan. Lansing: Michigan Department of Education, 1969. (Educational Resources Information Center, ED 039 000)

Crane, D. "Social structure in a group of scientists; a test of the 'invisible college' hypothesis." American Sociological Review, 34(3), 1969 (June), 335-52.

_____. Invisible Colleges: Diffusion of Knowledge in Scientific Communities. Chicago: University of Chicago Press, 1972.

Crawford, S. (ed.). Informal Communication among Scientists: Proceedings of a Conference on Current Research. Chicago: American Medical Association, 1971.

Cuadra, C. (ed.). Annual Review of Information Science and Technology. Chicago: Encyclopaedia Britannica, annual since 1966.

Doyle, J. and Grimes, G. H. "The progression of educational information," in Pierce Grove (ed.). Bibliographic Control of Nonprint Media. Chicago: American Library Association, 1972, pp. 44-47.

Ely, D. P. "The myths of information needs." Educational Researcher, 2(4), 1973(April), 15-17.

Garvey, W. D., Lin, N., and Nelson, C. E. "Communication in the physical and social sciences." Science, 170(3963), 1970(Dec. 11), 1166-1173.

Gerstberger, P. G. and Allen, T. J. "Criteria used in the selection of information channels by R & D engineers." Journal of Applied Psychology, 52(4), 1968(Aug.), 272-9.

Havelock, R. G. A Comparative Study of the Literature on the Dissemination and Utilization of Scientific Knowledge. Ann Arbor, Mich.: University of Michigan, Institute for Social Research, Center for Research on the Utilization of Scientific Knowledge, 1969. (Educational Resources Information Center, ED 029 171)

_____. and Havelock, M. C. Training for Change Agents. Ann Arbor, Mich.: University of Michigan, 1973.

Johns Hopkins University, Center for Research in Scientific Communication. Series 2, Report 1. Philadelphia: The Center, 1968.

Katz, W. A. Introduction to Reference Work: Vol. II, Reference Services. N.Y.: McGraw, 1969.

Kent, A. Specialized Information Centers. Washington, D.C.: Sparten Books, 1965.

Lancaster, F. W. Information Retrieval Systems: Characteristics, Testing, and Evaluation. N. Y.: Wiley, 1968, pp. 20-28.

Line, M. B. "The information users and needs of social scientists: an overview of INFROSS." Aslib Proceedings, 23(8), 1971(Aug.), 412-34.

Osgood, C. E. and Sebeok, T. A. Psycholinguistics, a Survey of Theory and Research Problems; with 'A Survey of Psycholinguistic Research, 1954-1964' by A. R. Diebold, Jr.; and 'The Psycholinguists' by G. A. Miller. Bloomington, Indiana: Indiana University Press, 1965.

Palmer, M. C. "Why academic library instruction?" in S. H. Lee, (ed.). Library Orientation, Papers Presented at the First Annual Conference on Library Orientation held at Eastern Michigan University, May 7, 1971. Ann Arbor, Mich.: Pierian Press, 1972.

Price, D. J. de Solla. "Some remarks on elitism in information and the invisible college phenomenon in science." Journal of the American Society for Information Science, 22(2), 1971(March/April), 74-75.

Rogers, E. M. Diffusion of Innovation. N. Y.: Free Press of Glencoe, 1962.

Schiller, A. R. "Reference service: instruction or information?" Library Quarterly, 35(1), 1965(Jan.), 58.

Shannon, C. E. and Weaver, W. The Mathematical Theory of Communication. Urbana, Ill.: University of Illinois Press, 1949.

Taube, M. (ed.). Studies in Coordinate Indexing, vol. III. Bethesda, Md.: Documentation Inc., 1956.

Taylor, R. S. "Question negotiation and information seeking in libraries." College and Research Libraries, 29(3), 1968(May), 178-94.

Uytterschaut, L. "Literature searching methods in social science research: a pilot inquiry." American Behavioral Scientist, 9(9), 1966(May), 14+.

INDEXES

Two indexes are provided: a general index and a title index. The title index includes all annotated reference resources in the book. Non-annotated titles are subject-indexed by category (e. g. , "Sociology periodicals, 77"). Title changes are included in the title index, if the former title is mentioned in the annotation. In some cases, shortened titles are used in the index for convenience. As a rule authors are not indexed, but, exceptions are made in the few cases where one thinks of the author more readily than the title (i. e. , Winchell, Katz).

GENERAL INDEX

TITLE INDEX